Favorite Hikes IN & AROUND
ZION NATIONAL PARK

Tanya Milligan and Bo Beck

- GRAND CANYON NATIONAL PARK
- BRYCE CANYON NATIONAL PARK
- CEDAR BREAKS NATIONAL MONUMENT
- DIXIE NATIONAL FOREST
- GRAND STAIRCASE-ESCALANTE NATIONAL MONUMENT
- PARIA CANYON WILDERNESS
- CANAAN MOUNTAIN WILDERNESS

Favorite Hikes IN & AROUND
ZION NATIONAL PARK

by TANYA MILLIGAN AND BO BECK

Published and distributed by
Sharp End Publishing, LLC
PO Box 1613
Boulder, CO 80306
t. 303.444.2698
www.sharpendbooks.com

ISBN: 978-1-892540-82-9-50
Printed in the USA

COVER PHOTO CREDIT
Summer and Kyra Milligan in Willis Creek by Tanya Milligan

OPENING PAGE PHOTO CREDIT
Bryce Canyon

UNLABELED PHOTO CREDIT
All photos by Tanya Milligan or Bo Beck

SPECIAL THANK YOU
To Gordon Milligan and Lisa Justet for all their editing help.

READ THIS BEFORE USING THIS GUIDE

HIking, scrambling, climbing and canyoneering are dangerous activities. Take all precautions and evaluate your ability carefully. Use judgment rather than the opinions represented in this book. The publishers and authors assume no responsibility for injury or death resulting from the use of this book. This book is based on opinions. Do not rely on information, descriptions, or difficulty ratings, as these are entirely subjective. If you are unwilling to assume complete responsibility for your safety, do not use this book.

THE AUTHORS AND PUBLISHER EXPRESSLY DISCLAIM ALL REPRESENTATIONS AND WARRANTIES REGARDING THIS GUIDE, THE ACCURACY OF THE INFORMATION HEREIN, AND THE RESULTS OF YOUR USE HEREOF, INCLUDING WITHOUT LIMITATION, IMPLIED WARRANTIES OF MERCHANTABILITY AND FITNESS FOR A PARTICULAR PURPOSE. THE USER ASSUMES ALL RISK ASSOCIATED WITH THE USE OF THIS BOOK.

It is your responsibility to take care of yourself while hiking or canyoneering. Seek a professional instructor or guide if you are unsure of your ability to handle any circumstances that may arise. This book is not intended as an instructional manual.

Child-friendly/Quick Hike
Day Hike
Technical Canyon/Route
Ideal for Backpack
Arch or Bridge
Petroglyphs or Ruins
Dinosaur Tracks

INTRODUCTION

Within these pages you will find directions to 50 incredible trails. Each one explores its own little piece of the rugged terrain, deep ravines and captivating vertical walls of southwest Utah and adjacent northern Arizona.

Zion National Park is the focus of this book, and with good reason. Zion has some of the most dramatic scenery in the entire western USA; visitors are rendered speechless time and time again when their eyes gaze upon the vast monoliths and sculpted sandstone precipices within this intoxicating natural wonder. The trails described here take you all over the park: some ascend to dizzying viewpoints and others wind their way into the deep, mysterious canyons for which the park is famed.

But there is more: to the north of Zion lies Bryce Canyon National Park. Within its 14 spectacular amphitheaters are found the most fantastic erosional formations on the planet; this is a unique place that leaves visitors breathless with lasting memories of its haunting features.

Southward is Arizona's Grand Canyon, a vast expanse of emptiness, a place where the hectic world seems to hold still as the sun gently peeks over the Colorado Plateau, illuminating with its warming sunrays ancient petroglyphs engraved on far more ancient rocks. The sun dazzles the limestone and worms deep into the huge chasm—finding, eventually, the Colorado River, a force of nature that has created this enormous wilderness.

We will also take you to less-well-known masterpieces of this red-rock desert. You will discover a treasure trove of fantastically shaped stones in Cedar Breaks National Monument, Ashdown Gorge Wilderness and Dixie National Forest's Cedar Mountain. Here is a magical world: sculpted hoodoos, windows and fins create a vivid contrast to the lush colors of the surrounding forest.

Lastly, we describe some explorations in the fabulous sandstone buttes and canyons of the Paria Canyon Wilderness-Vermilion Cliffs National Monument and the Canaan Mountain Wilderness. These trails visit the type of beauty that stops us in our tracks. Millions of years of raging storms have pitted ice, water and snow against rock to produce the wondrous creations now protected as public lands and kept pristine for the entire world to enjoy. The areas traversed by the trails in this book are unique and the land they sit on is a national treasure: Utah boasts that almost 75 percent of its sparsely populated, yet sizable state has been set aside for the public, protected by federal and state agencies.

We encourage you to explore and appreciate the tremendous variety of routes and locations described in this book. That said, however, it is obvious that the majority of the routes we describe are in and around Zion. This park and the adjacent land is a labyrinth of adrenaline-producing canyons and summits. The day-hikes and overnight adventures that explore this wilderness have held our interest for years—in truth, still not letting go. We continue to find and enjoy new hikes within its boundaries.

WHAT TO EXPECT FROM THIS BOOK

We describe a mix of trails: some are quick, easy, family-friendly paths; there is a selection of longer day-hikes, including some little-known gems; there are a handful of backpack trips. We also throw into the mix a few semi-technical and technical trips, some of which burrow deep into thrilling slot canyons, while some climb short cliffs en route to grand viewpoints.

Route descriptions include distances, expected completion times, elevations, difficulty rating, points of interest and recommended equipment and clothing. GPS coordinates are included for most routes.

USING THIS BOOK—WHAT THE DESERT EXPECTS FROM YOU

Many of the descriptions in this book require a map and compass, and the navigational skills to use both. Keep in mind that when driving, odometer readings vary from vehicle to vehicle. When hiking, realize that trails and even landscapes can change; new social paths may develop quickly. Sometimes paths change in order to get around a new obstacle, but trails (and cairns) may lure you in the wrong direction. Navigate with care. Always attempt to stay on existing footpaths and avoid creating detours.

You are responsible for your own safety and survival. This guide is to be used as an aid and is only to be used at your own risk.

DON'T BLAME US IF THINGS GO WRONG - We encourage you to research plans extensively from many sources. Outdoor recreation is potentially hazardous, by its very nature. Use good judgment, do not take kids where they should not go and be prepared for changes and complications. Use good decision-making skills. When hiking off-trail routes understand these are not maintained paths, but rather a way to get to a certain destination.

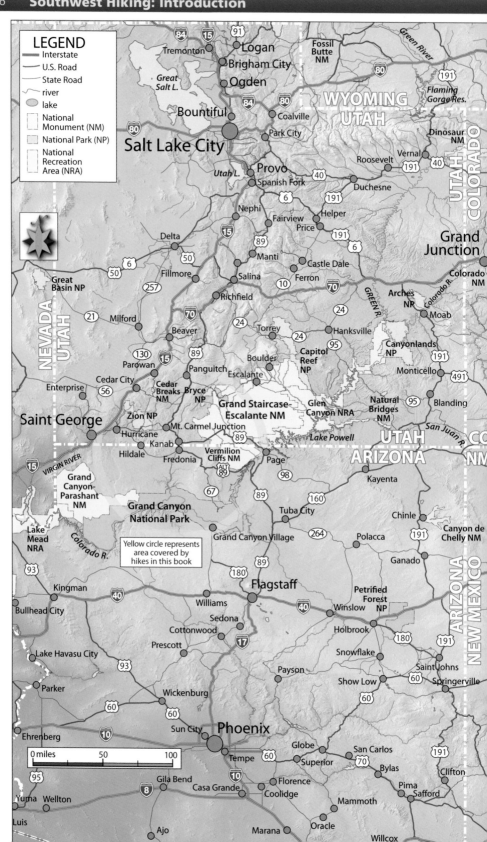

LEGEND
- —— Interstate
- —— U.S. Road
- —— State Road
- ⌁ river
- ◯ lake
- ▢ National Monument (NM)
- ▢ National Park (NP)
- ▢ National Recreation Area (NRA)

Yellow circle represents area covered by hikes in this book

0 miles   50   100

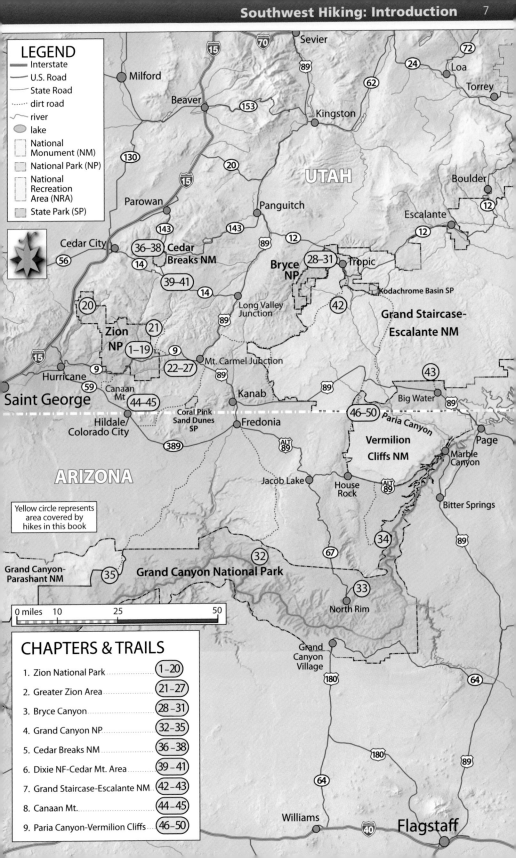

LEGEND

———	Interstate
———	U.S. Road
———	State Road
·········	dirt road
⋀⋁	river
⬮	lake
▢	National Monument (NM)
▢	National Park (NP)
▢	National Recreation Area (NRA)
▢	State Park (SP)

Yellow circle represents area covered by hikes in this book

0 miles   10   25   50

UTAH

Sevier · Loa · Torrey · Boulder · Escalante · Milford · Beaver · Kingston · Parowan · Panguitch · Cedar City · Cedar Breaks NM · Bryce NP · Tropic · Kodachrome Basin SP · Long Valley Junction · Grand Staircase-Escalante NM · Zion NP · Mt. Carmel Junction · Hurricane · Canaan Mt · Saint George · Kanab · Big Water · Paria Canyon · Page · Hildale/Colorado City · Coral Pink Sand Dunes SP · Fredonia · Vermilion Cliffs NM · Marble Canyon · Bitter Springs

ARIZONA

Grand Canyon-Parashant NM · Grand Canyon National Park · Jacob Lake · House Rock · North Rim · Grand Canyon Village · Williams · Flagstaff

Road markers: 15, 70, 89, 72, 24, 62, 153, 130, 20, 143, 14, 12, 56, 9, 59, 389, ALT 89, 67, 32, 33, 34, 35, 180, 64, 40

Hike markers: 36–38, 39–41, 28–31, 42, 1–19, 21, 22–27, 44–45, 43, 46–50, 34, 32, 33, 35, 20

CHAPTERS & TRAILS

Devil's in the Details: Suggestions for a Great Hike

Routes may present obstacles that require technical skills and techniques such as climbing, scrambling and even swimming. Heed all cautions when outdoors. Check weather conditions, wear appropriate attire and bring plenty of water and other supplies. Hiking may lead to places where rescue might be impossible and cell-phone or "Spot" coverage poor. A mishap like a sprained ankle, a snake bite or simply running out of water may incur serious consequences. Be aware that weather, flash flooding and other conditions can change a route and understand that hiking in extreme weather, either hot or cold, can change a simple hike into a dangerous situation.

Possibles Bag

Make yourself a "possibles bag" and take it with you hiking. Keep the weight and bulk low, but include those items that will keep you warm, dry and hydrated. Include things that are useful in an emergency and put them in an airtight bag so they stay dry. Pack a topographic map of the area you will be hiking in and a compass. Take a copy of the trail description; never rely on memory. Bring at least one headlamp per person and fresh batteries for each. Include a first aid kit with antibiotic ointment, pain killers, bandages, water purification tablets, sunscreen, chapstick, blister care and insect repellant. Also take high-energy food, socks, clothing, sunglasses, items for starting a fire, pocket knife, toilet paper, duct tape, candle, signal mirror, whistle, dental floss, needle, paper, pencil, 50 feet of 9/16" tubular webbing (to make a handline down or up an obstacle), and an emergency shelter such as a bivy sack. You can get bivy sacks under 4 oz that occupy a very small space in your pack. Choose one that is colorful (so you can be seen), waterproof, windproof and metalicized so that it reflects your own body heat back to you.

Other items may be useful or even necessary such as needed medication, but the basic list presented above may make the difference between a very uncomfortable night and a night with some comfort-providing commodities. If no one is hurt, water and warmth are your biggest issues.

Eat, Drink and Be Merry

Make sure you are well hydrated and eat well the day before and the morning of your planned hike. Water is heavy, weighing about 8 lbs per gallon, but bringing an adequate amount is essential for survival. Keep in mind that you can last about three weeks without food, but only a short time without water. If you are doing a loop route you can stash a water supply to be used on the return trip. If you are not certain that a water source is available then pack in the water you might need. Be sure you will have enough to stay hydrated the entire time you plan to be gone. Cattle and wildlife often frequent the scarce water sources, and giardia, cryptosporidium and other harmful bacteria can present a problem if water is not properly filtered or purified before consumption.

Spectra Ramp

Spot, GPS and Cell Phones

Spot, GPS units and cell phones do not work everywhere, especially in canyons. Bring extra batteries for the GPS and make sure phones are fully charged and turned off when not in use. Roaming uses more battery power than usual and your batteries might be dead once you are able to use the device. Many areas may not have cell coverage, but a phone can often help. The new emergency beacon devices, such as the SPOT, might be worth looking into and are some times very effective.

Possibles Plan

Leave a detailed description of your intended route, when you plan to be back and whom to contact in case you do not return when expected. Gauge your hiking and rest stops throughout the day to allow ample time for your return hike.

GPS Coordinates

Coordinates given in this book are only references and may or may not be accurate. Do not rely on GPS coordinates as the sole method of navigation. Always have a compass and a detailed map at hand. Practice proper map-reading and navigation skills before you embark on a difficult route. Many of the hikes listed in this guide travel into canyons where a GPS or Spot may have limited capabilities. Always check your position on a map before dropping into a canyon or attempting to locate a difficult location. The coordinate system we use is in degrees and decimal minutes in WGS84 datum. Online sites exist that can change this to your preferred datum.

Maps

While the maps in this book have been checked and were up-to-date at publishing, trails and routes can change over time due to natural occurrences.

TIME

The times listed are an average. Individuals may well go faster or slower. Experienced hikers maintain a moderate, steady pace throughout a hike. Beginners rush, get tired, then slow down and need extra rest breaks. In summer, begin hikes early in the day when it's cooler and in winter make sure to plan carefully so you return to your vehicle before dark.

CLOTHING

Wear sun-protective clothing that prevents sunburn, yet still breathes and allows comfort whether wet or dry. Using a layering system of lighter pieces rather than one thick layer allows for temperature changes through the day. Cotton clothing stays wet a long time and act as a evaporative cooler, which is tolerable if it's hot, but can be dangerous when it's cold. Hiking in wet cotton clothing can cause chafing. Modern synthetic clothes generally dry rapidly and make chafing less of a concern. Carry emergency clothing in the event your hike is unexpectedly extended. Study the weather report for the area that you will be hiking and use clothing that is appropriate.

SHOES

Good footwear is a must. Just as the tires on your vehicle are built for varying conditions, so is footwear for hikers. Many rescues in Zion are due to people slipping and falling. Choose shoes with sticky rubber that are suited for hiking on slick surfaces. Don't expect to buy shoes in the morning and use them in the afternoon for hiking. Be sure to give them several "test rides" so you know they will perform the way you want them to.

SOCKS

Buy and wear socks designed for hiking; they keep feet drier and help prevent blisters by wicking sweat away from your feet and reducing friction.

LOST AND FOUND

Always head out prepared to spend the night in case something unexpected happens. If you have your Possibles Bag and have set up your Possibles Plan, then everything should be alright. If you do become lost, remain calm, sit down and consult the trail description, map and compass that you brought along. Consider your situation. Do you know how to make it back to the last point where you did know where you were? How far away is it? Finding you is easier the closer you are to where you were supposed to be. If you have no idea where you are, then stay put and wait for

rescue and keep your group together. Use your signal mirror and whistle. If you know where you are but have run out of daylight, be calm, you have your headlamp in your Possibles Bag. Attempting to follow an off-the-beaten-path can be difficult or impossible at night. Never attempt to navigate dangerous terrain in the dark. Use your bivy sack and stay where you are until morning light. Stay warm and hydrated. Keep in mind, the more you eat, the more water it takes for your body to process it.

FLASH FLOODS

Do not camp in washes, or hike in a canyon if it is raining or it looks like rain is imminent. Also realize that an upstream storm can cause a flood many hours later, downsteam. Avoid crossing drainages with heavy water flow and do not park in potential flash-flood areas. Flash floods do occur in "dry" washes as well as those holding water.

Flash floods are just what the words describe, floods that appear in a "FLASH." Remember that water rarely rises slowly, but generally comes at once, resembling a "wall" of water. There may be little or no time to scramble to the safety of high ground. Watch the weather and be patient. The canyon will be there tomorrow, but if you make a wrong decision you may not be. Before starting a canyon hike, study the map; look for cloud build up around the catchment area upstream of the canyon.

MONSOON SEASON

Flash floods usually occur during the Southwest's monsoon season (from June until the end of September). Check weather reports for expected conditions. Watch daily cloud accumulation: if afternoon thunderclouds build up one day, there is a good chance they will do so the next day. Hikers need to avoid being caught by lightning strikes and flash floods caused by these afternoon storms.

Expect the Unexpected

Whatever weather reports predict, the desert still has a mind of its own. One year we hiked to Zion's Crawford Arch (page 47) in the month of June. This is a route that is best done in spring, but plans forced us to go later, when it is generally too hot. The morning began warm, but unexpectedly, the weather got steadily cooler during this long hike, and by the end, temperatures were frigid. Some in our party were prepared with rain gear and stayed dry and warm, but others, not so equipped, became dangerously cold. Make sure to take rain gear if there is even the slightest chance of precipitation.

Winter Hiking

Southern Utah and northern Arizona winters are exquisite. Swirls of rock meander with pockets of brilliant white snow and swelling storms fill blue skies with puffs of gray clouds, an ideal backdrop for dramatic photography. Rivers and streams are usually fuller in the winter and there are often waterfalls that exist at no other time of the year.

Although this is beautiful, it does add danger to hiking. Be careful, watch for patches of snow, ice and mud along the routes. Moss on rock can be dangerous at any time, but it is particularly treacherous and slippery in the winter when it is cold and frozen. Be aware that ice on high canyon walls will thunder down below where you are when the sun hits it and it begins to melt. In the winter stay even farther away from a cliff edge than you would feel safe in the summer. Moisture results in unstable rock. If hiking on snowy and icy paths wear crampons or some type of ice traction. Make sure your footwear insulates you from the cold and the wet. Be sure to leave plenty of time to finish your hike: a forced bivy in winter will feel endlessly long and be desperately cold.

Summer Hiking

Stay in the shade when resting—and even hiking when possible—to reduce the effect the sun has on you. Wear a ventilated hat and keep skin covered in loose, cool, light-colored clothing. Consume plenty of water and high-energy foods. Wear and reapply sunscreen as needed.

Water Sources

Keep water sources free of contamination. Do not bathe or wash dishes directly in a water source. Giardiasis is a dangerous microorganism in water that causes digestive upset, fatigue and dehydration. Purify all water: the most foolproof method is to boil water a minimum of two minutes, at a hard boil; otherwise, use a water filter or treat water with iodine or chlorine.

Dehydration

Carry enough water to stay hydrated even in the colder winter months. Utah and Arizona have arid climates and you will require lots of water. Be sure to have a cooler of liquids in your vehicle for after your hike. Know the signs and symptoms of dehydration.

Hyperthermia and Hypothermia

Hyperthermia (heatstroke) arises from overheating the body's core. Hypothermia is a condition where the body's core temperature is chilled. Study basic survival; know the signs and symptoms of both conditions and how to prevent them, and what to do in case they occur. Both conditions can produce lethargy, stumbling gait, confusion. Watch for such signs in other members of your party—and yourself. Be aware that by the time obvious symptoms arise, you are facing a serious medical emergency.

Snake Bites

Most importantly, keep the patient calm and get them to an emergency care facility as quickly as possible. Study the most current method of treating a snake bite; medical advice has changed over time. Don't try to extract venom. Keep the affected limb or part of the body below the heart if possible. If it can be done safely, kill the snake and bring it to the treatment facility for identification for appropriate antivenom selection.

Altitude Issues

Elevations of hikes in this book range from around 2,500 feet to 11,000 feet. When you hike at higher elevations (such as the Cedar Breaks plateau) and you are not use to it you might become surprisingly short of breath. A few days of acclimatization can make a big difference.

Cliffs

Stay away from cliff edges, keep hold of children when near edges, and stay on trails. Stone surfaces can be slippery and unstable. Extra caution should be taken near waterfalls, where rocks can be polished, mossy or wet and therefore very slippery.

Pests

Deer flies and gnats can be annoying along these hikes. Protect yourself against them and mosquitoes by using insect repellants and, if necessary, nets.

Dangerous Animals

Many species of birds, mammals and reptiles make their homes in the desert. Most species are generally docile; however they are wild and need to be respected. Snakes, mountain lions, tarantulas and scorpions are common, but humans seldom encounter them. Be aware of where you step, sit, or place your hands so you do not disturb a resting animal. Do not attempt to approach wildlife. Don't feed wild animals; they will learn to expect food from humans and can become aggressive when begging.

DANGEROUS PLANTS

Know which plants are dangerous in the area you are hiking and avoid touching them. Some are poisonous: among others, be wary of poison ivy and datura. Many other desert plants are spiky, particularly cacti.

PERMITS

Permits are usually required for camping and technical slot canyons. Requirements, correct for 2012, are given for each route in this book. Look online for up-to-date information. Wilderness permits for Zion National Park may be obtained in advance by logging on to the park website:

http://www.nps.gov/zion/planyourvisit/back-country-reservations-and-permits.htm

CAMPING

Always practice minimum-impact camping. If possible, make camp in an established campsite at least 200 yards from water. If there is not a site nearby then find a sandy or slickrock area with few plants. Refrain from making new trails around the campsite area and don't stay in one place too long. Even if campfires are allowed where you are camping use a backpacking stove for cooking. If you must make a fire, camouflage any signs of it before breaking camp. Repackage food and supplies to reduce trash and bring a trash bag, always packing out more than you pack in. Leave your site as clean and clear as possible. The organization "Leave No Trace" has a website with detailed, up-to-date information and suggestions on these and other ways to keep wild areas as pristine as possible:

http://www.lnt.org/programs/principles.php

Suggestions: Take extreme care with fires and stoves so you do not start a wildfire. Follow all posted rules for each particular area. Have enough gear and clothing to stay comfortably warm (or cool).

CANYONEERING

Slot canyons, in recent years, have gained enormous popularity. Please don't take slot canyons lightly. These watershed "avenues" rarely remain consistent in nature; monsoon rains, spring runoff and sudden, random rainstorms each send massive volumes of water through these drainages, bringing new debris, moving boulders and

logs, causing slot canyons to change frequently.

Never enter a technical canyon without the equipment, knowledge and skills needed to safely explore and return. Rappelling and down-climbing skills are required to navigate through many slot canyons. Do not jump! Jumping in canyons has resulted in broken bones, and rescues in slot canyons can be tricky. Excellent map-reading skills may be needed to locate the correct slot canyon.

EQUIPMENT FOR CANYONEERING

Technical slot canyons usually require specialized equipment: rope, harness, rappel device, carabiners, webbing and other gear. Specific needs are noted for each canyon described in this book.

Slot canyons often require crossing pools of water. These may be merely ankle-deep, or they might require swimming. Often the the depth is impossible to discern until you climb in. Long stretches of water might be encountered. Cold water may require that you wear a wetsuit or a drysuit. This may vary by season: wading a wet canyon in midsummer can be a welcome break from the heat, but in winter can be a fast way to get hypothermia. A wetsuit is cheaper and holds up better to the rugged demands of canyons but is heavier to carry. Specific needs are detailed in the relevant sections of this book.

When hiking in wet areas with a rope, special packs that drain rapidly are nice to have. You will also need a waterproof "dry bag" to keep extra clothing, maps, compass, GPS and other items dry.

ENVIRONMENTAL AWARENESS

Tread lightly; the desert is fragile and takes much longer to rebound than temperate forested landscape. Fragile rock, if broken, will never repair itself. Leave a wide berth around vegetation in sensitive sandstone gardens. Cryptobiotic-capped soil is nature's way of binding loose, sandy earth together and providing a foundation for fragile vegetation to take root. When possible, avoid disturbing this black crust and turning the "crust to dust." Stay on beaten paths and trails and always look for the path previously taken: there will be one if the route is in this book. If no trail is apparent, try to hike on hard, rock surfaces, rather than softer sand. Always aim to leave the desert as you found it.

Piles of rocks, known as cairns, can be useful along a route to keep hikers on a faint path so they do not get lost or trample the land. However, when overused they ruin the enjoyment of nature and the challenge of following a path. It's best to stay somewhere in the middle, keep cairns to a minimum, but do use them to avoid confusion.

DRIVING

Many of the routes described are not accessed from paved roads. Some trailheads are reachable with a regular high-clearance 2WD, but a 4WD is needed to get to other destinations in this book. Individual recommendations are noted in each section.

Dirt roads can become impassible when wet. They can become wet from rain, but less predictably, on a warm, dry day, melting snow may saturate the driving surface. Leave all gates as you found them and do not travel on property that is posted as private without the landowner's permission. Never drive in areas posted for no motor vehicles.

Make sure your vehicle is in good repair when traveling in remote areas. If you do break down, raise your hood and stay near your vehicle with your emergency water and food. Be sure of your skills before attempting to drive in deep sand, on slickrock, in mud or other difficult types of situations.

Cross streams with caution. Deep crossings require maintaining momentum while not creating too much of a bow wave (which can flood the air intake or electrical components and stall the engine). Get out and wade the creek first, to ascertain its depth and locate deeper holes or ruts to avoid.

Always pack the vehicle for emergencies. Keep the following in your vehicle: plenty of gas, spare tire, shovel, headlamp, air pump, jumper cables, rope, as well as whatever tools are needed to change a tire, get unstuck and perform minor vehicle repairs. For yourself, bring plenty of water and food, and overnight gear.

Bighorn sheep are a common sight along SR-9 (the Zion-Mt. Carmel Highway) on the east side of Zion National Park. Please drive slowly to avoid hitting these elegant creatures, and so you do not run into other vehicles that have stopped in the midde of the road due to a bighorn sheep sighting.

Labyrinth Falls

HISTORICAL SITES, CULTURAL RESOURCES AND ROCK ART

Do not disturb historical sites. On your travels you may stumble on historic artifacts—arrowheads, corn cobs, pottery shards, etc. There should never be any sign of your trek other than your footsteps. Federal law gives protection to such artifacts, particularly within our parks and monuments.

Please educate yourself and help to teach others to protect ancient forms of communication and artwork such as pictographs and petroglyphs. Please respect the outdoor museums of our public lands in the same way that you would an indoor museum.

Rock art is fragile! If you know of any vandalism to rock art, call the Archaeological Resources Protection hot line at 1.800.227.7286.

Don't touch rock art—Never make rubbings or touch the art with your hands. The oil from our bodies and the impact from touching rock art will cause damage.

Don't make a fire within a mile of any rock-art site. Smoke does cause damage. Report any sign of fire near rock art.

Do not camp near any rock-art site.

Don't dig near or climb above rock art.

The greatest danger to rock art is people!

WILDERNESS AND PUBLIC LANDS

Protect it, love it and most of all—do no harm. Pack out what you bring in. That includes toilet paper. Bring a trash bag with you for this purpose. Do not leave human waste on or near trails and never leave it near a water source. If you must leave waste, use a cat-hole 8 inches deep and at least 200 feet from any water, campsite or trail. On the trail, avoid building cairns and other markers. Let faster parties pass, and visit canyons in small groups. Never feed wild animals, pick them up, or chase them. When hiking in canyons, stay in the watercourse when possible to prevent land erosion.

Leave no trace.

"Take only pictures, leave only footprints, carve only memories."

Look for updates on our website:
www.zionnational-park.com

Bo Beck hiking the Many Pools route

Zion National Park

Zion National Park sits in a spectacular corner of southern Utah; a masterpiece of hiking and backpacking routes set amid towering cliffs, massive monoliths, mesas, buttes and deep, red canyons. Millions of outdoor enthusiasts flock to the park to enjoy slot canyons, daring trails and to backpack along the rim. In and around the park, you can explore low- and high deserts, waterfalls, sandstone wilderness, the river's lush riparian terrain as well as impressive, towering cliffs. Some of the best trails in the world are found here.

This "playground" is nestled in a serene setting full of protected secrets where you can take note of the small things and appreciate the delicacy of nature: observe fragile butterflies fluttering about, listen to the canyon tree frog's trilling song as it echoes through the canyon, and pay attention to the rush of the Virgin River that carved Zion Canyon. In this mosaic of monoliths and sandstone there are quiet places, unpeopled sanctuaries of stone. Some are in Zion Canyon, others are just off the road on the east side of the park, and many are in the elusive backcountry. This sanctuary has hidden secrets and even though the canyon itself is usually alive with activity, there are many places that few footprints will touch on any given day.

Getting There

Zion National Park is located on SR-9. There are two nearby towns: bustling Springdale, just outside the south entrance and peaceful Mt. Carmel Junction, 12 miles from the east entrance. See map, next page, for more details. Area map is on page 7.

Routes in Zion National Park

You can experience heights and panoramic vistas few Zion visitors ever see as we take you to the spectacular viewpoints on Angels Landing, Lady Mountain and Checkerboard Mesa. Then we will lead you to one of our favorite, easier, technical slot canyons: Orderville Canyon. We will also introduce you to the classic beauty of Emerald Pools and little-known routes such as Cockeye Falls, East Temple Saddle, Many Pools, The East Rim, Double Falls and Shelf Canyon.

Exploring canyons can begin at an early age: Gordon and Trey Milligan, Orderville Canyon, page 28

One of Zion's spectacular arches: Crawford Arch on Bridge Mountain, page 47

FREESTANDING ARCHES IN ZION

This magnificent park is known for its towering monoliths that surround and define Zion Canyon, but the most famous landmark of all is the world's second-longest arch, Kolob Arch. Other Zion arches are less well known, but they do display a dramatic variety of shapes and sizes, and there is nowhere on earth where arches are framed by such stunning beauty—the hikes to these natural wonders are some of the finest in the park. Eight of the 20 hikes in this chapter visit one of Zion's spectacular natural arches.

Some arches, like Two Pines Arch, can be reached by a short, family-friendly hike while others are more difficult to get to, like the one in Zion's famous Subway. Many require hiking off the beaten path, such as Checkerboard Arch, Jughandle Arch, Hepworth Arch and the magnificent Crawford Arch.

Note: Arches and bridges are formed in different ways. A natural arch is created by geological forces causing rock to fall away, leaving the arch structure standing. When sandstone blocks fall, they explode or crumble leaving little trace of their existence. A natural bridge, on the other hand, is formed by running water in a vertically-sided, winding canyon. If a bend in the canyon is sharp enough (a "gooseneck" shaped meander) that cliffs are surrounded on three sides by the creek, the water may erode a passage through to the other side of this projecting fin, leaving a natural bridge. Further, continued erosion by the watercourse can eventually leave the bridge high and dry.

A feature of both arches and bridges is that once they are formed, erosion continues, under and around the formations. This erosion enlarges and deepens the span and, over time, the resulting structure, made of stone yet seemingly floating weightless in the sky, defies belief.

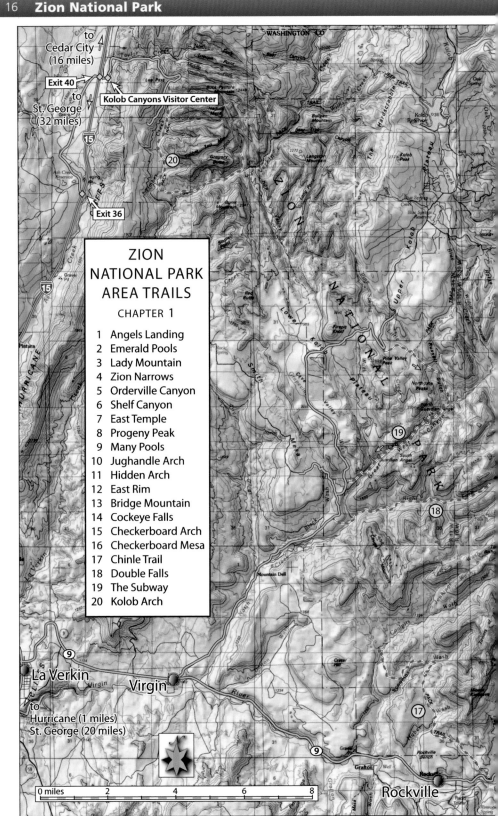

to
Cedar City
(16 miles)

Exit 40

to
St. George
(32 miles)

Kolob Canyons Visitor Center

Exit 36

La Verkin

Virgin

to
Hurricane (1 miles)
St. George (20 miles)

Rockville

0 miles   2   4   6   8

Angels Landing ①

While exploring Zion in 1916, Frederick Fisher exclaimed of one precipitous landmark, "Only an angel could land on it," and this pinnacle was henceforth named Angels Landing. This towering monolith is one of the most recognizable landmarks in the Southwest, and the trail to the summit, the Angels Landing Trail, is one of the most famous and thrilling hikes in the world.

Zion's pride and joy runs along a narrow rock fin with dizzying drop-offs on both sides. The trail culminates at a lofty perch, boasting magnificent views in every direction. Rarely is such an intimidating path so frequented by hikers. One would think that this narrow ridge with deep chasms on each of its flanks would tempt only the most intrepid of hikers. Climbers scale its big wall, hikers pull themselves up by chains and sightseers stand in awe at its stunning nobility.

—————— At a Glance ——————

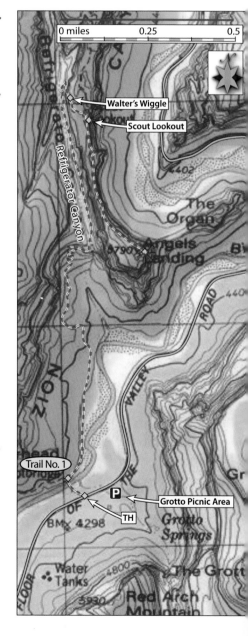

Day Hike: Yes.
Distance: 5-mile round-trip.
Average Hiking Time: 5 hours.
Difficulty: This is a strenuous, uphill hike, but on a well-maintained trail. Some sections, especially toward the end, are narrow with long, exposed drop-offs. There are some safety chains in the most precarious areas.
Equipment: A map to locate the landmarks surrounding Angels Landing, sticky-rubber-soled shoes, 2–3 quarts of water per person, energy snacks and sun-protective clothing.
Sun Exposure: Full sun in most places.
Permits: Not required.
Trail Conditions: The last half-mile traverses a narrow sandstone ridge above sheer cliffs. This trail is not ideal for children or those with a fear of heights. Do not hike the trail when it is wet, storming, or when high winds are present. The first 2 miles are well-maintained. Most of the path is sunny, but Refrigerator Canyon offers shade and often a cool breeze. This is a good early-morning hike. Be sure to allow time to be off the trail by dark if starting late in the day.
Trailhead: Grotto picnic area in Zion Canyon.
Trailend: Same as trailhead.
Trail Access: Year-round, either by the Zion Canyon Shuttle or by private vehicle when the shuttle is not running.
Best Season: March to October, but can be hiked year round as long as the trail is free of ice and snow.
Elevation Gain: 1,500 feet.
Summit Elevation: 5,790 feet.
Restrooms: Scout Lookout at the Angels Landing junction and at the Grotto Picnic area.

① ANGELS LANDING TRAIL DETAILS

WEST RIM TRAIL - Start at the Grotto Picnic area, cross Zion Canyon Road and head to the footbridge that crosses the North Fork of the Virgin River. On the other side of the bridge, take the north (right) fork to the West Rim Trail. This busy path travels through a riparian woodland of cottonwoods, pinyon pines and junipers. Next is a steady, 2-mile trek ascending switchbacks up the steep West Rim Trail. Much of the path hugs the side of the sun-baked mountain, offering an outstanding vista of a shimmering river, billowy cottonwood trees and a rich collection of stone. A few ambitious trees emerge tenaciously from cracks high on the sheer cliff, adding flecks of green to rock faces stained by iron oxide and desert varnish.

REFRIGERATOR CANYON - Just over a mile in, hikers get a reprieve from the constant, steep grade of the West Rim Trail and the blazing heat of the full sun. The path turns toward a gap between Angels Landing and Cathedral Mountain. A cool breeze blows through the shady canyon leading to its name: Refrigerator Canyon. In the cooler climate of this ravine, vegetation is more abundant.

WALTER'S WIGGLES - Just before the trail spills onto Scout Lookout, it's time to "squiggle the wiggles," as they ascend 21 steep, sharp zigzags. Walter's Wiggles was named after the first superintendent of Zion, who helped engineer this steep switchback section. The park was in its planning stages at this time and this section of trail was designed to enable horses to access Cabin Spring. His home, known now as the Worthington Gallery, still stands in Springdale.

SCOUT LOOKOUT - The Wiggles ascend to a broad, sandy area called Scout Lookout. This saddle marks the junction of the Angels Landing Trail and West Rim Trail. The views down into Zion Canyon from this vantage point are impressive. West Rim Trail continues north past Cabin Spring to Lava Point in the Kolob Terrace section of Zion, but the Angels Landing Trail turns southeast.

ANGELS LANDING - Navigate the next half-mile along a narrow sandstone isthmus with sheer cliffs on both sides. The precarious and arduous trail drops 1,200 feet on one side and 800 feet on the other. Chipmunks scurry carelessly along the ridge, finding bits of shade under the few trees that have found a weakness in which to burrow their roots. The summit offers incomparable, fairytale views. Almost 1,500 feet below, the Virgin River winds around the Organ. The Great White Throne seems only a stone's throw away. Northeast, across the canyon is Observation Point and to the east is Cable Mountain. Look closely to see the preserved cable-works structure on Cable Mountain.

Bo Beck eyeing up the final stretch of the Angels Landing Trail. The trail ascends the sunlit ridge

Emerald Pools ②

Emerald Pools is one of Zion's sweetest signature trails. Generously endowed with breathtaking scenery, this trail is one that children and adults alike will have fun hiking. Waterfalls, pools and a dazzling display of monoliths create the Emerald Pools Trail System. The trail was completed in 1925 and named for the green tint the algae gives the three pools. The pools and waterfalls are the attraction here, but the surrounding scenery is outstanding as well. The easy hiking along the Lower Emerald Pool Trail is a treat for kids and nice for parents pushing a stroller.

At a Glance

Day Hike: Yes.

Distance: 3-mile round-trip.

 To the Lower Pool: 0.6 miles one-way; 30 minutes; 69-foot ascent.

 To the Middle Pools: 0.8 miles one-way; 45 minutes; 150-foot ascent.

 To the Upper Pool: 1.5 miles one-way; 1.5 hours; 350-foot ascent.

 Kayenta Trail: 1 mile one-way; 1 hour; 150-foot ascent.

Accessible Trail: The Lower Emerald Pool Trail is nice for wheelchairs and strollers.

Equipment: Comfortable hiking shoes, water and sun-protection.

Difficulty: The Lower Pool Trail is paved and easy, ascending to the Upper Pool gets steep and is moderately strenuous.

Sun Exposure: This partially shaded path can be hiked comfortably throughout the day.

Permits: Not required.

Trail Conditions: Well maintained. Lower trail: paved until the ascent to Middle and Upper Pools. Kayenta Trail is dirt and rock.

Trailhead: Footbridge across the road from the Zion Lodge.

Trailend: Exiting on the Lower Emerald Pools Trail leads to Zion Lodge. The Kayenta Trail exit leads to the Grotto Picnic area.

Trail Access: When the shuttle is running, ride it and get off at Zion Lodge. The rest of the year, drive into Zion Canyon and park at the Emerald Pools parking lot

Best Season: Year-round.

Off the Beaten Path: No, this is a popular trail.

Restrooms: Zion Lodge and Grotto picnic area.

Water Availability: Water bottles can be filled at the Grotto picnic area or the Zion Lodge.

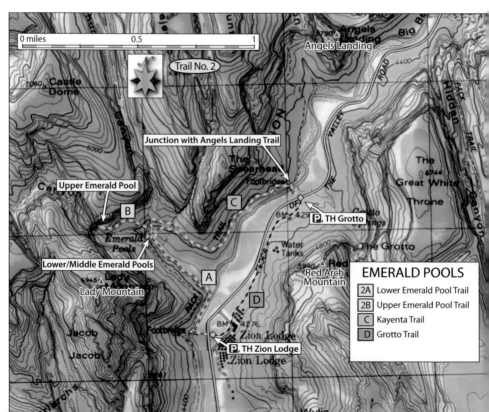

EMERALD POOLS

2A	Lower Emerald Pool Trail
2B	Upper Emerald Pool Trail
C	Kayenta Trail
D	Grotto Trail

② EMERALD POOLS DETAILS

LOWER EMERALD POOL - At the trailhead, follow the paved trail. Much of this trail is shaded by cottonwood and boxelder trees as it winds along the North Fork of the Virgin River. It's just over a half-mile to the lush alcove of Lower Emerald Pool. Moisture seeps from the sandstone and mist sprays from the falls, feeding lush hanging gardens in the recessed rock. Ferns and moss sprout from the mountainside with an occasional monkey flower, shooting star or columbine peering from more subtle vegetation. The trail ducks behind twin waterfalls; these spill from the Middle Pools, leaving black streaks of desert varnish. Droplets dance off boulders that have fallen from above, now lining the pool of mossy green water.

MIDDLE EMERALD POOLS - To access the Middle Emeral Pools, continue behind the falls on the Lower Emerald Pool Trail. The now-unpaved trail emerges into sunlight, leading toward the Middle Pools. A couple short switchbacks ascend nearly100 feet to the plateau holding the Middle Pools.

Note: The once-popular Middle Emerald Pools Trail is now closed due to a 2010 landslide and continuing instability.

At the Middle Pools, shallow streams cross the trail before the water spills over the lip to the Lower Pool. The first Middle Pool is formed by the Behunin Canyon watershed—one of Zion's drier canyoneering routes. Next, just over the ridge, the second Middle Pool is created by the Heaps Canyon drainage—one of Zion's most difficult canyoneering routes. After a storm, when water is flowing in Heaps Canyon and Behunin Canyon, the waterfalls become profuse. Watch that children don't stray near the overhanging edge beyond the chained areas, where algae and slippery rock create unsafe footing.

Waterfall into Upper Emerald Pool, with heavy winter runoff, viewed from the Kayenta Trail

A gallery of Zion landmarks is on display, and Red Arch Mountain is center stage. Lady Mountain towers almost 3,000 feet above the canyon floor. The route up this was one of the original trails in Zion Canyon. In the 1970s the park deemed this "via ferrata" overly hazardous, disassembled the chains and ladders, and stopped promoting it. However, the route to this magnificent summit can still be ascended, and is described on page 22. Looking north, glimpses of Mount Majestic and Cathedral Mountain can be seen.

UPPER EMERALD POOL TRAIL - The trail leading to the Upper Emerald Pool is on the ridge between the two Middle Pools. Most of the foot traffic ends at the spur to the Upper Pool (where the trail becomes more rugged and steep), but the Upper Pool at the end is worth every step. This secluded oasis is framed by colossal cliffs on three sides. Watch for canyoneers rappelling from Heaps Canyon down the backside of the boulder-rimmed pool.

RETURN - Backtrack to the Middle Pools. From here, return, via the Lower Emerald Pool Trail, to the lodge or follow the Kayenta Trail (see below) to the Grotto.

KAYENTA TRAIL OPTION - This trail provides an option for a loop hike (see map). The Kayenta Trail begins from the Grotto, a half-mile upstream from the lodge, and heads to the Emerald Pools. If the shuttle bus is running, you can easily start at the Lodge and finish at the Grotto. If exiting via the Kayenta Trail after the shuttles have shut down and your vehicle is parked at the lodge, follow the half-mile Grotto Trail back to the lodge.

Lady Mountain ③

Pioneers named most of the beautiful, lofty monoliths nestled within Zion Canyon long ago. Lady Mountain, towering above the Emerald Pools, was named for a supposed likeness to a female figure. At the Emerald Pools Trailhead, locate the blind arch near the top of the towering white monolith. Can you find the figure of a woman near the arch?

The now-obscure route to the summit of this Zion landmark was once a popular and maintained trail equipped with chains and other safety devices, much like those still found along the popular Angels Landing Trail. Completed in 1924, this amazing ascent up the steep mountainside was one of the first trails constructed by the park. Imagine adventurous women of the 1920s—in heels and long dresses—trudging up the route, leaving the roar of Zion's dramatic river-carved canyon far below, making their way to the lofty summit.

These days, the hardware is gone and this remarkable trip is not advertised by the park—but the route is as dramatic as ever. As you ascend, the blaring speakers from the commercial horse-riding concession fade and are replaced by the quieter sounds of nature. The never-ending stairway takes hikers up a seemingly impossible route—to finally reach the mountaintop after hours of breathtaking and diverse ascent.

At a Glance

Trail Distance: 2.6 miles one-way, and a 5.2-mile round-trip (which includes a portion of the now defunct Middle Emerald Pools Trail).

Average Hiking Time: 5–8 hours.

Difficulty: There are three short sections of technical climbing (up to 5.7), so at least one experienced climber needs to be in the group.

Sun Exposure: Full sun, most of the day, therefore carry plenty of water.

Permits: Not required.

Trail Conditions: This is a narrow trail with high-altitude drop-offs and technical climbing or scrambling sections (including several steep pitches) up to 5.7. Bring an 80-foot rope, and be sure you have the skills to use it.

Trailhead: When the shuttle is operating, take it to the Zion Lodge stop. The rest of the year, drive into the canyon and park at the Emerald Pools parking area. Use the footbridge to cross the Virgin River, then begin the hike up the Lower Emerald Pools Trail.

Best Season: This route should not be attempted in the winter. Depending on weather, March through October are usually good times to go. If you hike in the summer, begin early and complete as much of the route as you can in the cooler times of the day.

Elevation: Total elevation gain is 2,675 feet in 2.6 miles. Once you begin the ascent up the mountain, you will climb 2,345 feet in just 1.4 miles.

Summit Elevation: 6,945 feet.

Off the Beaten Path: Yes.

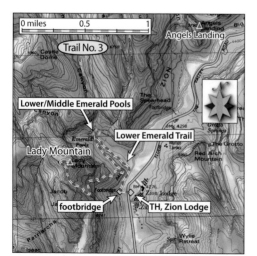

Tanya Milligan on Lady Mountain. Photo: Bo Beck

③ LADY MOUNTAIN DETAILS

TRAILHEAD - From the lodge, follow the Lower Emerald Pools Trail to the Middle Pools. At the southern-most pool there is a barrier thwarting hikers from continuing on the now-closed Middle Emerald Pools Trail. (This trail was damaged in a 2010 landslide and sections are still unstable). As of May 2012, the park has made a decision to allow hikers that wish to ascend Lady Mountain to continue beyond this barrier; however, hikers do so at their own risk. From the barrier, follow the now-unmaintained "trail" for 0.4 miles. You will cross a section of slide and soon you will see the footbridge below. A bit farther, around a corner, is a slight uphill rise and there should still be a sign or two on the trail's edge. About 20 yards before the signs, on the right, is a pinyon tree; just up and right from this is a pair of trees, a juniper and a pinyon. Locate a faint path that ascends steeply between these trees. Follow this as it steepens, then traverses right and then left. Soon, this rock and dirt path reaches the first cliffband. From here on, the journey ahead of you will ascend 2,345 feet in only 1.4 miles. You will be required to navigate slippery slopes and do a bit of technical climbing. There are moki steps (chiseled stairs) carved into the rock that make some uphill sections easier. One long set is dubbed the "Endless Staircase." Watch for faint arrows painted on the rocks; these will help you navigate the route.

OBSTACLES - The first obstacle is found just after the initial cliffband. A right-facing corner requires a 30-foot climb, made easier by carved "moki" steps. Due to the exposure, a rope belay or hand-line is strongly suggested. A rope will also be needed at the next obstacle—the chimney. This has an overhanging, 8-foot boulder move, rated at 5.3 YDS (Yosemite Decimal System). It is found a little less than 1.0 mile into the as-cent. The best climber in your group should take the rope up the unprotected section where they will find a rebar eyelet anchor. They can then belay less-experienced climbers—the exposure on this move is about 80 feet and the consequences of a slip could be severe. The third place a rope is needed is at a right-facing, 12-foot-high, off-width crack. This is a difficult section and is rated at 5.7 YDS. There is a ledge on top to belay from. Use a rope in the same three locations on the way back down. Beyond the right-facing off-width, the route becomes easier, with some 3rd- and easy 4th-class scrambling.

SUMMIT SECTION – Once past a short "V-slot," go north through the dense vegetation; a beaten path heads toward a precariously perched rock outcropping, where panoramas of the rims unfold. This scramble around the western side of the mountain reveals views of Isaac and Abraham. From here, stroll through a sandy clearing to a breathtaking vista: Zion literally opens up in front of you. In the far-southeast corner of the mountaintop is a human-made circular disc atop a rocky perch. This "compass" labels the cornucopia of peaks—the most delightful display of rock in the park. On a clear day the unobstructed 360-degree view allows you to see as far away as the Arizona Strip. North is Angels Landing, just beyond, Observation Point. To the east, locate Red Arch Mountain and the Great White Throne. To the south look for both East and West Temples, Deer Trap Mountain, Mountain of the Sun, and the Three Patriarchs.

Looking south from Lady Mountain's summit to the flat top of West Temple. The "compass" labels the peaks

GPS Coordinates
WGS84 Datum

Beginning off of the Middle Emerald Pool Trail
37°15.143 N, 112°57.553 W
First Cliffband and Start of Scrambling
37°15.174 N, 112°57.637 W

5.3 Chimney Problem
37°15.144 N, 112°57.792 W

5.7 Corner Crack Problem
37°15.061 N, 112°57.803 W

ZION NARROWS - VIRGIN RIVER NARROWS ④

Trekking through Zion's premier canyon, the Virgin River Narrows, is one of the most famou and breathtaking adventures in America. Extraordinary beauty and unique character describe this amazing gorge. Hanging gardens burst from dramatically colored precipices. Trickling water threads its way through moss-covered boulders on its journey southward. Gentle slope give way to sheer walls that funnel streams of water into fluted slides and twisting channels that cut deeper and deeper, year by year. Along the sandy perches of the banks, towering ponderosas send their roots downward, hungry for nutrients and water. The trip is wondrous—the Zion Narrows deserves its reputation as one of the best, if not THE best hike in the entire National Park System.

As a bonus, this hike passes by one of the rare Zion National Park arches. This one is a massive jug-handle-shaped arch, high on the canyon wall, just a couple of miles in.

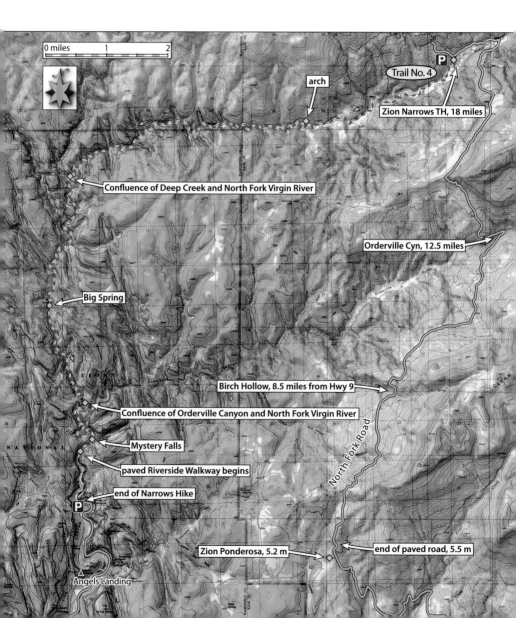

0 miles   1   2

arch

Trail No. 4

Zion Narrows TH, 18 miles

Confluence of Deep Creek and North Fork Virgin River

Orderville Cyn, 12.5 miles

Big Spring

Birch Hollow, 8.5 miles from Hwy 9

Confluence of Orderville Canyon and North Fork Virgin River

Mystery Falls

North Fork Road

paved Riverside Walkway begins

end of Narrows Hike

Zion Ponderosa, 5.2 m

end of paved road, 5.5 m

NATIONAL

Angels Landing

AT A GLANCE

Day Hike: The Narrows can be done as a long day-hike or as a relaxed overnight trip.

Distance: 16 miles.

Average Hiking Time: 13 hours. River hiking is arduous and time consuming; don't underestimate your time.

Equipment: Dry bags, sticky-rubber canyoneering shoes, neoprene socks, a pair of trekking poles (hiking with just a single stick is not as effective), emergency supplies, plenty of water, and bivy equipment. If camping bring overnight gear.

Difficulty: This is a strenuous route due to the demands of river hiking, slippery rocks and swift water crossings; however, the profile is a gentle downhill trek. Swimming is often required for short sections. Water current and volume is season-dependent, with the highest flow usually in spring and lowest in summer and fall.

Sun Exposure: Intermittent shade and sun. It's shady where canyon walls block the sun.

Permits: For the one-day, through-hike, Narrows trip, the current limit is 40 people per day. Of these, 24 spaces are available for reservations, 16 for the last-minute drawing and any remaining spaces are available for walk-ins. For backpackers, there are 12 designated sites; 6 for reservation, 6 for walk-ins. For reservation and permit information log onto the park's website (see web link info on page 27).

Note: Hikers are allowed to hike up the Narrows from the paved Riverside Walkway as far as Big Spring and return without a permit (as long as the riverflow has been less than 150cfs for the previous 24 hours).

Trail Conditions: Most of the route requires hiking in the river. There will be swift water and slippery rocks, but there are also some sandy and beaten paths on the side of the river that offer short reprieves. Be sure to check the weather and river flow before starting this hike, as flash floods can, and do, happen; a heavy current makes travel tedious and dangerous. The park will not issue permits unless the river is and has been flowing less than 120cfs (cubic feet per second) near Springdale for the previous 24 hours.

Trailhead: Chamberlain's Ranch, just off North Fork Road on the east side of the park. It's best to have a 4WD to navigate the dirt road to the trailhead, but high-clearance 2WD is adequate if the road is dry. Commercial shuttles can be rented that leave from Springdale or the east side of the park.

Trailend: The route ends at the Riverside Walk, at the Temple of Sinawava in Zion Canyon. From early spring until mid-fall, ride the Zion Canyon Shuttle from there to your vehicle, parked at the Zion Canyon Visitor Center (or in Springdale). From mid-fall until early spring you can drive all the way into the canyon and park at the Temple of Sinawava parking lot.

Best Season: The hike is best done in summer after snowmelt in the high country has subsided and when the air temperature is warmest. Weather information:

http://www.weather.gov/

Elevation Loss: 1,400 feet.

Off the Beaten Path: No, this is one of the most popular "trails" in the National Park System.

Big Spring in the Zion Narrows is a picturesque, lush oasis

④ ZION NARROWS DETAILS

1 **TRAILHEAD -** Set up your trailend transportation. Park one car at the Zion Canyon Visitor Center (if the Zion shuttle is running) or at the Temple of Sinawava if permitted. Drive a second vehicle to the east entrance and continue 2.4 miles past the entrance to the turnoff for the North Fork Road. Follow the North Fork Road for 5.2 paved miles; the next 13 miles to the trailhead are dirt and gravel: do not try to drive this road after a rain- or snowstorm as the clay content makes travel difficult or even impossible. Birch Hollow is bypassed at 8.5 miles, Orderville Canyon at 12.5 miles and a wooden bridge crosses the Virgin River at almost 18 miles. After the bridge, turn left onto the less-traveled road leading to Chamberlain's Ranch and leave the gate as you found it. Drive a little farther, taking the left fork in the road to get to the parking area for the Zion Narrows. Locate the NPS information sign, just above the parking area. The route crosses the river and follows a dirt road for the next 3.0 miles as it traverses privately owned meadows.

2 **ZION NARROWS -** The road ends and a short, beaten path drops into the river. The next 12 miles zigzag in and out of the water; put valuables into your dry bags. Keep your eyes peeled on the right bank during the next half-mile for a 50-foot jug-handle arch. Beyond the arch, Navajo sandstone walls progressively elevate and several narrow sections suggest the flavor to come. Soon, deep side-canyons make their entrance and the first of 12 campsites are seen. About 7.0 miles into the hike you will meet a seemingly impassable 20-foot waterfall. Getting around this is simple: walk up the left embankment and pass through a cleft in the rock.

Serious injuries have resulted from hikers plunging into the pool below this waterfall. Never jump off anything while in a canyon.

As you continue down the canyon, high walls rise on either side and filtered sunrays cast shadows and reflect mystical-colored light.

3 **CONFLUENCE OF DEEP CREEK AND THE NORTH FORK OF THE VIRGIN RIVER -** This marks the halfway point of the hike. The new water—crystalline and cold—spilling from the side-canyon almost triples the flow in your hiking path. If you have not used hiking poles yet, now may be the time. Farther downstream Kolob Creek enters from the right and may add yet more flow to the river "trail"—depending on whether the Washington County Water Conservancy District is releasing water from the Kolob Reservoir. The next side-stream is Goose Creek, which also enters from the right. Big Spring, located just past Goose Creek, is a picturesque oasis where water cascades through lush vegetation and tumbles to the river. This is a popular area to take a break and filter drinking water for the rest of the hike.

The amazing architecture of Zion Narrows

THE FINAL SECTION - Nearly 11 miles into the hike, crowds that have hiked up from the Riverside Walk start to appear. In this final section of the Narrows the lighting is almost eerie. A glowing spectrum of orange, red, and pink seems to radiate from within the rock itself. The best-known of the side-canyons, Orderville Canyon, will be on your left, 2.0 miles downriver from Big Spring. This canyon usually adds a gentle, cold flow into the churning water you are hiking in. (Orderville Canyon itself is an excellent, popular route described in detail on the next page). A little over a mile farther, Mystery Falls trickles down the steep sidewall. Now, with just 0.25 miles of river hiking left, the crowds will grow larger as curious tourists venture upstream from the end of the paved Riverside Walk. Take this trail south to the Temple of Sinawava and, depending the time of year, the Zion Canyon Shuttle or your vehicle.

PERMITS AND INFORMATION - Log onto the park's website for details about availability of, and information about, permits and reservations:

http://www.nps.gov/zion/planyourvisit/backcountry-reservations-and-permits.htm

GPS Coordinates, WGS84 Datum
Trailhead at Chamberlain Ranch: 37°23.105N, 112°50.327W
Trailend at Temple of Sinawava: 37°17.121N, 112°57.870W

Zion Narrows

ORDERVILLE CANYON ⑤

The sport of canyoneering has gained momentum in Utah the past decade as intrepid explorers have been lured into dimly lit passages—caverns recessed into the earth's thick crust. These channels form when flowing water detects a weakness in soft rock, then gnaws away at the stone, creating twisted labyrinths and misshapen formations as it forces a path downward. Fantastic things have resulted—imagine, if you can, vaulted cathedrals with towering arches, born of sandstone. But it is not just the structural architecture that captivates, it's also the intrinsic designs. Tiny whimsical waves, curves, and whirls are splattered throughout long tunnels, and in many places, layers of hardened sand have been stripped away revealing slashes of color. These are not dark caves, but fantastic slot canyons where light radiates from above and creates an eerie incandescence: these might just be the most seductive places in all of nature.

Permit and reservation information: Log onto the park's website:

http://www.nps.gov/zion/planyourvisit/backcountry-reservations-and-permits.htm

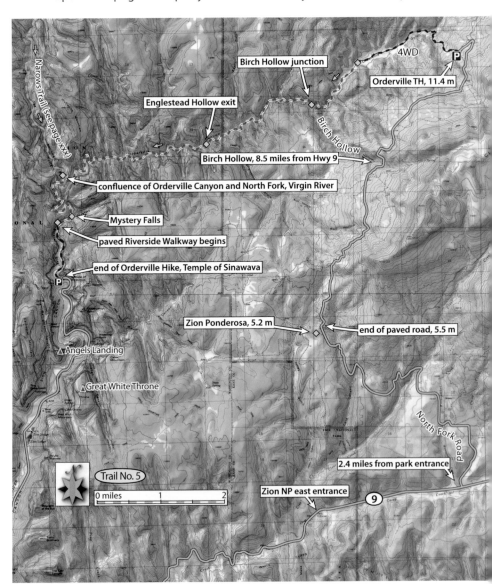

Narows Trail (see page xxx)

Birch Hollow junction

4WD

Orderville TH, 11.4 m

Englestead Hollow exit

Birch Hollow

Birch Hollow, 8.5 miles from Hwy 9

confluence of Orderville Canyon and North Fork, Virgin River

Mystery Falls

paved Riverside Walkway begins

end of Orderville Hike, Temple of Sinawava

Zion Ponderosa, 5.2 m

end of paved road, 5.5 m

△ Angels Landing

△ Great White Throne

North Fork Road

2.4 miles from park entrance

Trail No. 5

0 miles   1   2

Zion NP east entrance

⑨

AT A GLANCE

Day Hike: Yes.

Distance: 10–12 miles depending on where you are able to park.

Average Hiking Time: 8 hours.

Equipment: Bring water and a means of water purification, high-energy food, quick-dry (and extra) clothing, trekking poles, 50 feet of rope, canyoneering shoes with sticky-rubber soles, and emergency supplies.

Sun Exposure: Full sun in most places.

Technical: Short rappels and/or down-climbing.

Permits: The day-use limit for this canyon is 50 people per day from March 1 through August 30, 80 people per day for the remainder of the year. See the park website (use the link info on facing page) for details.

Difficulty: This is a technical slot canyon. Be prepared to rappel into cold pools of water and use a rope. River hiking is required.

Trailhead: East side of Zion, off the North Fork Road.

Trailend: Temple of Sinawava in Zion Canyon.

Trail Access: The dirt road to the trailhead may be impassable if wet.

Best Season: The hike is best done in summer after snowmelt in the high country has subsided and when the air temperature is warmest.

Elevation: Hike begins at 6,400 feet without a 4WD, or 5,800 feet with a 4WD.

Trailend: 4,470 feet.

Off the Beaten Path: This is a Zion classic, but only 80 users (only 50 fron March to August) are allowed to hike from the top down daily.

Weather Forecast: Weather information can be obtained at the visitor center or here:

http://www.weather.gov/

Warning: Orderville, like all slot canyons, presents a very real danger from flash flooding. Do not hike this trail if it is raining. A distant storm can trigger a nearby flash flood. Slot canyons can change dramatically in a short time due to flash floods and changing water levels. The directions given here are only a general reference; be prepared for variations in the canyon.

Bo Beck dwarfed by the high walls of Orderville Canyon.

⑤ ORDERVILLE CANYON DETAILS

1 **INTRODUCTION -** Orderville Canyon is an impressive slot-canyon adventure that requires some limited canyonering skills. At the start of Orderville, juniper and pine trees abruptly give way, and hikers drop into a brushy waterway and see their first glance of an intermittent waterfall. Rock walls and waterfalls slowly start to populate the stream as towering, vertical barricades enclose the canyon. A trip through this slot is not a meager undertaking: several obstacles requiring competent down-climbing skills, and rope-work complicates the 10- to12-mile trek. This one-way "hike" begins outside the eastern boundary of the park and ends at the Temple of Sinawava in Zion Canyon.

Warning: Hiking in slot canyons presents a danger from flash flooding. Do not enter this or any canyon if it's raining. A storm far off can trigger a flash flood where you are. Be prepared for variations in the canyon since flash floods rearrange obstacles.

2 **SHUTTLE SETUP -** Park one car at the Zion Canyon Visitor Center and drive another car to the Orderville Canyon Trailhead. To get there, go 2.4 miles past the park's east entrance, then turn left onto North Fork Road. Drive 5.2 miles on the paved road to the Zion Ponderosa. Beyond here, the road becomes dirt. The turnoff to the trailhead is 6.2 miles past the Ponderosa, or 11.4 miles from SR-9. From this point the actual trailhead is 2.5 miles farther, but beyond the gate, a 4WD is required even in dry conditions, so it may be best to park at the gate and walk down the road to the trailhead. Past the gate the road can be washed out, slippery and difficult to navigate; most 4WDs can go about 2.0 miles, leaving a half-mile of hiking to get to the riverbed where this route begins.

3 **ORDERVILLE CANYON –** Walk in the waterway for a little over a half-mile then follow the beaten path, heading left on top of the ridge, finally dropping into the canyon. The descent is about 175 feet. If water is flowing, look upstream to see the waterfall. Some canyoneers opt to rappel down this (usually dry) fall. Just over 1.0 mile into the hike, the canyon walls rise and move closer together.

4 **INITIAL OBSTACLE -** The first obstacle you should run into will be a large boulder. Locate the bolt on the right side and secure your rope. Those with proficient skills can go through the opening in the center of the rock, and then "chimney" when near the bottom. To chimney, put your back on one wall and feet on the opposite wall, then work yourself down. Never jump!

Beyond the first obstacle there are several down-climbs (or short rappels) to negotiate along the way to the intersection with the Zion Narrows, including the following:

5 **LOG LADDER -** There should be an anchor present for this 15-foot drop. Set up a rappel, a hand-line, or else climb down.

6 **LOGS -** Logs in the waterway tend to be very slippery, so take care when going down them. Hand-lines or rappels are safer than trying to otherwise navigate them.

7 **MOKI STEPS -** Use a rope to descend the carved stone steps, since this area tends to be mossy and slippery. Don't jump!

OPTIONAL BOTTOM ENTRY - To avoid obstacles, hikers can explore part of the canyon from the bottom. A permit is not needed to do this. From the Temple of Sinawava, take the casual stroll to the end of the Riverside Walk, then hike upstream 1.5 miles to the mouth of Orderville Canyon. You can explore this canyon as far as the Moki Steps.

Landmarks in Orderville Canyon:
  Birch Hollow: 2 miles – left side.
  Walker Gulch: 2.5 miles – right side.
  Esplin Gulch: 3.5 miles – right side.
  Englestead Gulch: 4 miles - left side.
  Bulloch Gulch: 5.75 miles – right side.
  Zion Narrows: 7.5 miles.
  End of Riverside Walk: 9 miles.
  Temple of Sinawava: 10 miles.

GPS Coordinates
WGS84 Datum

Turn Left from North Fork Road
37°20.224 N, 112°49.825 W

Gate
37°20.186 N, 112°49.902 W

Trailhead, End of Washed-out Road
37°20.074 N, 112°51.252 W

First Waterfall (descend slope on left side)
37°19.555 N, 112°52.217 W

SHELF CANYON ⑥

The road that heads east from Zion Canyon, SR-9, presents exceptional hiking opportunities in the maze of empty canyons on the east side of Zion (see map on next page, and Zion roadmap, page 17). The next 11 trails described all start from various locations along this highway and explore this fascinating, little-known landscape.

Shelf Canyon offers a fun little trek and a great introduction to the delights of the east side of the park. It takes a bit of boulder hopping to explore, but beyond some easy obstacles it's a short stroll and offers the visitor, who may have minimal hiking skills, equipment, and limited time, an opportunity to explore a true slot canyon.

Right from the start the canyon is decorated by tall, thin, rock spires called *hoodoos*, with the first attention grabber sitting high on a lofty perch to the left. During wetter times of the year, a refreshing trickle of water spills down the mountainside providing ferns below with just enough water to thrive in this shady little haven. Lush evergreens add a touch of year-round green to the spectrum of colors along the hike and contrast with towering cliffs of tangerine-colored rock. Toward the termination of the route, the walls close in, forming a short, yet impressive, slot; the path ends at a series of shelves—thus the name Shelf Canyon. Like much of the hiking on the east side of the park, this is a good winter excursion when the slickrock is dry.

AT A GLANCE

Day Hike: Yes.

Distance: 1 mile round-trip.

Average Hiking Time: 1 hour.

Difficulty: Moderate, with some simple bouldering.

Sun Exposure: There is enough sun for this to be an enjoyable winter hike and enough shade for it to be nice in the summer as well.

Permits: Not required.

Trail Conditions: Expect a sandy path through a short, usually dry drainage, with a couple of spots where rocks are difficult to pass and must be scaled. Like all slot canyons, this is a flash-flood hazard area.

Trailhead: Canyon Overlook parking lot.

Trailend: Same as starting point.

Trail Access: The Zion-Mt. Carmel Highway, SR-9 through the park, is open year-round and this trail begins just off the highway.

Best Season: March to October, but it's a good winter hike if the drainage is dry.

Elevation: Trailhead: 5,200 feet.

Trailend: 5,300 feet.

Off the Beaten Path: This canyon is near one of the most-used paths in the park, the Canyon Overlook Trail. But, after dropping into Shelf Canyon, you will usually have it to yourself; the slot itself is usually deserted. Parking can be a problem at busy times.

Restrooms: Located at the Canyon Overlook Trailhead.

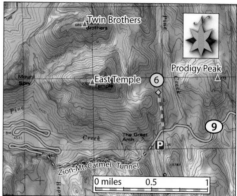

Bighorn Sheep are often seen around Shelf Canyon

⑥ SHELF CANYON DETAILS

Gordon Milligan in Shelf Canyon

1 TRAILHEAD - Look for the Canyon Overlook Trail parking lots near the east side of the Zion-Mt. Carmel Tunnel. Shelf Canyon is 250 yards east of the main parking lot and 300 yards west of the Upper Pine Creek drainage. The entrance to the canyon is an unsigned area on the north side of the highway, so peer over the edge to find the path of use, within the sandy drainage.

2 HOODOOS - Soon, you will see a group of hoodoos at the top of the sandstone cliff above and there are some fun rock formations to navigate around. A stone slab with lateral engravings is the first climbing obstacle.

3 SLOT - Toward the end of the path walls close in to make a short, narrow slot. Rocks clutter into the passage and a series of horizontal ledges and shelves prevent further exploration. Climbing at the end of the canyon is tempting but strongly discouraged.

GPS Coordinates
WGS84 Datum

Trailhead
37°12.898 N
112°56.343 W

Trailend
37°13.122 N
112° 56.376 W

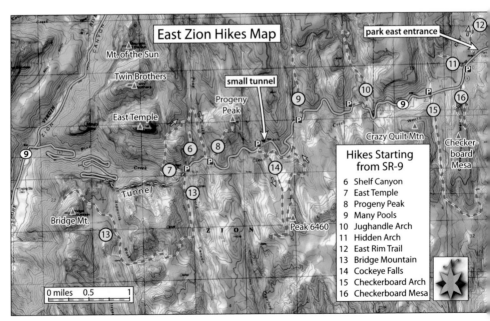

East Zion Hikes Map

park east entrance

Mt. of the Sun

Twin Brothers

small tunnel

Progeny Peak

East Temple

Crazy Quilt Mtn

Checkerboard Mesa

East Temple

Bridge Mt.

Peak 6460

Hikes Starting from SR-9

6 Shelf Canyon
7 East Temple
8 Progeny Peak
9 Many Pools
10 Jughandle Arch
11 Hidden Arch
12 East Rim Trail
13 Bridge Mountain
14 Cockeye Falls
15 Checkerboard Arch
16 Checkerboard Mesa

0 miles   0.5   1

EAST TEMPLE SADDLE LOOP (7)

Zion National Park is a land of enormous stone spectacles seen from many different perspectives throughout the park. The East Temple is one of the most massive of all. It was named by John Wesley Powell, and is best viewed from the east side of Zion, along the winding Zion-Mt. Carmel Highway (SR-9). East Temple's summit sits at 7,110 feet and towers 2,000 feet over the road.

Our East Temple Saddle Route will take you to a spectacular vantage point on the eastern slopes of East Temple where imposing slickrock prevails. The route begins by following the popular Canyon Overlook Trail to its end, and then climbs steeply northward into seldom-traveled terrain. This steep-but-rewarding hike ascends a stairway of red and white sandstone, skirts the flank of East Temple then leads to a hidden playground in Upper East Canyon, before dropping into the depths of Upper Pine Creek.

AT A GLANCE

Day Hike: Yes.

Distance: 2.25 miles.

Average Hiking Time: 4 hours.

Difficulty: This is a strenuous route. Slickrock scrambling is required. Wear proper footwear and do not go unless you are comfortable hiking on steep rock.

Equipment: Sticky-rubber shoes, plenty of water, food, sun-protection and the USGS 7.5′ Springdale East map.

Sun Exposure: Full sun.

Permits: Not required.

Trail Conditions: Unmaintained route, mostly on slickrock once past the Canyon Overlook Trail.

Trailhead: Canyon Overlook Trail, near the east end of the Zion-Mt. Carmel Tunnel.

Trailend: Upper Pine Creek.

Trail Access: The Zion-Mt. Carmel Highway is open year-round.

Best Season: Year-round. If it has rained recently and the sandstone is damp, patches of moss and lichen will be extremely slippery. Do not attempt this hike if snow or ice is present on northern slopes.

Elevation Gain: 1,100 feet.

Off the Beaten Path: The Canyon Overlook Trail is one of Zion's popular trails; beyond this section the East Temple route gets little use.

Bo Beck at the end of the Canyon Overlook Trail, looking down on the Zion switchbacks

⑦ East Temple Saddle Details

1 **Canyon Overlook Trail** - Park on the east side of the Zion-Mount Carmel Tunnel and locate the Canyon Overlook trailhead. Follow this trail as it ascends a well beaten path, winding west above Pine Creek for a half-mile and ending at an overlook above the Great Arch.

2 **East Temple** - Look north from the overlook and note the white hoodoos on the east, right, side of the East Temple. The hoodoos provide a landmark to hike toward. Keep in mind that the elevation gain of 1,100 feet takes place in a fairly short distance, so sticky-rubber hiking shoes are required. Now is the time to tighten up your laces and begin bearing north, following the path of least resistance. Do not attempt to go directly toward the hoodoos, but instead zigzag via ledge systems, and always avoid steep and dangerous areas. Cairns, if present, can provide a path to follow, nevertheless use your own judgement to pick the easiest route between the rock markers. At the saddle the views of the West Temple, Bridge Mountain, Progeny Peak and Deertrap Mountain are outstanding.

3 **Upper Pine Creek** - This route is a loop, so you will not be turning around to head back to the Canyon Overlook Trail. The backside of the saddle exposes a large bowl of trees and slickrock. The easiest path into the bowl is to traverse and descend the ledges, until arriving in a wash that flows east. The total descent to the wash, from the saddle, is 550 feet. Follow the wash 0.3 miles to the east, until it abruptly spills into a deep slot canyon below. You are now standing on the edge of a long drop-off and peering into the depths of Shelf Canyon. Turn left (north) and walk along the edge of this small canyon for 100 yards. After arriving at the head of Shelf Canyon carefully contour around its head and gain the slickrock ridge on the opposite side. Follow the ridge back down Shelf Canyon's eastern side until it is possible to descend left (northeast) to the easier terrain below. Try to remain at a constant elevation as you now walk north in the direction of the head of Upper Pine Creek. Be aware of the cliffband on the right, which is the east wall of Upper Pine Creek. Note: Shelf Canyon itself provides a short but excellent hike, described on page 31.

4 **Exit** - Examine the wall for the vertically streaked, water-stained pour-off. About 100 yards upstream of the stain, pick the easiest route down the steep slickrock as it drops into Upper Pine Creek. From here it's a leisurely quarter-mile stroll back to the road, and your vehicle is just another 100 yards or so down the road.

GPS Coordinates
WGS84 Datum

East Saddle:
37°13.068 N
112°56.680 W

Head Of Shelf Canyon:
37°13.272 N
112°56.437 W

Descent into Pine Creek:
37°13.398 N
112°56.323 W

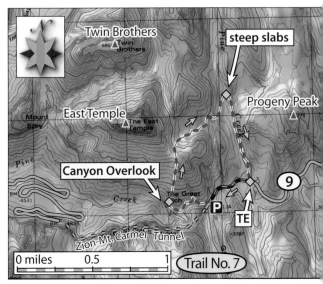

TWO PINES ARCH AND PROGENY PEAK ⑧

On the east side of Zion National Park the wind has swept the blond slickrock into intricate patterns, embedded with subtle tints of yellow, pink, and green and geological processes have twisted and tortured rock and sand into magnificent arrangements. Uplift and erosion created spires, domes, hoodoos, mountains—and a few notable arches. Arches may be more common in other areas of southern Utah but there is no place that surrounds them with such utter perfection as Zion.

Two Pines Arch is a highlight of this trail and a beautifully framed treasure (the hike to the arch is easy with the exception of one short section that requires scrambling). The mountain above the arch, Progeny Peak, has a fine summit with a majestic panorama in every direction.

Bo Beck near the summit of Progeny Peak, enjoying the fine view of Zion's East Temple

AT A GLANCE

Day Hike: Yes.

Arch Distance: 0.4 miles one way.

Progeny Peak Distance: 0.8 miles one way. Total hike distance to summit and back: 1.6 miles.

Average Hiking Time: 3 hours to Progeny Peak and back.

Equipment: Carry at least 2 quarts of water per person, energy foods, basic first aid kit, emergency supplies and proper clothing for the season. Always wear sturdy sticky rubber shoes when scrambling on slickrock.

Sun Exposure: Full Sun.

Permits: Not required.

Difficulty: The hike to the arch is a quick jaunt. The Progeny Peak hike is moderately strenuous with exposed slickrock scrambling.

Trailhead: The trailhead is on the north side of the Zion-Mt. Carmel Highway (SR-9) and just east of the Zion-Mt. Carmel Tunnel. Look for the small wash, identified, at the time of writing, by a yellow sign that says: "Caution Delays Possible Be Prepared to Stop."

Trailend: Same as trailhead.

Trail Access: The Zion-Mt. Carmel Highway is open year-round.

Best Season: It's possible to do this route in spring, fall and winter. Summers are hot, so begin early in the morning to reduce sun exposure.

Starting Elevation: 5,200 feet.

Arch Elevation: 5,600 feet.

Summit Elevation: 6,275 feet.

Total Elevation Gain: 1,075 feet.

Off the Beaten Path: Yes.

⑧ Two Pines Arch and Progeny Peak Details

1. TRAILHEAD - Park at the Canyon Overlook parking lot. If this is full, more parking is available just east of the Zion-Mt. Carmel Tunnel. The trailhead is on the north side of the road, 0.4 miles east of the Canyon Overlook parking lot, and is identified by a small wash and the yellow sign that currently says, "Caution delays possible be prepared to stop."

2. WASH ROUTE - Enter the wash on the north side of SR-9, hugging the mountain to the east, until a path of use is visible leading down into the wash. Once in the bottom, hike north for 150 yards where the drainage splits into two. The prominent drainage veers to the northwest, and a less prominent wash goes to the right in a more northerly direction. Go right (north). The wash soon becomes larger. Continue hiking in the watercourse, and soon a small, layered dryfall is encountered. Beyond the dryfall the wash opens up, and you should spot Two Pines Arch, surrounded by ponderosa pine trees.

3. HIKE TO THE ARCH - About 0.3 miles into the hike, the route leaves the easy terrain of the wash. Steep directly up the slickrock toward the arch. The climb is moderately steep, but it is only 0.1 miles. Now that you know where the arch is it will be easy to spot it from a distance after you return to your car.

NOTE: Scrambling on slickrock should only be attempted by experienced hikers. Wear sticky-soled hiking shoes to help grip the rock. Slickrock is dangerous when wet and even more so if icy. The rock is often dotted with moss, which holds water and can be as slippery as ice.

4. PROGENY PEAK - From Two Pines Arch, the scramble to the summit of Progeny Peak gets steep and tricky, so finding the easiest path is important. Hike north from the arch, to the left side of the buttress. Almost immediately there is a steep slab to negotiate. Use the ridges in the "slabby" rock to your advantage and travel will be easier. You should soon be on top of the saddle. From here, to the west sit some hoodoos; to the northeast towers the summit of Progeny Peak.

From here, walk east, in the general direction of the summit and work through the ledge systems. It's a bit easier if you angle slightly right and up the slabs toward the shoulder on the south side of the summit. The slabs further north (left), are steeper. Some small ledges will need to be negotiated on the way. Once on the south shoulder, head north up the short scramble to the summit.

5. SUMMIT - The view from the top of Progeny Peak is truly spectacular, well worth the 0.8-mile hike and 1,000-foot elevation gain. Looking southwest, Zion's East and West Temples are visible, as well as the Zion-Mt. Carmel Tunnel. To the west and north you can see the Twin Brothers, Mountain of the Sun, Deertrap Mountain and the East Rim. Peering east, Crazy Quilt Mesa and Checkerboard Mesa partially hide the white cliffs bordering the Grand Staircase.

Two Pines Arch

GPS Coordinates
WGS84 Datum

Trailhead
37°12.911 N
112°56.090 W

Two Pines Arch
37°13.117 N
112°55.980 W.

Progeny Peak
37°13.297 N
112°55.836 W

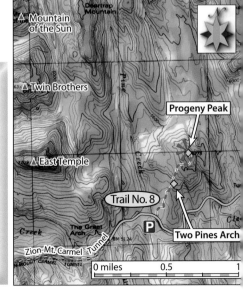

MANY POOLS ⑨

This delightful and hidden excursion in Zion National Park meanders gently up a particularly scenic section of slickrock on the east side of the park. On a topographic map, the two drainages east of the small tunnel resemble a root canal and thus when mentioned together are often called the "Route Canals" or "Twins," but when considered alone, Many Pools is the more common name for the "trail" presented here. The canyon is wide with sandstone mountains crowding closer as the path reaches the eastern rim of the park. Rainstorms and snowmelt on the high plateaus provide intermittent, running water which cascades down the smooth rock and spills into the many hot-tub-sized potholes etched into the sandstone. These potholes capture and store water until evaporation and permeation empty the sculpted "desert tanks."

AT A GLANCE

Day Hike: Yes.

Distance: It is 2 miles to the end of the Many Pools route and back, but if you continue to the East Rim it is a 4.4 mile round-trip.

Average Hiking Time: Plan on 2 hours to get to the end of the Many Pools route and back; and 6 hours to the East Rim and back.

Equipment: For both trips make sure you wear sticky-rubber hiking shoes and if you plan to go to the East Rim take at least 3 quarts of water per person, energy food, sun-protective gear, extra clothing for possible changes in the weather and emergency bivouac gear.

Permits: Not required.

Difficulty: Moderate, with a gentle uphill climb, to the alcove; plan for a strenuous hike if you continue to the East Rim.

Sun Exposure: Full sun for most of this route.

Trail Conditions: The path is mostly hiking over slickrock, but there are sections requiring easy scrambling. Beyond the pool features, rough, loose, steep scrambling is prevalent.

Trailhead: 0.9 miles east of Zion's smaller tunnel.

Trailend: Same as trailhead.

Trail Access: Zion-Mt. Carmel Highway (SR 9) is open year-round and the route begins right off the highway.

Best Season: The best times are winter and spring, when it is wetter; or in the summer and fall after a rainstorm.

Starting Elevation: 5,391 feet.

Highest Elevation: 6,833 feet.

Off the Beaten Path: Yes.

Restrooms: There are vault toilets at the park's east entrance station, or at the Canyon Overlook Trailhead at the east side of the Zion-Mt. Carmel Tunnel.

Bo Beck on the Many Pools route

⑨ MANY POOLS DETAILS

1 TRAILHEAD - Drive along the Zion-Mt. Carmel Highway, heading east from the small tunnel and look for the second drainage on the north side of the road. Large white monoliths are notable landmarks visible from the road, as well as the hiking route that passes between a small dome-like mountain and a larger mountain to the right. There is a pullout 0.8 miles from the end of the small tunnel: park here.

2 TRAIL - Hike 150 yards east along SR-9, then drop down into the bowl on the north side of the highway. Stay in the drainage, going away from the 1930s-built culvert. The terrain changes from soft sand to smooth, washed stone and walls open up as northerly travel leads to potholes, and big slabs of flat stone make a nice walking path. A big rock, that appears to be laying on its side, forms a short slot canyon on the right. Two large ponderosa pines and two large juniper trees offer a momentary reprieve from the sun while a huge boulder provides a charming backdrop for a dwarf waterfall about a half-mile into this scenic stroll. Soon the "trail" gets steeper as water-gnawed tanks become more common. To the east is a black-capped hoodoo and impressive views are revealed in all directions. Some distant slickrock is carved with cross-bedding similar to that on Checkerboard Mesa and there are many water-filled basins.

3 ALCOVE - You will approach a lovely alcove 0.7 miles into the hike where, in wet conditions, you will find a waterfall and hanging garden. A pinyon and two juniper trees should help find the landmark. Navigate around this obstacle by taking the sandy path to the west. The canyon widens to expose a broad sandstone bowl and brilliant blue skies before sheer rock walls close in. Towering slickrock begins

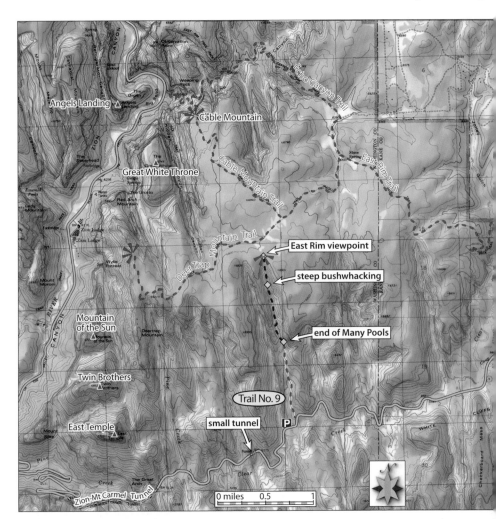

to rise higher on both sides of the route. Streams of water have carved a winding path through the hard surface below, while above, red stains and striations steal the show. Prickly pear and yucca cactus, ponderosa and pinyon pines, manzanitas, junipers and shrub live oak dot the landscape. One mile into the hike is the top of the pools sitting at an elevation of 6,209 feet. Most hikers will turn around at this point.

EAST RIM - The next part of the "trail" is strenuous and should only be attempted by experienced hikers. This section is marked in blue on the map. If you choose to forge ahead, expect steep ascents, bouldering, loose plates, talus and scree scrambling as well as some serious bushwhacking. The canyon will narrow and can be treacherous in the winter when large slabs of ice and huge icicles slough from the smooth, adjacent mountainsides and crash into the narrow passage below. Therefore, do not attempt this route if ice is present on the mountains. Stay in the drainage all the way to the rim. It is 2.2 miles from the start of the hike to the East Rim and will take about 3 hours. The elevation at the top is 6,833 feet: there is a nice viewpoint to look back down into Eastern Route Canal. At the top of the mountain you are on the East Rim. (But not the classic East Rim Trail, described on page 44, which begins near the east entrance of the park and terminates at the Weeping Rock parking lot).

TRAIL EXTENSIONS - If you have time and would like to explore a bit more, a choice can be made to continue to other prominent and historic landmarks on the east side of Zion (also see map, previous page, for more details):

1. DEERTRAP MOUNTAIN - Proceed north 0.2 miles to where you will find the east-west running Deertrap Mountain Trail. Upon arriving at this well-used trail, turn left and go 2.0 miles west to the viewpoint atop Deertrap Mountain where you will see Mountain of the Sun, the Twin Brothers, and the Court of the Patriarchs as well as Zion Canyon far below.

2. CABLE MOUNTAIN - Instead of turning left at the intersection of the Deertrap Mountain Trail, turn right and walk east 0.4 miles to the Cable Mountain Trail. Follow this path north for 1.75 miles until it ends at the historic cable-works and an impressive point to look down upon the Great White Throne, Angels Landing, Observation Point, and the West Rim of Zion.

3. EAST RIM TRAIL - A third option would take you onto the East Rim Trail, exiting either at Weeping Rock or at Zion's east entrance. Once again, at the intersection with the Deertrap Mountain Trail, turn right and travel 1.5 miles east to the junction with the East Rim Trail at Stave Spring, bypassing the spur trail to Cable Mountain, on the left. At the East Rim Trail intersection, turn left and travel the mostly downhill 4.2 miles into Echo Canyon, ending at Weeping Rock in Zion Canyon; or turn right and walk 5.8 miles to the trailhead near the east entrance to Zion National Park on SR-9. For a full description of the East Rim Trail, see page 44.

The beauty of Many Pools

GPS Coordinates
WGS84 Datum

Many Pools Trailhead
37°13.392 N, 112°54.876 W

End of Many Pools Hike
37°14.211 N, 112°55.099 W

Top Of East Rim
37°14.803 N, 112°55.244 W

JUGHANDLE ARCH ⑩

There are numerous natural arches in Zion National Park. Some are mentioned in this book, like Hepworth, Crawford, Two Pines, Hidden Canyon, Hidden Arch, Checkerboard, and the enormous Kolob Arch. Jughandle Arch is an oddly shaped, propped arch which is hard to spot unless you know right where to look—therefore, few have ever seen it.

Although it can be viewed from the road, a half-mile round-trip gains a much better viewpoint, or you can do the strenuous 3.0-mile round-trip hike and scramble up to the arch itself. The structure is nestled within the beautiful slickrock that is so prevalent on the east side of the park.

During the summer the mounds of rock east of the Zion-Mt. Carmel Tunnel can be a forbidding furnace: the pillars of fairyland-like rock outcroppings and sparse trees offer only isolated pockets of shade. Winter is an ideal time to hike in such a parched environment and by adding the right clothing you can be very comfortable. Dress in layers. Begin with a wicking base, then a light, insulating fleece, add a light wind-stopper and top all this with a waterproof shell. Your body temperature, based on physical exertion, can be regulated by removing or adding one item at a time.

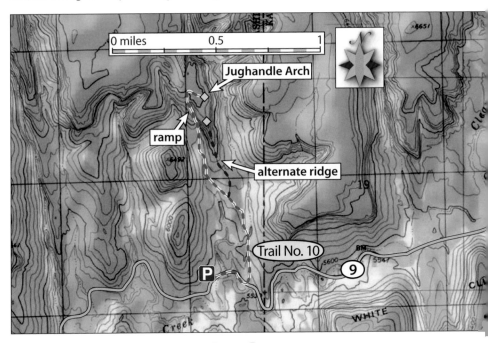

AT A GLANCE

Day Hike: Yes.

Distance: 3-mile round-trip.

Average Hiking Time: 4-hour round-trip.

Equipment: Sticky-soled shoes, energy snacks, at least 3 quarts of water per person, sun-protective clothing and emergency supplies.

Difficulty: Strenuous, some steep uphill hiking.

Sun Exposure: Full sun in most places.

Permits: Not required.

Trail Conditions: This is an unmaintained route and is in full sun. Do not hike midday in summer or if there is snow or ice on the rock. After rain the rocks are loose. Do not climb down near the arch.

Trailhead: 2.0 miles east of the smaller of the two tunnels in Zion.

Trailend: Same as trailhead.

Trail Access: The Zion-Mt. Carmel Highway is open year-round, and the trail begins just off the highway.

Best Season: Spring and fall.

Elevation Trailhead: 5,412 feet.

Elevation Gain: 1,032 feet.

Highest Elevation: 6,444 feet.

Off the Beaten Path: Yes

Restrooms: The closest restrooms are on the east side of the large tunnel; also at the east entrance station.

⑩ JUGHANDLE ARCH DETAILS

PARKING - The parking area and viewpoint for Jughandle Arch is on the south side of the Zion-Mt. Carmel Highway, 2 miles west of the east entrance or 1.9 miles east of the small tunnel. There is also a small pullout 100 yards east of the main parking area. From the parking area, look north to the skyline and try to locate the arch on the right side of the large peninsula.

TRAILHEAD - Hike east along the highway, passing a drainage on the left side of the road. There is a sweeping left curve around a blind corner, so use caution and stay off the road to avoid traffic. About 200 yards from the parking area (100 yards from the small pullout), a drainage appears on the left, identifiable by a large slickrock bowl and dome-shaped hoodoo located at the top of the wash.

VIEWPOINT - Walk down into the wash, then hike up toward the hoodoo ahead of you. Soon the sand yields to a steep slickrock scramble. After a 150-yard ascent up the sandstone, you will arrive at a saddle. Look north to see an unobstructed view of Jughandle Arch and the terrain to be covered on the way to the structure. This viewpoint is a convenient turnaround spot if you are not doing the entire hike.

KEYHOLE CANYON - If you wish to continue past the half-mile, round-trip viewpoint, then drop down the steep slope into Keyhole Canyon 150 feet below. This is your chance to peek at one of Zion's most popular canyoneering routes. To enter this slot requires canyoneering skills and equipment, a wet- or drysuit, and a permit from the park.

RAMP- From the bottom of the slope that you just descended, look upstream. About 75 feet away is a steep, vegetated ramp on the left, just before the canyon constricts to a narrow slot. Work up this ramp about 200 feet to the top of the ridge, which bears north toward the arch. Keep your eyes open for bighorn sheep which are often spotted in this area.

OPTIONAL SCRAMBLE - As the route continues toward the arch along the relatively level ridge, you will see a steep buttress of white sandstone. It is possible to go slightly to the left and work up this 3rd-class slope to an ideal viewpoint for taking photos of the arch.

Note: never scramble past where you are comfortable. Keep in mind, also, that if the rock is wet, or moss on the rock is moist or frozen, it can be as slippery as ice.

THE ARCH - This second option heads north and eventually follows another ridge to the right, going up a steep chute on the western side of the peninsula that the arch sits upon. Instead of scrambling up the steep buttress toward the arch, drop left and down into the wide, open wash below. Walk up the drainage a short distance and scramble up the slickrock watercourse. At the top of the slickrock, steer right through some pines and other vegetation then up another steep sandstone scramble. Soon the rock yields to talus and bushes. Look for a beaten path that bears left and up towards a chute. There is one steep, 3rd-class section partway up the loose ramp that requires the use of hands to negotiate. Once at the top of the chute, double back on the sparsely vegetated plateau and steer toward the eastern side. The rocky outcropping is Jughandle Arch. The best place to stand to photograph the arch is 50 feet north of the outcropping. Don't get too close to the edge because the rock there is fractured and could crumble. Keep in mind that sandstone is more hazardous when it's wet.

Jughandle Arch

GPS Coordinates
WGS84 Datum

Parking for Jughandle Arch
37°13.4750N, 112°54.1610W

Jughandle Arch
37°14.2298W, 112°54.2719W

HIDDEN ARCH (11)

It's just over one mile to Hidden Arch and back. This fun hike is located on the far east side of Zion National Park, near the impressive Zion landmark, Checkerboard Mesa, and starts from the Checkerboard Mesa parking lot (a half-mile from the east entrance station). The route travels through a wash and over slickrock to an impressive jug arch, and then returns back on the same route to SR-9. The east side of Zion is characterized by slickrock and hoodoos with a few natural arches among its treasures.

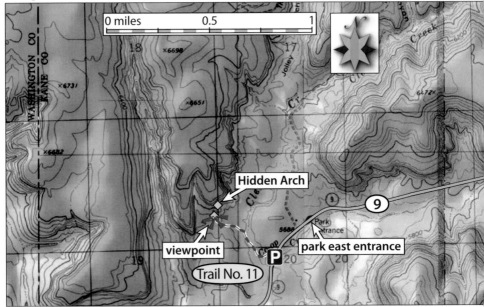

AT A GLANCE

Day Hike: Yes.
Distance: 1.4-mile round-trip.
Average Hiking Time: 2-hour round-trip.
Equipment: At least 2 quarts of water per person, comfortable, sticky-rubber hiking shoes, energy food, clothing appropriate for the weather, first aid and emergency gear.
Sun Exposure: Full sun in most places. This is a hot trail when hiking in the summer, but it's nice early or late in the day.
Difficulty: Moderate. Route-finding skills are required. There is a short section of easy scrambling. If hiking in winter, moss on the slickrock can be as slippery as ice.
Permits: Not needed.
Trail Conditions: Sandy, rocky wash with intermittent sections of slickrock.
Trailhead: Checkerboard Mesa parking lot, located just southwest of the east entrance to the park.
Trailend: Same as trailhead.
Trail Access: The Zion-Mt. Carmel Highway (SR- 9) is open year-round.

Best Season: This is a year-round hike, but take care not to hike in the hottest hours of a summer day.
Starting Elevation: 5,700 feet.
Highest Elevation: 5,900 feet.
Elevation Gain: 200 feet.
Off the Beaten Path: Yes.
Water availability: None. This hike is in full sun, do not go without plenty of water.
Restrooms: Vault toilets are located off the road by the east entrance station.

GPS Coordinates
WGS84 Datum

Checkerboard Mesa Viewpoint
Hidden Arch Parking:
37°13.8176N
112°52.6910W

Hidden Arch Viewpoint:
37°14.0371N
112°53.0235W

⑪ HIDDEN ARCH DETAILS

TRAILHEAD - Park at Checkerboard Mesa. The parking lot is just south of the east park entrance. The trail begins at the far northeast corner of the rock wall. Look over the end of the wall to locate the path of use. Follow a sandy trail down into the (usually dry) waterway. Once in the creekbed, turn left (downstream). Shortly, the creekbed will split. Take the right fork, not the fork that parallels the road.

HIDDEN ARCH - Walk up the creekbed for about 0.75 miles until the dry streambed turns northeast. A low-angle slickrock wash enters from the left. Leave the creekbed and hike up the slickrock wash, toward the mountain on the left, staying in the watercourse. After 0.25 miles the path gets more difficult to follow. Leave the shallow wash and steer left, toward the ridgetop. There is some minor scrambling over slickrock. Walk to the top of the hill and hike to the fallen tree. From that point, examine the mountain to the right. The arch is high at the top and angled so it is not easy to see at first.

EXIT - Return back on the same path, staying on the "trail." This area has cryptobiotic soil* that is easily damaged by straying off the trail.

Important: To keep destinations like this open, please stay in the watercourse when possible. This prevents soil erosion, stops social trails and keeps cryptobiotic soil* from being damaged.

*CRYPTOBIOTIC SOIL - This is recognizable by its dark, crusty, lumpy appearance. It provides a simple but slightly harder surface to the desert, to keep moisture in, and prevent wind from blowing material away. If damaged it can take several decades to repair itself. This crusty ground cover is made up of mostly cyanobacteria, but algae, lichens, moss, bacteria and microfungi are also involved in the makeup. Long ago, it is thought, cryptobiotic organisms were responsible for changing the earth's original atmosphere to one that is filled with life-sustaining oxygen.

The approach to Hidden Arch

EAST RIM ⑫

The East Rim Trail in Zion is exceptionally scenic and is on many lists as "one of the best hikes in Utah." With all the trail competition in the state, like the Zion Narrows and Angels Landing, that is saying a great deal.

This trek climbs, steadily and gently, 1,400 feet to the magnificent slickrock rim. Here, towering pine trees bring a marked change of scenery and a visit to the the elusive, spectacular Echo Canyon gives a tantalizing peek into the bowels of one of Zion's best-known slot canyons; technical skills, canyoneering gear and a permit are required to explore this canyon. Beyond here, the hike begins its descent into Zion Canyon. The downhill finish is spectacular, showcasing an almost constant view of some of the park's greatest landmarks including Angels Landing, the Organ, Great White Throne and in the distance, Cathedral Mountain.

The East Rim Trail follows an old Paiute route to the top of the mesa called the John Winder Trail. Winder was a Mormon rancher with a goal to link Zion Canyon to what is now the east side of Zion National Park. In 1923, Winder led surveyors to where the Zion-Mt. Carmel Tunnel was built.

AT A GLANCE

Day Hike: Yes, but it can also be done, and is often enjoyed, as a backpack.

Distance: 10 miles, one way, with the use of a shuttle (or by hitchhiking, which is allowed within Zion's boundaries). It is a 20-mile round-trip without a shuttle.

Average Hiking Time: Plan for a 6-hour hike from the trailhead at the east entrance to the trailend at the Weeping Rock parking lot.

Difficulty: Strenuous for a maintained and classic ZNP trail.

Sun Exposure: Full sun on most of the hike. The start is a somewhat strenuous and sandy uphill slog with little shade. Bring plenty of water and begin hiking early in the day.

Permits: These are not needed for day hike, but if you plan to backpack, an overnight camping permit is required.

Trail Conditions: Expect a maintained, dirt and rock path for the first 8.5 miles and pavement on the last 1.5 miles. Toes can take a beating on the downhill trek if your shoes do not fit properly. Lace them tightly during this section to help. If you have "bad knees" take care in your hiking. Wear a brace or ace bandage wrap and don't tense your muscles when hiking downhill. Trekking Poles may assist immensely to reduce impact on the knees. The trail can get icy and muddy in the winter and may become impassible. There are long drop-offs along the last part of the trail, but the path is nice and wide for the most part.

Water Availability: Stave Spring is an unreliable water source and water from it must be treated before drinking. During wet years there is an intermittent waterfall at Jolly Gulch.

Restrooms: Restrooms are located right next to the east entrance fee booth. They are off the road and hard to see, but they are there. There are also some at the trailend at the Weeping Rock/Observation Point parking lot.

Trailhead: 150 yards west of the east entrance.

Trailend: Weeping Rock parking lot.

Trail Access: Usually this trail is okay to hike from late March until early November depending on snow and ice conditions. For a one-way hike, if the shuttles are running, station a vehicle either at the Zion Canyon Visitor Center or Canyon Junction. If there are no shuttles, then park one car at the Weeping Rock parking lot and drive a second vehicle to the East Rim Trailhead just inside the East Entrance of the Park where you will begin the hike.

Off the Beaten Path: This is one of Zion's main backpacking trails and parts of the trail are shared with those hiking the classic and busy trails such as Observation Point and Hidden Canyon. Canyoneers also use parts of this path to get to Echo Canyon.

Elevation Gain: 1,400 feet up, then a gradually steepening downhill descent of 2,400 feet.

Peak: 6,700 feet.

⑫ EAST RIM DETAILS

EAST RIM TRAILHEAD - After positioning a vehicle or making shuttle arrangements watch for the small "trailhead" sign along the Zion-Mt. Carmel Highway, just west of the east entrance booth. Initially the trail follows the intermittently flowing creek bed of Clear Creek; BLM land will be just to your right. On this first section of the hike, the view looking back toward the road elegantly frames Checkerboard Mesa with its distinctive, deeply etched crossbedding. The next 5 miles follows an old wagon road trail, the Winder Stock Trail, which ascends gradually through junipers, pinyons, and small ponderosa pines. Some sections of the trail are sandy, but the steady climb to the top of the mesa is fairly moderate.

JOLLEY GULCH - Jolley Gulch, 2.8 miles into the hike, is the first signed area the trail passes, with a nice view down into a canyon. When water is flowing in Jolly Gulch there is a magnificent waterfall.

STAVE SPRING - Continue the uphill climb to Stave Spring. The spring is not much more than a pipe in the ground during years of drought, but during wet years there are streams flowing about Stave Spring. Look for the remnants (old posts) left over from logging. This is the 5.7-mile mark. Another half-mile and there is a sign directing the way to finish the East Rim Trail and giving the mileage for other options at the top of the mesa. The turnoff to Deertrap and Cable Mountain is just past Stave Spring (5.8 miles from the trailhead) and it is signed. Check the NPS website for current conditions on this spring.

ECHO CANYON - With 4.3 miles left in the hike, the East Rim Trail reaches the top of the mesa and begins to flatten out. Watch for cairns (stacks of rocks) that, usually, mark the trail. It now edges the Echo Canyon slot canyon—the views down into Echo Canyon are incredible. The slickrock displays vivid patterns on ancient, twisted, and uplifted sand dunes. A steep descent begins, down into what must be one of the most sensational sections of Zion. Once down and inside Echo Canyon the trail becomes a charming, rock-lined path that winds around towering obstacles that display the incomparable magnificence of Zion's geology. Fossilized sand dunes glitter in the sun and giant monoliths are seen in every direction.

DOWNHILL TREK ON A PAVED TRAIL - The East Rim and Observation Point Trails combine with the lower portion of the Observation Point Trail. Less than a half-mile farther is the narrow passageway through Echo Canyon and the charming "Echo Canyon Walkway" followed by a steady downhill hike into Zion Canyon.

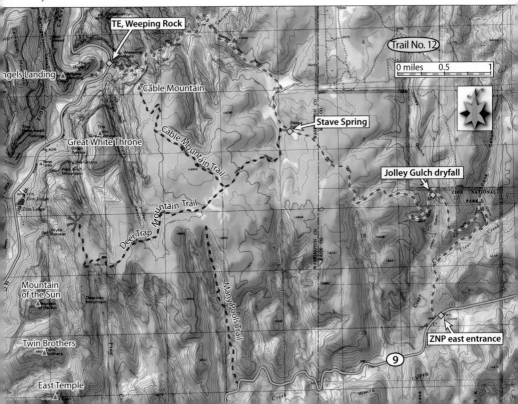

6 Detour to Observation Point Option - If your body and mind are willing, you might want to hike up to Observation Point from the spur in the trail. Keep in mind that it is a steep 2-mile climb up and then a 2-mile downhill hike back the same way.

7 Echo Canyon Walkway - The Walkway allows for a close-up look into a pretty part of Echo Canyon and also leads to the entrance to Middle Echo Slot Canyon. When dry, this is a fun and easy slot canyon, but entering it requires a permit. From the Walkway, the trail descends steeply for 1.5 miles. To the right of the trail is Lower Echo Canyon. During the winter and wet years water flows here.

8 Big Bend and Trailend - As the East Rim Trail descends from the mesa, the panorama of Zion Canyon and Big Bend takes center stage. This is one of the best views in the entire park. The Virgin River is forced around the Organ and the outline of the Angels Landing Trail is seen from its side. The Great White Throne and Cathedral Mountain loom in the background. The steep path continues to switchback downward, past the spur to Hidden Canyon and finally to the trailend at Weeping Rock parking lot.

East Rim Side–Trip/BackPack Options:

1. Cable Mountain - This is a 6-mile round-trip from the junction with the East Rim Trail. There are incredible views of the Great White Throne, Angels Landing, Observation Point and the West Rim of Zion.

2. Deertrap Mountain - This is an 8-mile round-trip from the junction with the East Rim Trail, with nice views of Mountain of the Sun, Twin Brothers and the Court of the Patriarchs.

3. Backpack Option: East Rim, Cable Mountain, Deertrap Mountain - A backpacking option includes camping at Stave Spring and then a day-hike to Cable Mountain. You would then double back to the Cable Mountain-Deertrap Mountain junction (not Stave Spring) and continue to Deertrap Mountain (see map, previous page) before finally going back to Stave Spring. The final part of the hike would be the downhill trek ending at the Weeping Rock parking lot. Total mileage: 20 miles.

GPS Coordinates WGS84 Datum
Trailhead
37 14.027N
112 52.621W
Stave Spring
37 15.672N
112 54.288W

4. Observation Point - This trail is a 4-mile round-trip from the Observation Point/East Rim junction. Marvelous views of Zion Canyon can be seen along much of this hike as well as at the viewpoint at the end of the trail.

Spectacular views on the descent from the East Rim Trail

CRAWFORD ARCH ON BRIDGE MOUNTAIN ⑬

This excellent hike accesses two very different freestanding arches: massive Hepworth Arch and delicate Crawford Arch.

For those that want a leisurely stroll, the beginning of this route will take you through beautiful and secluded Gifford Canyon. Part 2 of this hike involves strenuous slickrock scrambling and ends at Hepworth Arch. Hardcore adventurers can go a step farther to Crawford Arch, a spectacular, freestanding arch that is 3 feet wide and 156 feet long. It can be seen at a distance from the information plaque in front of the Zion Human History Museum, but its full splendor is best appreciated from close up.

AT A GLANCE

Day Hike: To Crawford Arch, a long day-hike or an overnight trip.

Distance: 3-mile round-trip to Gifford Canyon; 10-mile round-trip to Crawford Arch.

Average Hiking Time: 12–16 hours.

Difficulty: Extremely strenuous, uphill hiking.

Equipment: Sticky-rubber hiking shoes, energy snacks, at least 3 quarts of water per person, emergency clothing and route map. For the last section to Crawford Arch, 100 feet of climbing rope, harness, rappel device and extra webbing.

Sun Exposure: Expect full sun during most of the hike. Begin early in the morning when it's cooler.

Permits: Not needed for day hike, but if you plan to backpack and camp, an overnight permit is required.

Technical: Technical climbing is necessary (up a 5th-class, 30-foot-high chimney with no anchors) to complete the route to Crawford Arch.

Trail Conditions: The steep slickrock can be precarious at the start and end of the route and the chimney can have ice in it during the colder months of the year. There is a generous amount of slickrock scrambling on this "trail." The slickrock in Zion can be dangerously slippery when wet; even after the stone dries, moss retains moisture and can be very hazardous. There are sections of exposed, cliffside, slickrock crossings.

Camping: Open camping (permit required).

Trailhead: The Canyon Overlook parking lot near Gifford Canyon.

Trailend: Same as the trailhead.

Trail Access: SR-9 is open all year, so the parking lot is accessible all year. If water is running in Clear Creek it can be difficult to cross, and crossing is required to get into Gifford Canyon.

Best Season: Late spring is best. A hot summer day would be brutal. Fall would be pleasant but the days are shorter. Winter and early spring there is often ice in the chimney.

Starting Elevation: 5,124 feet.

Elevation, Crawford Arch: 5,300 feet.

Highest Elevation: 6,180 feet.

Off the Beaten Path: Yes.

Water Availability: Usually none.

Restrooms: At the Canyon Overlook parking lot.

Bridge Mountain route. Hiking through Hepworth Wash, with Hepworth Arch visible in the distance

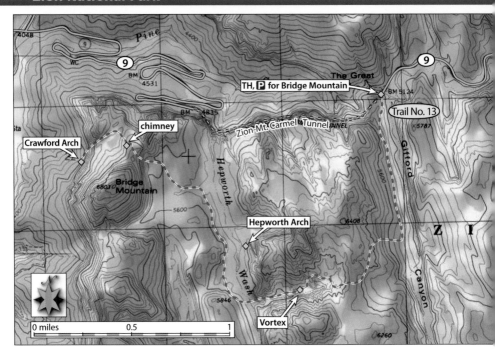

⑬ Crawford Arch on Bridge Mountain Details

1 Gifford Canyon - Park at the east side of the Zion-Mt. Carmel Tunnel then follow the beaten path that runs alongside the road-bridge and descends into the Clear Creek drainage. Head upstream for 100 yards, looking for signs of use through the trees at the alcove on the right. Once up top, the "trail" traverses and then switches back until it drops into the north end of Gifford Canyon. If Gifford Canyon is as far as you are going, it is a casual 3.0-mile stroll to the end of the trail and back. The turnaround point is obvious—a box canyon with a blank 200-foot wall.

Be aware that slickrock hiking in wet or freezing conditions is dangerous. The slickrock in Zion can be dangerous when wet due to the moss absorbing water and becoming as slick as ice.

2 Continuation toward Hepworth Arch - If you plan to continue to Hepworth Arch, look for a drainage entering Gifford Canyon from the right, about 0.75 miles from the trailhead. Head up the slickrock mountain, staying to the right where it's less steep. Zigzag upward via ramps and ledges for about 0.25 miles. Look for some 60-foot-tall cliffs dotted with pine trees; head for the base of these cliffs, then locate a small drainage beneath the cliffbase that leads to a ridge. Scramble up and to the left of it as you progress steadily upward. Soon *cairns* (piled-rock markers) lead the way into a massive (one-quarter-mile-wide) sandstone bowl just beneath the rim. Enter the bowl then bear west, picking the easiest route to the plateau above.

3 The East–West Canyon - On the plateau-top, go north and locate a major east-west canyon. Enter this by descending north and west. You will soon reach the top of a cliffband. Hike above and north of this cliff until you find a weakness through it. Drop into the main drainage below, then navigate downward. Look for another wash entering the canyon from the right. Walk up this wash. A 40-foot-high wall will appear on the left; look for a weakness to scramble to the ridge above. From the top of the ridge walk 100 feet north to a steep ramp that goes down and to the south and then descends into the major east-west canyon. Once at the bottom of the canyon travel downstream, looking for a hidden slit on the left, the Vortex, in the canyon wall located at the head of the wash. If temperatures are hot outside the rapidly moving air in the slot will be chilly, making it a great place to cool off. Next, walk downcanyon until the path connects with Hepworth Wash.

HEPWORTH WASH - Once in Hepworth Wash, head right (north). An intermittent stream is often flowing and filled with toads and other delightful creatures. Hepworth Arch is a little more than a half-mile down Hepworth Wash, on the right. This is an enjoyable camping area or a destination for a day-hike.

To continue to Crawford Arch you need 100 feet of rope, a rappel device, and a harness for the 5th-class climbing in the chimney. There are also two very narrow, exposed areas to be crossed.

CRAWFORD ARCH APPROACH - If you are continuing to Crawford Arch, hike north through Hepworth Wash for about a mile to a drainage entering from the west. Proceed into it, but soon veer up and right (northwest) through trees and cacti. Head toward the "V" notch right of Bridge Mountain and left of a smaller rock outcropping. Don't be lured to the larger notches farther right. After gaining some elevation, drop into the next wash you encounter and follow it west. Near the head, look up and to the right to locate a steep, bushy ramp. Scramble up this to the saddle on top, and descend an even steeper drainage on the backside of this saddle. At the bottom of the drainage, there is a beaten path on the left side that hugs the rock slab. Soon a steep right-sloping rock slab with an exposed drop-off is encountered. Sticky-rubber-soled shoes will be helpful for this short traverse. Beyond this, scramble up the buttress ahead to gain the chimney.

Crawford Arch

6 THE CHIMNEY - This is the technical climbing section, requiring 100 feet of rope. There is currently a log wedged 6 feet up in the chimney that makes it easier to get started. From the log, work upward and to the right 40 feet to a ledge (see photo). Note: the chimney on the left is much harder, though doable if you go deep inside and squeeze up a slot in the rear. Once one person is above the chimney they can belay from an anchor of webbing slung from trees on the ledge just above the climb itself, in order to safely bring other members up. From here, continue up the steep rock- and tree-filled ramp system 300 feet to a couple of 30-foot-tall ponderosa trees. At this point there is one more tricky section, a narrow, low-angle, slickrock ledge traverse. Beyond this is the final destination, a beautiful hanging valley.

7 CRAWFORD ARCH - From the two ponderosas, hike 15 feet up, then bear right along the narrow ledge. The ledge gains elevation, but be careful not to go too high, because you will need to come back down once you sight the hanging valley. Head for the obvious weakness taking you into this desert oasis of dunes and ponderosa. Walk to the south, toward the bottom of the valley, then steer left around the dryfalls, aiming for the steep, tree-covered slope. Scramble up the slope and then bear right to Crawford Arch.

Hepworth Arch

Bo Beck climbing the technical chimney

**Bridge Mountain
GPS Coordinates
WGS84 Datum**

Parking at Tunnel
37°12.778 N, 112°56.457 W

Ascent from bottom of
Gifford Wash to the west:
37°12.021 N, 112°56.274 W

Descend into east-west canyon
37°11.919 N, 112°56.655 W

Intersection of east-west canyon
with Hepworth Wash
37°11.873 N, 112°57.198 W

Saddle
37°12.555 N, 112°57.792 W

Chimney
37°12.608 N, 112°57.832 W

Crawford Arch
37°12.414 N, 112°58.107 W

COCKEYE FALLS

Don't be afraid to lace up your boots and hit the trails when it's chilly outside. Learn to embrace cool temperatures and warm up to hiking during every season. Unfortunately winter is when many people close their doors, crank up their heaters and hibernate until they feel the warmth of spring, but winter is a magical time that holds a special beauty that you cannot find during spring, summer or fall. Get out and get some sun, admire the contrast of snow and brilliant blue skies, find icicles tucked away in shady alcoves, enjoy views that are usually obscured by dense vegetation, but most of all see the beauty of Zion when it has been transformed into a winter wonderland. Although mornings can be brisk, you could actually find yourself throwing off your jacket and rolling up your sleeves in the afternoon.

One ideal winter route begins just off the Zion-Mt. Carmel Highway on the east side of Zion, where weathered earth claims the land, showcasing acres of multicolored domes streaked with crimson hues and dotted with whimsically shaped hoodoos and evergreen trees. The Cockeye Falls "trail" traverses slickrock on the way to a remote viewpoint overlooking Parunuweap Canyon, then descends into a surprisingly beautiful drainage that culminates at the twisting, polished flute referred to by locals as Cockeye Falls. During much of the year the pour-off is dry, but in the winter you might discover a partially frozen cascade as it works its way into the wash. After heavy rain it's delightful to see water zigzagging urgently down fluted channels of porous sandstone and dropping into Clear Creek.

Cockeye Falls: an intermittent, wintertime waterfall, seen here from the Zion-Mt. Carmel Hwy

AT A GLANCE

Day Hike: Yes.
Distance: 4.5-mile round-trip.
Average Time: 6 hours.
Difficulty: Steep slickrock scrambling and route-finding.
Equipment: Carry at least 3 quarts of water per person, extra clothing, emergency supplies, energy foods, map and compass. Wear sticky-rubber-soled footwear for scrambling on slickrock.
Sun Exposure: Full sun.
Permits: Required.
Trailhead: South end of the little tunnel.
Trailend: Same as the trailhead.
Trail Access: The Zion-Mt. Carmel Hwy is open year-round. If there is water in Clear Creek the trail may not be accessible.

Best Season: Spring, fall and winter if conditions are dry.
Starting Elevation: 5,275 feet
Highest Elevation: 6,200 feet
Elevation: +/- 925 feet.
Off the Beaten Path: Yes.

Check the weather report before attempting this canyon. Do not go if it looks like rain or if there is ice on the slickrock. Hiking in slot canyons presents a danger from flash flooding. Remember, a storm far off can trigger a flash flood. Weather info:

http://www.weather.gov/

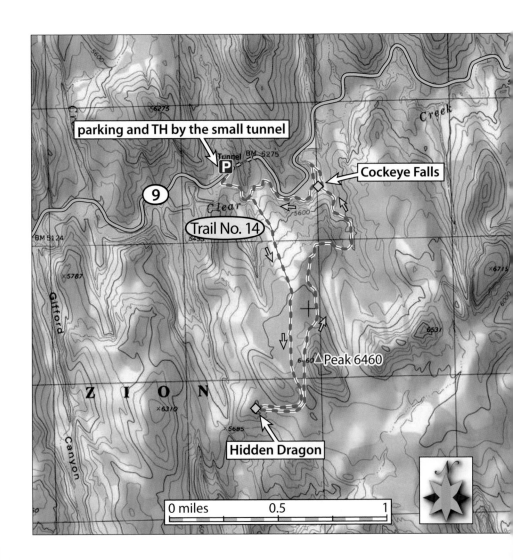

⑭ COCKEYE FALLS DETAILS

TRAILHEAD - Park at the west end of the small tunnel, which is 1.5 miles east of the longer Zion-Mt. Carmel Tunnel. Follow the steep, worn path south and down into the drainage below. Travel the generally dry wash for 150 yards until it intersects with Clear Creek.

CLEAR CREEK - If the creek is fairly dry, head upstream through the sand-and-cobblestone streambed (after a rainstorm the creek can be a raging torrent and you will not be able to continue). From the trailhead it is 0.35 miles to the entrance of Hidden Garden. The somewhat apparent opening to this short slot canyon is on the right and is partially blocked by a large ponderosa tree. Continue past this landmark and up the creek 200 yards, looking for a less prominent drainage (also on the right). Follow this cleft a short distance before working your way up and onto the slickrock slab on the left.

SLICKROCK ASCENT - Scramble up the slickrock slab. You will ascend 900 vertical feet in the next 0.7 horizontal miles. This is steep, but manageable—by scanning for weaknesses before proceeding upward, you should be able to find easier passages. Sparsely scattered pine trees and sculpted bowls create a road map as the path steers toward the right side of the nearing sandstone butte. Moki-marbles can be found here. The sandstone butte's summit is listed as Peak 6460′ on topographical maps.

Warning: Never scramble on slickrock without the proper footwear and skills required to keep you safe. Remember, you are responsible for your own safety.

VIEWS - Vistas to the north and west reveal ridges, valleys, slot canyons, and towering summits. You should be able to locate the East and West Temples, East Rim, Deertrap Mountain, Bridge Mountain and Progeny Peak (6,275 feet).

THE SADDLE - As you travel beyond the right (west) side of Peak 6460′ the slickrock slabs yield to a flat valley of low brush, grass and cacti. Deer and sheep wandering south toward the expanses of Parunuweap have worn trails through the vegetation, cutting paths through the thickets. From the point where you left the creek, it is 1.0 mile to the saddle on the western flank of Peak 6460′. Impressive views open to the south revealing the plateaus on the north and south sides of Parunuweap Canyon.

HIDDEN DRAGON - From the saddle, bear slightly southwest and down into the slickrock bowl. Descend toward a white dome that is just a few hundred feet away. Once there look above and to the northwest 200 yards and locate the rock that locals have dubbed Hidden Dragon.

EXIT - Retrace the route you came in on until you reach the saddle. From this point, skirt around the base of Peak 6460′ in a generally northerly direction until you get to an obvious north-south ridge. Stay on top of the ridge as it steers toward Clear Creek where it will twist northeasterly after a half-mile. The ridge narrows and begins to fall off steeply to left and right as well as straight ahead. Carefully pick a route off the right side of the ridge and switchback downward to reach the floor of the canyon.

COCKEYE FALLS - Follow the canyon floor as it descends north toward the highway and the creek. Along the path there will be some dryfalls to negotiate. It's easiest to bypass them on the right (east) side but you will have to do some careful down-climbing on the steep slickrock. Once past the obstacles, the wash makes a quick turn to the left where you will see the highway and creek below. Cockeye Falls, which can actually be seen from the road, winds through sculpted sandstone and touches down into Clear Creek. Be careful not to walk too far down the falls as the grade becomes very steep.

CLEAR CREEK - If you head downhill in a northeasterly direction the grade becomes manageable so that you can descend the slickrock and enter the creek. Once down, it is an enjoyable 0.75-mile stroll through the sometimes open and sometimes slotted riverbed back to your vehicle.

GPS Coordinates, WGS84 Datum

Trailhead	Begin Ascent	Hidden Dragon
37°13.30450N, 112°55.4260W	37°12.9244N, 112°55.3265W	37 12.1020N, 112 55.3140W
Brown Petroglyphs	Saddle at Ridge Summit	Descent into Cockeye Falls Wash
37°12 9810N, 112°55.4480W	37°12.2496N, 112°55.0852W	37 12.8105N, 112 54.9787W
Hidden Gardens Entrance	Hoodoo in Bowl	Cockeye Falls
37°12.9160N, 112°55.3760W	37°12.0570N, 112°55.1550W	37 12.9660N, 112 54.9560W

CHECKERBOARD ARCH ⑮

Zion's east side is dominated by a myriad of nameless domes, hoodoos and valleys. These are works of art, patiently provided by nature's insurmountable havoc. In its wake, nature turned lofty piles of sand into a magnificent gallery of textured slickrock. Water-filled potholes, twisted rock and alabaster stone dot the arid landscape. The signature landmark on the east side of the park is the vertically and horizontally striated Checkerboard Mesa and a number of great hikes are centered around this dramatic mountain.

The path to Checkerboard Arch has a little bit of everything: slickrock scrambling, bushwhacking, route-finding, and soft-sand hiking. Blind arches, which are seen along the trail, are common on the east side of Zion. Beauty abounds along the trek with Checkerboard Mesa to the east, Crazy Quilt Mesa to the west and expansive vistas above Parunuweap Canyon ahead.

AT A GLANCE

Day Hike: Yes.
Distance: 4-mile round-trip.
Average Hiking Time: 5 hours.
Difficulty: This route is moderately difficult and route-finding skills are required.
Equipment: USGS 7.5′ Topographic Map "The Barracks." At least 3 quarts of water per person, clothing appropriate for the weather, sticky hiking shoes and emergency equipment.
Sun Exposure: Full sun in most places.
Permits: Not needed.
Trail Conditions: This is an unmaintained route, rather than an actual trail. The path goes through a wash and along slickrock to an arch in Zion's backcountry wilderness.

Trailhead: The second pullout south of the Checkerboard Mesa parking area.
Trailend: Same as trailhead.
Trail Access: Zion-Mt. Carmel Hwy (SR-9) is open year-round.
Best Season: Year-round.
Starting Elevation: 5,530 feet.
Highest Point: The Saddle is at 6,100 feet and the Checkerboard Arch Viewpoint is at 5,800 feet.
Off the Beaten Path: Yes.
Restrooms: There are vault toilets at the east entrance station.

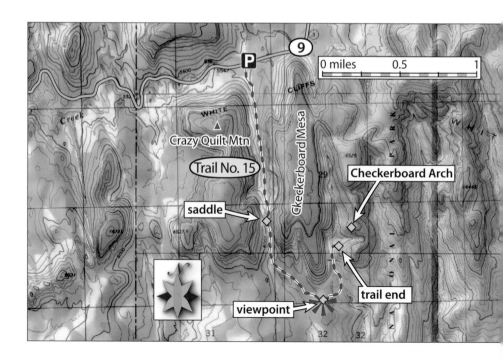

⑮ CHECKERBOARD ARCH DETAILS

TRAILHEAD - Park at the second pullout which is located just southwest of the main Checkerboard Mesa viewpoint. Cross the highway, to the south, and look for the path of use along the narrow drainage.

Follow the drainage that is west of Checkerboard Mesa and east of Crazy Quilt Mesa (the mountainous mesa just west of Checkerboard Mesa). There are two drainages, and the one closer to Crazy Quilt Mesa affords the easiest travel. This is not a maintained trail so be prepared to climb obstacles such as fallen trees. Follow the wash until, about a half-mile in, a beaten dirt path becomes obvious on the left. The "trail" will cross the drainage several times, but it is generally easy to find on either side of the wash. Travel directly in the watercourse when possible to prevent soil erosion. A mile in, the "trail" steepens, and soon reaches a saddle (6,100 feet). South is a magnificent view of the plateau above Parunuweap. From the saddle, hike south (downhill). It's about 0.35 miles and 150 feet vertically to the bottom and into the wash below.

CHECKERBOARD ARCH - From the wash, turn to the east (left), and look for the beaten path. Continue east and hug the southern tip of Checkerboard Mesa. While rounding the tip and looking east and north, three mountains will come into view. The center mountain is topped with juniper trees. We will call this unnamed mountain Peak 6273', since this is how it is identified on some USGS 7.5-minute topographic maps. Checkerboard Arch is the large, freestanding arch on the left (west) edge of this mountain. Continue toward the arch, going up and over the saddle. Cross the main wash between Checkerboard Mesa and Peak 6273' for a close-up view of the arch.

EXIT - There are two options. Return the same way or take a more difficult optional exit described below. The optional loop exit is not marked on the map.

LOOP EXIT OPTION - For hikers that want to loop rather than double back there is an option, but it's not easy. Continue north up the drainage between Checkerboard Mesa and Checkerboard Arch. Most of the route is steep, with a slippery downhill descent on the north side of the saddle. Expect bushwhacking, except in winter. This alternate exit is 2 miles long, the same distance as the primary exit.

Checkerboard Arch

GPS Coordinates
WGS84 Datum

Parking
37°13.602N, 112°53.080W

Saddle between Checkerboard Mesa
and Quilt Mesa
37°12.719N, 112°52.998W

Viewpoint
37°12.312N, 112°52.411W

Checkerboard Arch
37°12.681N, 112°52.411W

CHECKERBOARD MESA (16)

Entering Zion National Park from the east entrance immediately reveals a colorful display of orange, brown and white slickrock that includes one of the park's main landmarks, Checkerboard Mesa. This majestic mountain towers 900 feet above the Zion-Mt. Carmel Highway and resembles a giant, extended chess- or checkerboard. The vertical and horizontal fissures are best displayed on the north side of the mesa—a photographer's delight. The deep, left-to-right scratches were eroded by the prevailing north-to-south winds, while the vertical cracks result from repeated cycles of water freezing and thawing. This erosion is ongoing—change still continues in the park, and the massive monoliths will eventually break down and once again become great dunes of sand.

Immediately west of Checkerboard Mesa is Crazy Quilt Mesa, another wonderful example of cross-bedding. Checkerboard Mesa was once known as Rock Candy Mountain but Preston Patraw, park superintendant from 1932–1938, renamed it in 1938.

The route described here will take hikers on a fascinating hike that few have done. You will venture up the side of Checkerboard Mesa to the northern tip where you can look down upon the nearby magnificent, smooth, stone hills. In addition, this view encompasses desert tanks and odd-shaped outcroppings of twisted and manipulated sandstone, in a myriad of shapes and sizes.

AT A GLANCE

Day Hike: Yes.
Distance: 2-mile round-trip.
Average Hiking Time: 4 hours.
Equipment: Sturdy hiking shoes with sticky-rubber soles should always be worn when hiking on slickrock to ensure safe footing. Bring emergency equipment, plenty of water and energy snacks.
Difficulty: This is a strenuous, uphill route with a lot of bushwhacking. On the other hand it's relatively short. Navigation skills are required.
Sun Exposure: Full sun most of the hike.
Permits: Not required.
Trailhead: Checkerboard Mesa viewpoint parking lot.
Trailend: Same as the trailhead.

Trail Access: SR-9 (Zion-Mt. Carmel Highway) is open year-round, but the route itself can be difficult during the summer when vegetation growth restricts the trail.
Best Season: Spring, summer and fall. Snow and ice on the north- and east-facing chutes and ledges of this trail can make travel extremely dangerous during winter and early spring.
Elevation Gain: 900 feet.
Off the Beaten Path: This is one of Zion's main landmarks, but few venture past the viewpoint or parking lot just off the side of the road; therefore the route gets little use.

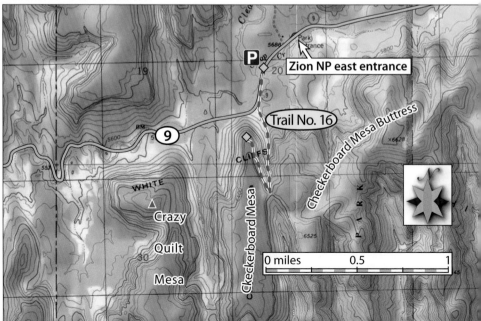

⑯ CHECKERBOARD MESA DETAILS

PARKING - Park at the Checkerboard Mesa pullout and viewpoint, found just east of the east entrance station.

THE WASH - Walk west along SR-9 until you are at the base of Checkerboard Mesa. On the east side of the mesa, follow the drainage that runs along the slickrock, bypassing several potholes. Before long the path becomes a sandy wash, winding south and ascending to the saddle that separates the more popular area north of SR-9 from the less visited plateaus above Parunuweap. Stay in the wash as much as possible, passing the social trails that split off to the left and head into the shrubbery on the hillside above. You will find the travel easier if you stay against Checkerboard Mesa; also, your hiking will result in less erosion to the hillsides on either side of the drainage. There will be a few dryfalls along the route that can usually be avoided by going left, up and then around.

SADDLE APPROACH - The ascent steepens as the top of the saddle becomes more obvious. Watch for a beaten path that emerges and ascends through the trees. This "trail" will take you out of the drainage; watch for where it branches to the right before reaching the actual saddle highpoint. The path requires a scramble up a short 8-foot cliffband. Soon you will come to the forested ledge just below, and east of the Checkerboard Mesa tabletop.

PROMONTORY - Now it is necessary to switch direction and travel north, back toward SR-9, hiking on top of the ledge. Stay to the right, and just above the developing cliff so that you avoid the even denser foliage up high. The use of game trails will make travel easier. This way is simpler than trying to ascend to the base of the caprock that comprises the Checkerboard Mesa tabletop. Continue north for several hundred yards to the promontory just north of and below the actual tabletop. Soon the terrain will level out and spectacular views appear. There is a good flat area to sit and have lunch. After lunch walk around and marvel at the expansive views of slickrock country.

> **GPS Coordinates**
> **WGS84 Datum**
> Parking
> 37°13.762 N, 112°52.739 W
> Hike End and Viewpoint
> 37°13.530 N, 112°52.807 W

Looking toward the West Temple from near the top of Checkerboard Mesa

CHINLE TRAIL

Winter in Utah's southwest desert leaves many popular backpacking areas inaccessible due to snow, ice, and other obstacles. But in turn winter opens up a diverse array of hiking routes that are ideal for cold-weather adventure. The low-desert routes, best avoided when temperatures soar in the summer, make top-notch winter treks.

The Chinle Trail, located outside the highly touristed section of Zion, traverses a sun-baked bench and comes into its own during the winter. This hike offers lofty mountain vistas throughout, including views of the West Temple, Mount Kinesava, Towers of the Virgin, Sundial and the eerie spires of Eagle Crags. At the end of the route, hikers are graced with views of remote Cougar Mountain and Smith Mesa. Treasures, such as petrified wood, can be found in select areas of this hike, but remember you are in a National Park and collecting petrified wood (or any other rock) is forbidden by the National Park Service.

AT A GLANCE

Day Hike: This route can usually be accomplished as a long day-hike, but if hiking in the winter keep in mind the short days and make sure you have enough time to return. This is an ideal overnight trip.

Distance: 16-mile round-trip.

Average Hiking Time: 8 hours is average. If hiking in the winter, allow yourself enough time to get back to your vehicle in daylight.

Difficulty: This is a long-but-moderate route lacking major elevation changes.

Permits: A permit is only required for camping.

Trail Conditions: The path is sandy and easy to walk on if it's dry. There is little reprieve from the sun on this low-altitude trail: it is not recommended in the summer. The clay content in the soil makes the footpath difficult after a rain- or snowstorm. Hiking when the path is wet also leaves deep footprints which are uncomfortable for others to hike on once the trail dries.

Trailhead: The trailhead is located outside the south entrance of Zion National Park, about a block south of the "Springdale Fruit Company" in Springdale. Enter the commercial area, at the Anasazi Plateau housing development, and take the immediate right located at the top of the hill. The hill is steep, making the turnoff difficult to see, but be sure you do not go into the housing section.

Trailend: Same as trailhead.

Trail Access: Year-round access. The trailhead is just off SR-9.

Elevation Gain: 650 feet.

Starting Elevation: 3,800 feet.

Highest Elevation: 4,450 feet.

Off the Beaten Path: Yes.

Best Season: This is a good trail for winter hiking but it's long—not all hikers will be able to complete it during the short winter days. This is a good route for trail runners when the weather is cool.

Water Availability: Coalpits Wash generally has flowing water. Coalpits Spring is located in Coalpits Wash, 0.2 miles downstream from the junction of Chinle Trail and Coalpits Wash. Water from both sources should be filtered or purified.

Sacred Datura

⑰ CHINLE TRAIL DETAILS

TRAILHEAD - Drive 3.5 miles from Zion's south entrance booth and look for the turnoff on the north side of SR-9, just past the fruit stand. There are homes (Anasazi Plateau Subdivision) on the north hill above the trailhead parking lot. Turn onto the steep Anasazi Road, drive uphill for a short distance and look for an immediate righthand turnoff. The turnoff to the Chinle Trailhead is currently unmarked. Park in the large, flat, dirt area. There is a trail information kiosk at the parking area.

CHINLE TRAIL - To begin the trail, follow the switchbacks uphill, cross the paved road and continue up the wash, following the beaten path under the bridge. Continue to the hikers' gate and kiosk, passing through and closing the gate behind you. Once inside the gate you are within Zion National Park boundaries. Please remember to remain on the obvious trail so fragile cryptobiotic soil is not destroyed. Follow the narrow, sandy path as it crosses the northern edge of the Rockville Bench and passes through the low-desert juniper forest. After 3.0 miles the trail crosses Huber Wash, which flows south and eventually drains into the Virgin River. As the trail slowly gains elevation, pinyon trees increasingly cover the land and the views to the north, west and south unfold.

PETRIFIED WOOD - While crossing the Rockville Bench and before arriving at Scoggins Wash, notice how the Petrified Forest is sprinkled with all sorts of wood and crystal treasures. This section of the trail, along the Chinle formation, is where the hike gets its name. Chinle is a Triassic shale that has shards of petrified wood.

Please don't collect the petrified wood within the National Park; leave it for others to enjoy!

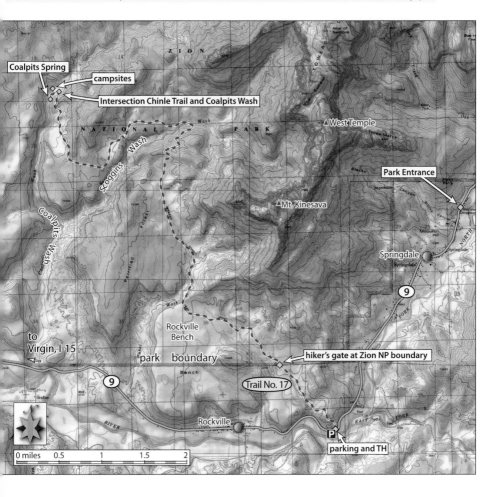

4 SCOGGINS WASH CONFLUENCE - The next wash, located 5.0 miles into the hike, is Scoggins Wash, another drainage of the Virgin River. The trail bears southwest between the Scoggins and Coalpits washes and soon meets the junction of the Old Scoggins Stock Trail.

5 OLD SCOGGINS STOCK TRAIL INTERSECTION - Almost a mile and a half (1.35 miles) after rounding the head of Scoggins Wash is the intersection of the Old Scoggins Stock Trail, which descends steeply into the bottom of Scoggins Wash. At this intersection, follow the righthand trail that leads to Coalpits Wash. It is only 1.3 miles to Coalpits from this intersection.

6 COALPITS WASH - The Chinle Trail ends at Coalpits Wash, yet another drainage of the Virgin River. The campsites are located across the wash and downstream 50 yards (where there is a trail that turns right and away from the wash). There are some level campsites in this area and the spring is nearby making it an ideal area to spend the night. This is the end of the Chinle Trail but if time allows, hikers can explore Coalpits Wash. This drainage is probably the most enjoyable of the southern Zion hikes due to water running in the wash.

7 COALPITS SPRING - From the junction of Coalpits and Chinle walk downstream in Coalpits Wash for a short distance (0.2 miles) and look on the right bank for flowing water. Be sure to filter or purify any water found in Coalpits Wash or the spring.

8 LOOP TRAIL OPTION - A car shuttle could be placed at Coalpits Wash and SR-9. Hike the Chinle Trail from the trailhead and once arriving at Coalpits Wash, walk in the wash to the south for 3.6 miles to arrive at SR-9. There is usually running water in Coalpits Wash, so have appropriate footwear and clothing for the season.

View of Cougar Mountain from Coalpits Wash

GPS Coordinates
WGS84 Datum
Parking and Trailhead
37°09.671 N
113°01.133 W

Chinle Trail-Coalpits Wash
confluence
37°12.948 N
113°04.638 W

Coalpits Spring
37°12.911 N
113°04.746 W

Coalpits Campsites
37°12.952 N
113°04.693 W

DOUBLE FALLS - BARRIER FALLS ⑱

The mention of Zion National Park conjures up images of vertical sandstone walls enclosing a magnificent desertscape dusted with a scattering of trails leading to water within the arid land of the park. One such trail is this one, which follows the Right Fork of North Creek.

Along this hike, a meandering stream is framed by wide, welcoming walls; cattails, moss, and ferns provide nutrients for the abundant wildlife that thrives in this rich, riparian habitat. Cliff swallows and canyon tree frogs harmonize in melody and cascades of cool water spill over slabs of layered sandstone. The destination is a pair of delicate waterfalls tucked deep in the canyon. Hikers can make their way behind picturesque Double Falls and gaze through streaming sheets of water to the calm pool below. Visitors who partake in this challenging and exhilarating trek will find a magical beauty in this quiet corner of Zion.

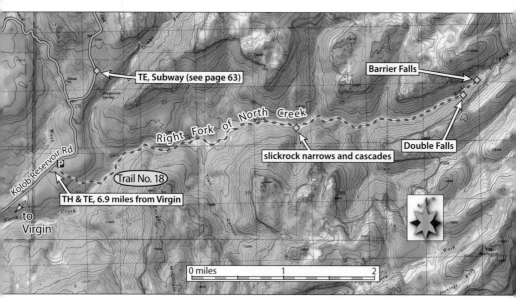

AT A GLANCE

Day Hike: Yes.

Distance: 11.6-mile round-trip.

Average Hiking Time: 11 hours.

Difficulty: Expect: boulder hopping; steep, slickrock scrambles; wet, slippery, stream crossings; and bushwhacking. Route-finding skills are required. Possible swimming. Be careful to avoid the poison ivy along the creek.

Equipment: Neoprene socks, sticky-sole shoes, dry clothing, hat, 3 liters of water per person and/or a water filter, energy food, map, compass and emergency gear.

Sun Exposure: Full sun most of the hike.

Permits: A permit is not required for this route. Weather information:
http://www.weather.gov/

Trail Conditions: Route-finding decisions and stream crossings are required, and possibly swimming.

Trailhead: Lower Right Fork Trailhead located off the Kolob Reservoir Road, 6.9 miles northeast of Virgin.

Trailend: Same as the trailhead.

Best Season: Summer or autumn. Cold rivers and heavy current will deter most hikers in the winter months. Spring runoff in both the Left Fork and Right Fork often results in swollen stream flow and may make stream crossings difficult or impossible.

Elevation: Trailhead: 4,500 feet. Trailend: 5,000 feet.

Off the Beaten Path: Yes.

> **Be sure to check the weather report before attempting this canyon. <u>Do not go</u> if it looks like rain. Hiking in slot canyons presents a real danger from flash flooding. Remember, a storm far off can trigger a flash flood.**

⑱ DOUBLE FALLS/BARRIER FALLS DETAILS

1 DRIVING INSTRUCTIONS - Start from the town of Virgin on SR-9. Set your odometer and turn north onto the signed Kolob Reservoir Road. Drive for 6.9 miles to the Lower Right Fork parking lot.

2 HIKING - Begin by traveling through junipers and cacti for the first 0.25 miles until you arrive at a basalt bluff overlooking North Creek. The trail becomes steep the next 0.25 miles as it winds through the basalt cliffband, requiring some short down-climbs. Soon the terrain eases, leading to the bottom and arriving at North Creek. Once at North Creek, head upstream for roughly 200 yards, passing a waterfall carved through a slickrock slab. Just upstream is the confluence of Right Fork of North Creek and Left Fork of North Creek. Cross the stream to the east side, staying on the beaten path, and make your way up the Right Fork of North Creek. The beaten path crisscrosses the gently flowing stream many times during the trek east toward Barrier Falls. Stay in the watercourse when possible or on the most-well-beaten paths to minimize impact to the fragile environment. Several years ago a landslide created a rather deep lake. The slide remains active. The lake should be swam through rather than navigated around because rocks are continuing to come down.

3 TRAIL CANYON - After 2.5 miles, you will pass Trail Canyon on your right. There are some wonderful cascades a little over one-third of a mile past Trail Canyon. At 3.75 miles the first 5-foot-tall waterfall slices through the slickrock and creates a beautiful pool. Just beyond 4.25 miles the canyon narrows, forming pools and waterfalls. Lush hanging gardens, cattail and horsetail adorn a short section of narrows.

4 DOUBLE FALLS - A mile past the narrows is Double Falls. This is a wonderful place to stop and shoot pictures, absorb the desert oasis, and recover for the last 0.35 miles of scrambling, bouldering, and bushwhacking required to reach the end of the trek at Barrier Falls.

5 BARRIER FALS - To get to Barrier Falls, head up the steep embankment on the right side, navigating the 4-foot rock ledge, then traverse upstream above and on the right side of Double Falls. On top of Double Falls the route becomes more difficult. Scramble up the slabs in the stream to eventually come to another waterfall which can be bypassed on the left side. Barrier Falls is now just a short distance through the boulders and up the ledge on the left. The mileage at this point is 5.8 miles. You will know you are at Barrier Falls when you can go no farther. Although not as photogenic as Double Falls, the trip wouldn't be complete without a glimpse of the "Barrier." Don't attempt to scale up this steep, slippery rock beyond here: a fall could result in serious injury and a very slow, complicated rescue. Be sure to start back (retracing your path) at least 5 hours before the sun goes down.

The idyllic desert oasis of Double Falls. Photo: Bo Beck

GPS Coordinates
WGS84 Datum

Parking At Right Fork Trailhead
37°16.247 N
113°06.185 W

Right Fork Trailhead Entry
and Exit at North Creek
37°16.056 N
113°05.720 W

Trail Canyon Intersection
37°16.464 N
113°04.507 W

Double Falls
37°16.872 N
113°01.438 W

Barrier Falls
37°16.996 N
113°01.222 W

THE SUBWAY ⑲

The mystical journey through the Left Fork of North Creek involves route-finding, plunging cautiously into chilly pools, sloshing—sometimes frantically—through frigid water over and through difficult obstacles, and even a seldom-seen natural arch. The narrow Subway section of this hike forces hikers through a unique tunnel sculpted by the Left Fork of North Creek. Churning water chisels the rock floor, forming shallow potholes that fill to the brim with frosty water. Silhouettes dance freely on multi-colored walls where only a trickle of sunlight penetrates into the Subway's curved chamber. Falling water echoes in the tunnel. Dragonflies dart, frogs laze about and shimmering emerald pools tempt cold hikers to dawdle. Before long, the promise of daylight urges an exit to the warmth of the sun waiting outside the shaded walls. As the canyon widens, hikers cross back and forth across the creek, making their way to the grueling uphill exit.

If you want a glimpse of the canyon, but prefer to stay away from uncomfortable obstacles, you can get a taste by entering from the bottom, where thin sheets of glistening water cascade over mossy stair-step slivers of rock.

The bizarre geometry of the Subway

One of the many colorful pools in the Subway

AT A GLANCE

Day Hike: Yes.

Distance: 9.5 miles.

Average Hiking Time: 8 hours.

Equipment: Neoprene socks, rope, harness, sturdy sticky-rubber hiking shoes, 3 liters of water per person or a purification method, energy food, dry clothing, emergency equipment and a headlamp. Spring and autumn may necessitate the use of wetsuits. Use a dry bag for electronics and extra clothing—ziplock baggies and other such household items will NOT keep gear dry. Bring a 60-foot length of rope.

Difficulty: This is a technical canyon where rappelling and down-climbing skills are required. These obstacles can be avoided by hiking into the Subway from the bottom.

Sun Exposure: There are some cold areas that get no sun, but most of the hike is in full sun.

Permits: A permit is required. Demand can be high, so it's best to plan well ahead. See the park website for details (link info on page 67). Note: In heavy-snowpack years the Left Fork may be impassible and the NPS may not issue any permits; the park website will have up-to-date information.

Trail Conditions: Swimming is usually required through at least three pools of cold water and there are usually four obstacles that must be down-climbed or rappelled with the use of a rope.

Trailhead: Wildcat Canyon Trailhead is located on the Kolob Reservoir Road, 15.5 miles north of Virgin.

Trailend: The Lower Left Fork Trailend is also on the Kolob Reservoir Road, 8 miles north of the town of Virgin.

Trail Access: Begin the Subway at the Wildcat Canyon Trailhead.

Best Season: In the summer when the water and air are warmer. Heavy winter snowfall, and spring runoff may render hiking the Subway impossible. It's cold in this canyon and only experienced canyoneers with proper gear should attempt it in the spring, winter or late fall.

Elevation: Parking: 6,985 feet.

Elevation: Trailend: 5,100 feet.

Off the Beaten Path: This is a popular, classic wilderness hike with 80 hikers a day maximum.

Water Availability: In the later section of the hike, there is one major spring entering from the right (north) and several seeps that may be present depending on conditions. Purify all water before use.

Note: The enclosed nature of the Subway creates a flash-flood danger. In addition, there are numerous slippery rocks and obstacles to down-climb. Swimming in ice-cold water can cause hypothermia. The lower section of the canyon is slippery due to moss. Slot canyons can change dramatically in a short time due to flash floods.

Brandon Beck rappels in the Subway

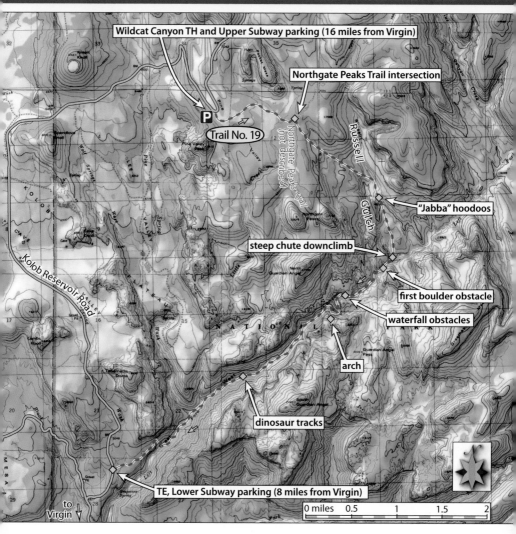

Wildcat Canyon TH and Upper Subway parking (16 miles from Virgin)

Northgate Peaks Trail intersection

P

Trail No. 19

"Jabba" hoodoos

steep chute downclimb

first boulder obstacle

waterfall obstacles

arch

dinosaur tracks

TE, Lower Subway parking (8 miles from Virgin)

to Virgin

0 miles   0.5   1   1.5   2

9 SUBWAY DETAILS

SHUTTLE SETUP - You will need to arrange to leave a vehicle parked at both ends of the hike. First drive two vehicles to Virgin, which is 12 miles from Zion's south entrance (see map on page 16). Toward the end of town, turn onto the Kolob Reservoir Road and head north for 8.0 miles. Park one vehicle at the Left Fork Trailend (the bottom end of the Subway) then continue 8.0 miles north to the Wildcat Canyon Trailhead to park the second vehicle and begin the route.

WILDCAT CANYON TRAILHEAD - Walk east on the Wildcat Canyon Trail for 0.85 miles until it meets the Northgate Peaks Trail. Head south on the Northgate Peaks Trail for less than 0.2 miles to where a Subway Trailhead sign marks the route. The trail is now over slickrock. Look for a metal post with a footprint placard, as well as occasional cairns marking the proper path. Traverse down and right, staying on the cairned slickrock path until it enters a short winding trail through manzanita. The route will once again require some slickrock travel and eventually enter a wash strewn with basalt talus. By following the cairns and remaining on the path of use, impact to surrounding sensitive soils will be mitigated. Eventually the path arrives at a buttress overlooking the depths of Russell Gulch. One last steep descent of 200 feet will bring you into the bottom of the gulch.

3 RUSSELL GULCH - Once at the bottom of the gulch, hike to the slickrock on the east side of Russell Gulch. Look for a cross-bedded, dome-like "Jabba the Hut" hoodoo high in the saddle, to the south. Continue hiking slickrock toward the domes and, at the saddle, pass between the domes. Hike south, down the large slickrock bowl, and look for where the trail enters the vegetated area at the end of the bowl. Continue a short distance on the trail to a small wash. This wash lures some hikers to the right; instead, keep an eye out for a cairn to the left that indicates where the correct route goes: ascend to a small saddle and then descend into another wash. The trail then ascends a short distance and traverses for a couple hundred yards before the steep, final descent into Russell Gulch. You are now close to the very bottom end of Russell Gulch. Watch for a pine tree next to a slab of rock on the right. This seems like an improbable chute to maneuver; however, by carefully stepping down the rock-and-root stairway and picking through the loose rock for 300 vertical feet, the bottom of Russell Gulch is obtained. At the bottom of this steep chute, turn left and walk 100 yards to find the confluence of Left Fork of North Creek and Russell Gulch. Turn right at this confluence.

4 BOULDER OBSTACLE - About 300 yards down the Left Fork of North Creek is the first obstacle. Scamper up this 12-foot boulder and locate the sling anchor on its right side. Secure a doubled rope so the last person in the party can pull it free. This is an easy and straightforward rappel. There is also a chimney on the right side of the boulder that can be rappelled. Do not jump! Search and Rescue teams are often called to the Subway for those that are unprepared to navigate obstacles and get hurt jumping.

Bo Beck swimming in the Subway

SPECIAL WARNINGS FOR THE SUBWAY:

1. Pack cameras and other sensitive items into good quality dry bags (TWO dry bags, one inside the other, is best).

2. If the temperatures outside are cool, wetsuits are required—the water is frigid even in the middle of the summer, and in spring and fall can be dangerously cold. Even when it is hot outside, wear quick-dry clothing and keep some dry clothes to wear for the shady, cool Subway section that follows.

3. Navigate with care through or around the potholes. Never jump into a pothole—there may be barely-submerged rocks! Also note that each flash flood changes the character of the route and the depth of the pools.

5 CANYON ROUTE - Continue downcanyon. Be prepared to swim! The first pool is generally about 30 feet long, followed by a shorter pool. At the end of the first pool there is a submerged window that some choose to swim through.

6 KEYHOLE FALLS - Yet another waterfall in the narrow slot will necessitate the use of a rope. The drop only 8 feet to the water, but, once again, submerged rocks make jumping dangerous. To the right, an o bolt with a hanger is used as an anchor that allows a hand-line or rappel through the crack.

7 BOWLING BALL OBSTACLE - Bolts in the now-narrow slot canyon may have a webbing sling attache that aids in the 8-foot drop to a small ledge. This is followed by another 3- to 4-foot drop into the poc below. Do not jump into the water, there is a hazardous submerged rock just 3 feet below the surface. This is a difficult obstacle for many to navigate without some aid. Swimming is required after climbing into this pool of water. The next two chambers present wonderful photo opportunities—if you can kee your camera dry!

THE SUBWAY - The quarter-mile passage through the Subway is the most charming segment of the adventure. Deep inside the tubular tunnel glimmers of sunlight trickle into the darkness, allowing algae to grow in water-filled potholes. The green flora creates an eerie turquoise glow that radiates throughout the spectacular chamber. The crystal-clear water splashing through this picturesque setting meanders over polished rock to the open canyon below.

LOG CHAMBER AND SUBWAY ARCH - Inside the Subway, just past Keyhole Falls, is a chamber where there may still be a log perched against the wall—it is amazing how long it has stayed without a flood washing it away. Ten yards upstream of the log, a freestanding arch can be seen—look up and left.

FINAL OBSTACLE - A few yards past the leaning log is a 6-foot waterfall. Stay right, on a rock ledge, to bypass this. Continue downstream 50 yards, where the canyon turns to the left and arrives at the final obstacle. A log jammed in a narrow crack in the rock waterway forms a short bridge over the waterfall. Cross to the slickrock ledge on the left. Walk 20 yards downstream on this ledge and locate a two-bolt anchor just 6 feet below, inside a small bowl. A 60-foot rope is required for the 30-foot rappel from these bolts. Take care here, as the the rock is often wet and slippery from moss and the rock is quite vertical near the bottom. The best climber should rappel first to help the others in the party.

WATERFALL ROOM - Once below the final obstacle, be sure to wade, swim and work through the potholes back upstream to see the waterfall room. This is the waterfall you walked over by using the wedged log bridge. Stay and enjoy the many desert tanks in the once-again tunneled Subway. This waterfall room is the turn-around spot if you hiked up from the bottom. The canyon now opens up and follows the streambed for most of the remaining hike. Please do not be tempted to create new trails; either stay in the streambed or follow the cairn-marked path. Over the years multiple social trails have caused a great deal of erosional impact, and the park service is attempting to mitigate this impact by creating a single, sustainable path of use.

CASCADES - Shortly after leaving the Subway there are several notable cascades. Use caution since the falls are extremely slippery. Enjoy the beautiful cascades and often crystalline water. Beyond the last cascade, the route crosses back and forth from one side of the creek to the other—and occasionally travels in the center of the watercourse.

DINOSAUR TRACKS - Seven miles into the hike, on the right (north), are two large slabs of white rock, angled toward the creekbed, with embedded prints of a dinosaur, most likely a Grallator-type therapod.

CANYON EXIT - The exit from the Left Fork of North Creek is downstream from the dinosaur tracks. As of 2012, there is a well-established trail for this exit. Please follow this. The exit scrambles up to the top of the basalt ridge that appears in front of you. It will look impossible to climb, but the steep route ascends up and to the right of the 100- to 200-foot-high basalt cliffs. Once at the top of the basalt ridge a trail meanders through a juniper and pinyon forest for 0.5 miles and arrives back at the lower Left Fork trailend.

PERMIT AND RESERVATION INFORMATION - Demand for permits for this popular hike is very high so it's best to plan ahead. Log onto the park's website for details:

http://www.nps.gov/zion/planyourvisit/backcountry-reservations-and-permits.htm

Subway GPS Coordinates
WGS84 Datum

Parking at Wildcat Canyon Trailhead: Elevation 6985'
37°20.401N , 113°04.544W

Junction of Wildcat Canyon Trail and Northgate Peaks Trail
37°20.411N , 113°03.566W

Trail to Russell Gulch
37°20.235N , 113°03.500W

Cross Russell Gulch to the east side
37°19.837N , 113°02.682W

Slickrock Saddle
37°19.647N , 113°02.599W

Entry Trail to Left Fork
37°19.096N , 113°02.417W

Dinosaur Tracks
37°17.986 N , 113°04.207 W

Exit from Left Fork
37°17.378 N , 113°05.084 W

Parking at Trailend:
37°17.080 N , 113° 05.761 W

Kolob Arch ㉒

Kolob Arch flaunts one of the longest freestanding arches in the world. This massive sandstone span towers over a beautiful canyon in a far corner of Zion National Park. Built on a classic, monumental scale, this is a must-see feature that is just far enough from the nearest road to preserve a primitive, remote feel.

The Natural Arch and Bridge Society, after measuring in 2006, came to the conclusion that Kolob Arch is the second-longest natural arch in the world measuring 287.4 feet. This leaves Zion's arch about three feet shorter than Arches National Park's pride, Landscape Arch. If the long debate over which is the longer of the two arches is not over now, it could end in the near future since Landscape Arch is near the end of its lifecycle. Kolob Arch is an adult-alcove, natural arch perched high on an exposed cliff. It was created as a result of vertical joint expansion, wall collapse and erosion.

Kolob Canyons, where the arch lies, is in the far northwestern and less visited section of Zion National Park, accessed off I-15 at exit 40 near Cedar City (see roadmap on page 16). The 14-mile round trip to the landmark can be done as a leisurely backpack or a long day-hike. No permit is needed for hiking, but a permit is needed to camp: see the park website for details:

http://www.nps.gov/zion/planyourvisit/backcountry-reservations-and-permits.htm

Kolob Arch can be seen, from afar, by hiking though Hop Valley, located off the Kolob Terrace Road.

Kolob Arch—magnificent, massive, monumental—a must-see feature of Zion National Park's backcountry

AT A GLANCE

Day Hike: The Kolob Arch hike can be done as a long day-hike but many take two days—or even stretch it into a multi-day backpacking trip.

Distance: 14-mile round-trip.

Average Hiking Time: 12 hours, round-trip.

Equipment: Take at least 3 quarts of water per person as well as a means to purify or filter it, energy food, comfortable hiking shoes that would dry quickly if they get wet, dry socks, sun-protective and extra clothing for possible changes in the weather, insect repellent and emergency gear. Bring camping gear if plans are to stay the night.

Difficulty: This is a strenuous hiking trail when done as a day hike, but only moderately strenuous as a backpack. Much of the path is soft sand leading to some leg fatigue. There may be several stream crossings.

Sun Exposure: Expect full sun during most of the hike.

Permits: A permit is required for camping, but not needed if you plan to day hike. There are 13 campsites: 6 are available by reservation and 7 are saved for walk-ins. The maximum group size is 12. For more information and campsite availability visit the park website (see link info on facing page).

Trail Conditions: This is a maintained dirt path.

Trailhead: Park at Lee Pass parking area, in the Kolob Canyons section of Zion, 3.7 miles up the scenic drive from the Kolob Canyons Visitor Center (see map p16).

Trailend: Same as the trailhead.

Trail Access: Snowpack, slick, wet, and steep trail conditions generally deter most hikers in the winter months; however, in low-precipitation winters the hike may be possible.

Best Season: The best time to hike this trail is in the spring and fall. Summer is also nice if you get an early start, otherwise it can be a hot day due to lack of shade, even though it is usually about 10 degrees cooler in Kolob Canyons than Zion Canyon. If you choose to do this hike in the winter, keep in mind that the road leading to the trailhead might close temporarily due to snow.

Elevation: Trailhead: 6,100 feet, Trailend: 5,400 feet, Lowest Elevation: 5,000 feet.

Off the Beaten Path: No.

Water Availability: Water is generally available a mile into the hike at Timber Creek, but in dry years you may have to hike to La Verkin Creek, about 4 miles from the trailhead. Once at La Verkin Creek, water will be abundant until the intersection with the final 0.5-mile spur trail to Kolob Arch. Water should always be purified and/or filtered before drinking.

20) KOLOB ARCH DETAILS

LEE PASS TRAILHEAD - Drive 16 miles south of Cedar City on I-15 or 32 miles north of St. George on I-15 and take Exit 40 (see roadmap on page 16). Exit 40 leads to the Kolob Canyons Visitor Center and a scenic drive with breathtaking views of the towering cliffs of the Kolob "fingers." A short but impressive drive up the road from the visitor center reaches the parking lot for the Lee Pass Trailhead. The views of Tucupit Point, Paria Point and Beatty Point are delightful but less well-known than Zion's main landmarks, since this side of the park is less frequented than the main section of Zion.

TIMBER CREEK - The first mile of the hike, from the Lee Pass Trailhead, descends a moderately steep ridge. The next 2 miles contour in and out of Timber Creek, then it rounds Shuntavi Butte and bears to the east around the western tip of Gregory Butte. Eventually the trail winds through pinyon and juniper trees and descends into the lush, east-west oriented La Verkin Creek drainage.

Butterfly. You may see lots of wildlife on the scenic hike to Kolob Arch

3 LA VERKIN CREEK - At La Verkin Creek the path is relatively flat, but sand makes the progress tedious at times. Halfway through the meander, alongside La Verkin Creek, the trail crosses a flowing spring-fed stream. After 2 miles of hiking along La Verkin Creek, you will arrive at the junction of the Kolob Arch Trail. Here, head left (north) and leave the sandy travel behind. A half-mile past the junction, you will reach a fine viewpoint where you will get your first glimpse of the impressive Kolob Arch, high up and on the left. The structure rests on the sheer cliffband walls northeast of Gregory Butte Formation.

DAY HIKING - If doing this as a day-hike, this viewpoint is a great place to get out of the sun, take a lunch break, relax and regenerate for the hike back out. La Verkin Creek may entice you to take a quick refresher dip and cool off before the hike back begins.

BACKPACKING - There are 13 designated campsites. Three sites dot the first 3 miles of the hike from the trailhead. The remaining 10 are within the next 4 miles. Camping is allowed only in designated sites.

GPS Coordinates
WGS84 Datum
Trailhead
37°27.125N, 113°11.480W
Kolob Arch Viewpoint
37°25.370N, 113°09.134W

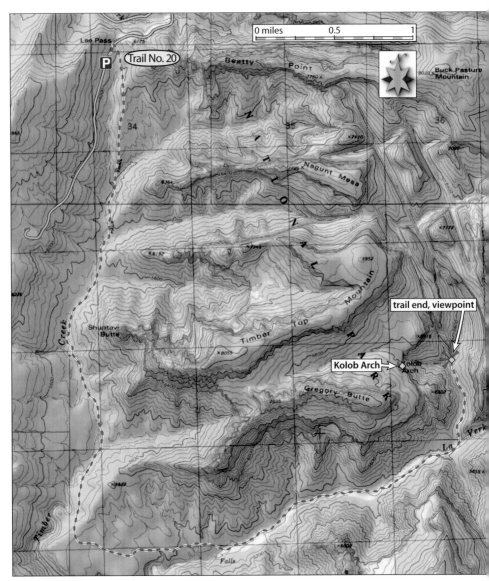

Tanya Milligan rappelling. Photo: Bo Beck

GREATER ZION AREA

The beauty seen along the Zion-Mt. Carmel Highway (SR-9) and explored in the previous chapter does not stop at the park boundaries. Drive east out of Zion National Park to Mt. Carmel Junction and you reach the terminus of SR-9, and a T-junction with US-89. A left turn here leads north to spectacular Bryce Canyon, a right turn takes you to the North Rim of the Grand Canyon. US-89 is a gateway to a vast and little-visited world of sculpted sandstone, vermilion cliffs, forests, hoodoos, slickrock plateaus, windswept canyons, and slickrock.

Closer at hand, US-89 accesses canyon adventures such as Peek-a-Boo and Red Hollow, tucked away in secret locations not too far from Zion. Other routes in this chapter are accessed from SR-9 just beyond the park boundaries, and represent the best of the delights found in this corner of southwest Utah. Birch Hollow is just northeast of Zion, Eagle Crags sits just southwest of the park, while Parunuweap Canyon and the classic Fat Man's Misery explore hidden canyons immediately southeast of the park. Area map is on facing page. Zion NP map, pages 16–17, may also be helpful. Regional map is on page 7.

Red Canyon (Peek-a-boo) is a fun, dry, non-technical slot canyon. Here, Tanya Milligan explores its mysteries. Photo: Bo Beck

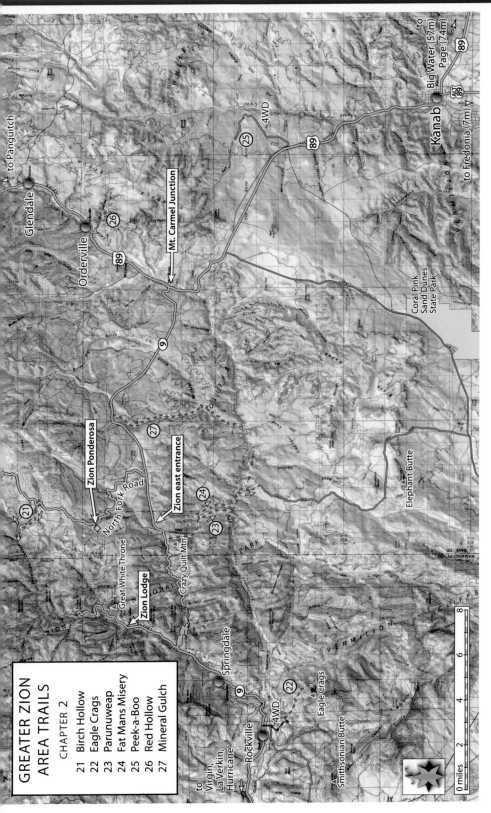

GREATER ZION
AREA TRAILS
CHAPTER 2

21 Birch Hollow
22 Eagle Crags
23 Parunuweap
24 Fat Mans Misery
25 Peek-a-Boo
26 Red Hollow
27 Mineral Gulch

BIRCH HOLLOW ㉑

Imagine an impossibly narrow canyon with sinewy, curved, and wind-swept paths, lit with mysterious shadows and hints of light; a canyon that tempts canyoneers to wiggle, slither and climb to its finish. Birch Hollow is such a canyon, yet it's a forgotten gem in the canyoneering world because it doesn't hold the distinction of being within Zion National Park's boundaries.

Not only does Birch Hollow offer some of the best canyoneering to be had anywhere, it can be combined with two of Zion's classic canyons, Orderville Canyon and the Zion Narrows, to create a magnificent canyoneering adventure.

Technical Canyoneering Warnings: Birch Hollow is a technical canyon requiring ropes and the skill to use them. Never enter a technical canyon without the equipment, knowledge and skills needed to safely explore and return. Many technical canyons require excellent map-reading skills. Hiking in slot canyons presents a very real danger from flash flooding. Do not hike this trail if it's raining—even a distant storm can trigger a flash flood. Birch Hollow has a high flash-flood danger. Remember, slot canyons can change dramatically in a short time due to flash floods and water levels. The directions given here are only a general reference; be prepared for variations in the canyon. Weather information: http://www.weather.gov/

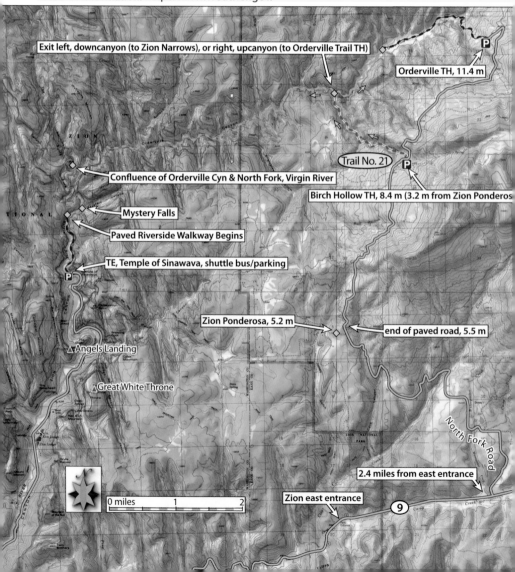

Exit left, downcanyon (to Zion Narrows), or right, upcanyon (to Orderville Trail TH)

Orderville TH, 11.4 m

Trail No. 21

Confluence of Orderville Cyn & North Fork, Virgin River

Birch Hollow TH, 8.4 m (3.2 m from Zion Ponderosa

Mystery Falls

Paved Riverside Walkway Begins

TE, Temple of Sinawava, shuttle bus/parking

Zion Ponderosa, 5.2 m

end of paved road, 5.5 m

△Angels Landing

▲Great White Throne

North Fork Road

2.4 miles from east entrance

0 miles   1   2

Zion east entrance

9

AT A GLANCE

Day Hike: Yes.

Distance: 10 miles.

Average Hiking Time: 12 hours.

Difficulty: This canyon is strenuous. It requires technical canyoneering skills and has numerous rappels. The down-climbs are hard but not overly difficult.

Equipment: Two 100-foot ropes (or one 200-foot rope), 20 feet of webbing, harness, rappel device, map, dry bag, sticky-rubber soled canyoneering shoes, quick-dry clothing, energy foods, 3 liters of water per person, water purification or water filter and emergency gear.

Sun Exposure: The canyon section offers shade, but there is some hiking in full sun in areas as well.

Permit: A permit is required for Orderville Canyon but not for Birch Hollow; so you only need to obtain one if you plan to exit via Orderville Canyon and the Zion Narrows.

Technical: There are about 10 rappels, with the longest at 100 feet, and there are several short down-climbs.

Trailhead: 8.4 miles north of SR-9 on the North Fork Road, located just outside the east side of Zion.

Trailend: Temple of Sinawava in Zion Canyon; or at the Orderville Canyon entrance on the North Fork Road.

Trail Access: Cold river temperatures and heavy current in the Zion Narrows and Orderville Canyon will deter most hikers in the spring and winter. Dirt roads leading to the trailhead may be impassable when wet. This hike requires a car shuttle.

Best Season: Mid-June to mid-September when the water is warmer in the canyons.

Off the Beaten Path: Yes.

Bo Beck rappelling in Birch Hollow

㉑ Birch Hollow (with Zion Narrows Exit) Details

1 Driving Instructions - Park the first vehicle at the Zion Canyon Visitor Center if the park shuttles are running; if they are not running, park the first vehicle at the Temple of Sinawava in Zion Canyon. Drive the second vehicle to the Birch Hollow Trailhead.

2 Birch Hollow Trailhead - Leave Zion National Park from the east gate and drive 2.4 miles. Turn left at the junction of North Fork Road and SR-9. Drive 5.2 miles up the paved road to the Zion Ponderosa. Don't drive in, but reset your odometer and continue on the now-dirt North Fork Road. When your odometer hits 3.2 miles you are at Birch Hollow. There is a place to pull over on the left side of the road. The wash on the left is where the hike begins.

3 Birch Hollow - Drop immediately into the Birch Hollow wash and bushwhack downstream. Follow the somewhat vegetated wash for about 20 minutes, passing remnants of an old ramp made of 4x4 timbers. The canyon soon becomes less densely vegetated and travel becomes easier.

4 Obstacle - The first large obstacle will soon present itself: a large bowl headed with a dryfall. Negotiate this by rappelling on natural tree anchors on the right side, or scrambling up, around and down on the left side. There is loose rock in this section and it might be wiser to down-climb rather than rappel. After completing the first obstacle, continue downstream where there are several short down-climbs. Soon the canyon walls come closer together, revealing a glimpse of the fluted and narrowing sandstone that lies ahead. Before long you will be walking in an open canyon floor.

5 First Rappel - Just a short distance away is a second large bowl and the first required rappel. This rappel is usually done from a natural boulder anchor smack in the middle of the watercourse, but may also be done from one of the many anchor opportunities that exist nearby. This rappel is about 50 feet, and lands in a grotto at the bottom of the wash—a genuine slot canyon now lies ahead.

6 Rappels 2–4 - Continuing downstream, the canyon will begin to close in and demonstrate fluted sandstone, which will be evident for the rest of the canyon. Next comes a couple of 15-foot rappels using a chockstone anchor 20 feet upstream from the drop. Soon after is another 15-foot rappel using a pinched chockstone anchor. Just a short distance further comes a 25-foot rappel off a two-bolt anchor.

7 Rappels 5–6 - The canyon widens for a bit and an amazing fir forest sprouts on the sloping sides of the canyon. There are possible escapes on the left if needed. After 0.25 miles of this beautiful landscape the canyon floor abruptly drops out, and a twisted slot canyon below beckons to canyoneers. A 100-foot rappel from a tree anchor on the left side will bring you to a bowl below. A short walk through the bowl reveals a two-bolt anchor for another 45-foot rappel as the canyon becomes deeper and deeper.

8 Seventh Rappel - Just around the corner comes another 45-foot rappel leading to a sandy wash below. Another possible escape route becomes evident after this rappel.

9 Eighth Rappel - Continue downstream to encounter a 7-foot down-climb and soon the eighth rappel. This 35-foot rappel begins from the bolt anchor on the right. This rappel can be down-climbed using the two large logs wedged in the watercourse, but this is not recommended.

10 Ninth Rappel - Now, near the end of Birch Hollow is the grand finale. The final two rappels are absolutely amazing as the canyon twists and deepens. The ninth rappel drops 65 feet into a bowl. Look up to view a large, round boulder wedged in the tight canyon above and the light filtered through the twisted, sculpted rock.

11 Tenth Rappel - The tenth rappel, of 40 feet, puts you within a stone's throw of the famous Orderville Canyon.

12 Exit - Take Orderville Canyon downstream to where it connects with the Zion Narrows. Orderville Canyon is a technical canyon, requiring some down-climbing and possible rappels, though less complicated rappels than those found in Birch Hollow. At drop-offs, either rappel or carefully down-climb—never jump! Follow the Zion Narrows to the Riverside Walk, which ends at the Temple of Sinawava. If shuttles are running, catch the Zion Canyon Shuttle and ride back to your vehicle; otherwise you should have a vehicle parked here.

ALTERNATE BIRCH HOLLOW OPTION
(QUICK TRIP EXITING AT THE ORDERVILLE CANYON TRAILHEAD)

AT A GLANCE:

Distance: 6.2 miles.
Hiking Time: 6 hours hiking time.
Trailend: Orderville Canyon Trailhead.

ALTERNATE BIRCH HOLLOW OPTION DETAILS

DRIVING INSTRUCTIONS - Park the first vehicle at the Orderville Canyon Trailhead. To get there, drive two vehicles on the North Fork Road. Drive past the Birch Hollow Trailhead and continue another 3.0 miles north, on the road, to the Orderville Canyon Road on the left. The Orderville Canyon Trailhead turnoff is 6.2 miles past the Zion Ponderosa (11.4 miles from the turnoff from SR-9).

Note: this road can be washed out, slippery and difficult to navigate; keep in mind that rain can make the dirt road conditions impassable—make sure you can get out from where you drive to. If driving a 4WD, pass through the gate and then close the gate behind you. Most 4WDs can make it in about 2.0 miles, leaving about a half-mile hike to Orderville Canyon. If you don't have two 4WD vehicles, park the shuttle vehicle at the gate before dropping into Orderville Canyon.

Park the second vehicle at the Birch Hollow Trailhead (see instructions on facing page for driving to Birch Hollow).

BIRCH HOLLOW - Begin hiking at the Birch Hollow Trailhead, as described on the facing page.

EXIT - At the intersection with Orderville Canyon, turn right (up-canyon) until the 4WD road becomes evident. Follow the road to your vehicle.

GPS Coordinates
WGS84 Datum

Birch Hollow Trailhead
37°18.584N
112°51.371W

Parking at Orderville
Canyon Gate (trailend
for alternate exit option)
37°20.089N
112°49.067W

A rappel in Birch Hollow. Note use of climbing harness for comfortable descending

Eagle Crags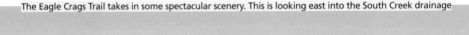

The beauty of Zion National Park reaches beyond the park's boundary. To the southwest of the park and across the Virgin River is a sprawling expanse of desolate, colorful cliffs and mesas, the Vermilion Cliffs, which stretch southward into Arizona. Towers of misshapen rock and eerie crags nest in the lofty tops of the Vermilion Cliffs. Juniper forests thrive in this parched environment; they survive by hoarding precious moisture while soaking up the abundant sunshine.

The 5-mile round-trip route described here, to Eagle Crags, begins at the end of a dirt road where the tiny town of Rockville gives way to BLM land (see map on facing page. Map on page 73 and area map on page 16 may be helpful). The trail runs along a wide, sandy path winding through a labyrinth of desert vegetation, taking you deep into this wild land.

Most of the trail ascends gently, except for a few steeper sections near the end. Sturdy hiking shoes or boots will help prevent slipping and injury along the more difficult portions of the trek.

The Eagle Crags Trail takes in some spectacular scenery. This is looking east into the South Creek drainage

At a Glance

Day Hike: Yes.

Distance: 4.8-mile round-trip.

Average Hiking Time: 4 hours.

Difficulty: Moderate. An easy trail until the final, steeper sections.

Equipment: Wear appropriate clothing for the weather and take emergency supplies. Sturdy hiking shoes are recommended. Be sure to carry at least 2–3 quarts of water for each person.

Sun Exposure: Full sun.

Permits: Permits are not required, even if camping, since this trail is on BLM land outside Zion National Park.

Trail Conditions: This path is wide and sandy, strewn with rocks, in full sun and on the arid, hot side of Zion National Park. It is a popular route for horseback riders and is well-suited for trail runners.

Trailhead: Rockville - South of the south entrance to Zion National Park.

Trailend: Same as the trailhead.

Trail Access: It's best to use a high-clearance 4WD. The road can be impassable if wet. The trailhead is in a remote area so ensure your 4WD has a good spare tire, a full tank, and a jack. Bring extra water.

Best Season: The best time to do this hike is in the spring, fall and winter. This is not an ideal hike in the heat of summer—it will be hot (though starting very early in the morning should make it bearable).

Starting Elevation: 4,380 feet.

Highest Elevation: 5,200 feet.

Elevation Gain: 900 feet.

Off the Beaten Path: Yes.

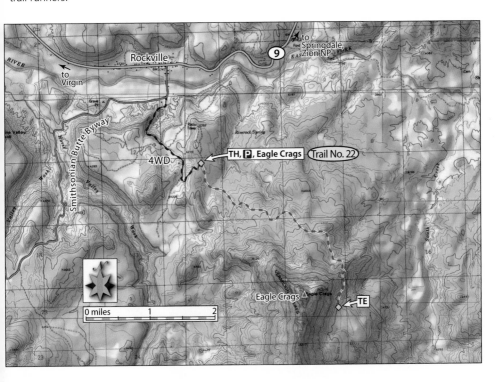

㉒ Eagle Crags Trail Details

Trailhead - A high-clearance 4WD vehicle is recommended, but even so the road may be impassible when wet. Drive to Rockville, which is located on the south side of Zion just past Springdale. Once in town, turn south on Bridge Road, set your odometer and drive south across the old bridge spanning the Virgin River. Soon after the bridge the paved road takes a hard right turn. Don't follow this turn; instead, go straight here onto the dirt road. You will climb a steep grade before traversing up to the head of a large bowl. One mile from SR-9 there is a three-way intersection; drive straight instead of turning. Drive past the dwellings on both the right and left as you begin the short, rocky, uphill climb to yet another junction. Turn left at the intersection and pass over the wash then follow the road up the hillside to the northeast. At 1.9 miles there is a small pullout on the right and a narrow ATV path doubling back to it. This is where you will leave your vehicle. On the southeast edge of the parking area should be a BLM trailhead sign; however, it is often vandalized and missing, so don't count on it being there.

2 EAGLE CRAGS TRAIL START- The route bears southeast for the first half-mile as it slowly traverses and descends into the wash below. Next comes a gradual ascent, still headed southeast, up the opposite side of the drainage, revealing views of the massive "laccolith" of Pine Valley Mountain to the west and the main canyon of Zion to the north. The outcrop of sandstone known as Eagle Crags appears to grow in elevation as each step draws you closer to the base of the towering, magnificent pinnacles.

3 EAGLE CRAGS - The trail follows a ridge to the south where you pass through a hikers' gate; a mile farther the path begins to head east. You will see wonderful views of Parunuweap basin unfold to the northeast, and a large private reservoir can be seen below to the east in the South Creek drainage. Hiking becomes harder here as elevation increases and you switchback up and toward the eastern tip of the crags. After some huffing and puffing, you will make it to the top of a ridge and the end of the 2.5 mile route. The views to the south show the slickrock cliffs that rim Lower Mountain. Beyond the ridge, the beaten path becomes faint and difficult to follow. This is where most people will stop and turn around.

The Eagle Crags themselves are a ridge of the Vermilion Cliffs, extending north of Lower Mountain, sitting on the plateau of Canaan Mountain. There is ample space and a level area at the end of this trail to settle back for a nice picnic so you can relax and prepare for the downhill hike back to your vehicle.

While resting, see if you can spot the historic Shunesburg settlement in the distance and the slickrock plateau of Canaan Mountain. You should also be able to see many other peaks extending all the way to the skyline including: Shunesburg Mountain, Johnson Mountain, De Mille Peak and Zion's Watchman, Mount Kinesava and West Temple. If you are lucky, you might even see a climber scaling the sheer stone of the Eagle Crags, making their way to the top of the crag via the climbing route known as Mrs. Butterworth.

Eagle Crags

4 BACKPACKING OPTION - Past this point is the "Old Cattle Trail" which was once used by cowboys to move cattle to and from Lower Mountain and Canaan Mountain, as well as to access the old sawmill on top. For the backpacker this route is the end of one of the authors' favorite trails, which begins in Hildale, Arizona, travels through Water Canyon, up Canaan Mountain and exits here (see Hike No. 44, page160, for details).

**GPS Coordinates
WGS84 Datum**

Eagle Crags Trailhead
37°08.862N, 113°01.866W

Hikers' Gate
37°08.552N, 113°01.439W

Eagle Crags Trailend
37°07.647N, 113°00.396W

PARUNUWEAP CANYON TRIP 1 ㉓

One of the most magnificent slot-canyon experiences in southern Utah is the descent into Parunuweap Canyon. This book describes two journeys into this entrancing place; the trip described here begins at the Zion-Mt. Carmel Highway (SR-9), just inside Zion National Park, near Checkerboard Mesa. It follows the first part of the Checkerboard Arch Trail (see page 54) then forges deep into BLM land, eventually meeting the canyon of the East Fork of the Virgin River. This trip returns the same way. (The other journey, described on page 85, is a more technical route that starts in the same place but continues south to an independent exit, thus requiring two vehicles).

The explorer John Wesley Powell named this area Parunuweap, meaning "Roaring Water Canyon." Along this hike you can view the memorial plaque dedicated to Powell's historic journey and envision the difficulties and sheer excitement that was confronted during his trip through this magical wilderness. Sheer canyon walls envelop the meandering—yet sometimes violent—flow of the East Fork of the Virgin River, as it makes its way west to join the North Fork of the Virgin River in Springdale.

At the trail's end, a short stroll upstream along the East Fork accesses the warm desert oasis and spring-fed, lush pool known as Sulfur Spring, located just outside the popular technical canyon route of Fat Man's Misery. Along the way, revel in the narrow passage cut in the Navajo sandstone, a slot that rivals the famous Zion Narrows. With some effort it is possible to go downstream a short distance and look at Labyrinth Falls from above and wonder how, over a century ago, explorers conceived of continuing beyond this point.

Parunuweap Canyon

At a Glance

Day Hike: Yes.

Distance: 4.3 miles from the Checkerboard Mesa approach to the the Powell plaque memorial on the river. The optional hike upriver to Sulfur Spring is 0.3 miles, and the hike downriver to Labyrinth Falls is an additional 0.4 miles. Allow time to explore, which adds mileage to the entire hike. The round-trip of about 10 miles includes over 1,500 feet elevation gain and loss, making for a difficult day: but this is one of the authors' favorite hikes in this book and well worth the effort.

Average Hiking Time: 12 hours.

Equipment: All hikers will need plenty of water or a method of water purification or filtration, topo maps (Springdale East and the Barracks USGS 7.5´), dry bag, sun-protection, sturdy sticky-soled shoes, and energy food. If planning to go to Labyrinth Falls you will also need a 50-foot-long rope, webbing, harness, rappel device and a means of re-ascending the rope at a 12-foot vertical chockstone.

Difficulty: There is strenuous hiking in sand and over slickrock, as well as river hiking. You will encounter one tenuous "slab" down-climb and traverse during the descent to the river. This hike is not for the timid and requires good physical stamina, conditioning and route-finding skills. Poison ivy is present in many places along the river.

Sun Exposure: Expect to be in full sun most of the hike.

Permits: A permit is not required.

Trail Conditions: Mostly, the path is not too hard to locate and helpful cairns appear here and there, but careful route-finding IS required in places, especially on the slickrock sections.

Note: Be aware that cairns may lead to destinations other than the Powell Plaque—including the entrance to the technical slot canyon, Fat Man's Misery. Needless to say, do not enter this slot canyon without the skills and equipment needed to safely navigate it.

Parunuweap Canyon slot

Trailhead: This depends on where parking is available. If the small pullout just southwest of the main Checkerboard Mesa viewpoint is full, park at the Checkerboard Mesa parking lot.

Trailend: Same as trailhead.

Trail Access: The parking area can be accessed year-round via the Zion-Mt. Carmel Highway (SR-9). Cold river temperatures, heavy current and frozen patches on the "trail" will deter most hikers in the winter months.

Best Season: This hike is more comfortable when the water temperatures are warm, as in mid-June to mid-September. However, the approach and exit for this hike are in full sun and can be brutal in the summer. It helps to do the approach in the early part of the day and the exit in the later part of the day.

Elevation: Trailhead: 5,560 feet; highest elevation at saddle: 6,120 feet; Labyrinth Falls and Lowest Elevation: 4,500 feet.

Off the Beaten Path: Yes.

Check the weather report before hiking this route. Do not hike if it looks like rain at or near the trailhead or if it looks like rain in the Alton area, which is near the head of the East Fork of the Virgin River.

㉓ PARUNUWEAP CANYON DETAILS

TRAILHEAD - Park your vehicle at either the Checkerboard Mesa viewpoint parking area, just north of Checkerboard Mesa, on the east side of Zion National Park, or, better, locate the pullout a half-mile to the west on the Zion-Mt. Carmel Highway (which accommodates just four vehicles). The latter parking area cuts off one mile of hiking to the round-trip.

APPROACH - Locate the slickrock wash separating Checkerboard Mesa and Crazy Quilt Mesa, just to the west. Follow this wash south past several potholes. Soon the canyon closes in, creating a shady path to travel. Stay in the slot as the "trail" gradually ascends. There will be a seemingly impassable dryfall partway up the canyon—get around this by taking the slickrock "ramp" on the left, prior to the dryfall. Shortly after, a ridge divides the canyon. Ascend the ridge until the trail descends left and back into the wash below. Continue up the drainage trying to avoid "social trails" that might lure you up and out of the wash. At 1.3 miles the path is no longer gradual in its ascent. It is now necessary to scramble to your right and ascend the dirt path as it rises toward the saddle 400 feet above. This part of the route is steep and sandy, but it is the last major uphill ascent before the trail begins the long descent to Parunuweap. At the top, stop and take in the fabulous, panoramic views of the East Rim of Zion, Parunuweap and the numerous plateaus. After taking a breather, descend to the south following the obvious path. The "trail" will follow the drainage below but will eventually steer left and out of the wash onto the plateau at the south end of Checkerboard Mesa.

CHECKERBOARD ARCH - The path now bears southeast, with Checkerboard Arch visible to the north and some large, white sandstone ridges to the east. (For those that want a shorter hike, Checkerboard Arch is a great destination before turning around and heading back to the trailhead; see the trail description in this book, page 54, for detailed directions to this arch.)

SLICKROCK RIB - Head toward the south end of the farthest white sandstone ridge. You will travel through several small washes en route. Sometimes the "path" is very prominent where it has been worn into the sandy terrain, other times it is necessary to search for cairns marking the direction across the

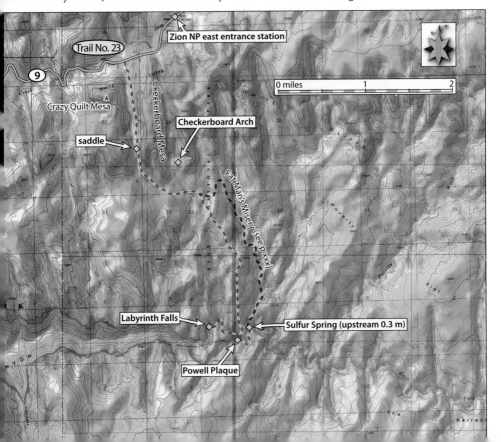

sandstone. It is important to stay on the correct "trail" steering south, contouring the ridge above a popular, but deep, technical slot canyon called Fat Man's Misery.

5 RIVER DESCENT - At 3.5 miles into the hike, the path begins a fairly steep descent, just as Parunuweap is seen to the south and Fat Man's Misery to the east. At 4 miles there is a tenuous "slab" down-climb and traverse just prior to the steep 3rd-class scramble to the river.

6 EAST FORK VIRGIN RIVER - Having descended to the river, locate the Powell Plaque which will be found at the west end of the peninsula, somewhat buried by overgrowth. There is a beaten path through the vegetation. You could reach it by walking downstream but then it is easy to miss.

7 UPSTREAM TO SULFUR SPRING - The hike to Sulfur Spring requires no special equipment and ends at a unique desert oasis. A truly magnificent section of narrows is located 0.3 miles upstream, between the Powell Plaque and the mouth of Fat Man's Misery. During the summer months, warm water pooled at the end of a rock "slide" is a welcome finale to canyoneers exiting the cold, wet, and dark caverns of the technical slot canyon. Here you will find an almost tropical ecosystem which makes a great spot to relax and rejuvenate for the hike downstream and the long ascent back out.

8 DOWNSTREAM TOWARD LABYRINTH FALLS - After visiting Sulfur Spring, turn around, hike downstream past the Powell Plaque and explore as far as you can comfortably go. There is a technical section before reaching Labyrinth Falls, requiring a 50-foot rope. If you are not intending on doing the technical section leading to Labyrinth Falls, turn around at this point. If you are going farther, bear in mind that the hike out will be mostly uphill and in full sun; it is extremely important to gauge your time so you are done before dark.

9 OPTIONAL TECHNICAL SECTION - To get to Labyrinth Falls it will be necessary to use a rope. Head downstream approximately 0.4 miles from the Powell Plaque, bypassing several obstacles including a 12-foot down-climb on the right side of the two-falls watercourse. Farther downstream there is a 7-foot down-climb off the left side of a sloping boulder. Near Labyrinth Falls the river has cut a narrow slot in the rock. Carefully traverse the left side on a narrow ledge for 20 yards before arriving at the top of the falls. A rope is needed for this section to aid non-climbers. Once at Labyrinth Falls, it is difficult to look down the entire waterfall, but the location is magnificent nonetheless. Note: the canyon below Labyrinth Falls is officially off-limits.

GPS Coordinates WGS84 Datum	Powell Memorial Plaque 37°10.885N, 112°51.757W
Trailhead 37°13.562N, 112°53.150W	Sulfur Spring 37°11.001N, 112°51.636W
Saddle and Highest Elevation 37°12.716N, 112°53.007W	Labyrinth Falls 37°10.985N, 112°52.086W

The Powell Memorial Plaque

MEMORIAL
MAJOR JOHN W. POWELL (1834-1902), EXPLORER-SCIENTIST
STEPHEN V. JONES (1840-1920), TEACHER-TOPOGRAPHER
PRES. JOSEPH W. YOUNG (1829-1873), MORMON PIONEER LEADER

DESCENDED LABYRINTH FALLS 1/2 MILE BELOW-MON. SEP 30, 1872
DURING FIRST PARUNUWEAP CANYON TRAVERSE.

POWELL NAMED THIS CANYON FROM THE PAIUTE INDIAN WORD
PARUNUWEAP WHICH MEANS "ROARING WATER CANYON"

DEDICATED SEP. 30, 1972

Parunuweap Canyon Trip 2–
Fat Man's Misery ㉔

This extended journey into Parunuweap Canyon is a one-way hike that includes the technical slot canyon Fat Man's Misery. The West Fork of Fat Man's Misery is a delightfully twisted crevice that winds its way through slickrock fields. This technical canyon is filled with short rappels and down-climbs over rock slides, boulders, and an array of interesting obstacles.

Once past the technical section of the narrow slot, towering canyon walls enclose the river in much the same manner as the Zion Narrows. However, unlike the popular Zion hike, this route is through a wilderness area where other hikers are rarely encountered.

The end of Fat Man's Misery is marked by the warm-water oasis of Sulfur Spring, followed by entry into magnificent Parunuweap Canyon. About a half-mile downstream from this point is the Powell Plaque (see photo on facing page). The exit described requires a 4WD shuttle vehicle, but is a great independent finish, highlighting the dramatic scenery of Parunuweap Canyon.

Bo Beck in the dark depths of Fat Man's Misery

AT A GLANCE

Day Hike: Fat Man's is usually done as a day hike, but it would make a nice backpack.

Distance: 9.0 miles from Checkerboard Mesa to the Elephant Butte trailend.

Average Hiking Time: 12 hours.

Equipment: 140 feet of rope, webbing, harness, rappel device, sticky-soled canyoneering shoes, map, dry bag, helmet, emergency supplies, and plenty of water.

Difficulty: Strenuous river and steep, uphill hiking. Technical canyoneering through Fat Man's Misery slot canyon. Down-climbing and route-finding skills are required. Poison ivy grows in many places on the river and in the exit canyon.

Permits: No permit is required because the technical section is on BLM land, outside the park.

Technical: There are at least 4 short rappels or down-climbs. One optional rappel is 70 feet long. The longest required rappel is 35 feet and overhanging. Two shorter rappels can be down-climbed with a hand-line.

Trailhead: Park and begin hiking at either one of the two roadcut pullouts west of the main Checkerboard Mesa viewpoint.

Trailend: The Powell Plaque in Parunuweap Canyon is the midpoint of this trip. From here the route continues up Parunuweap Canyon to the Elephant Butte exit. If you can't or don't want to set up a shuttle vehicle, you can head back to the Checkerboard Mesa trailhead via the Parunuweap/Checkerboard Arch Trails; see pages 83 and 54 for more details.

Trail Access: The Zion-Mt. Carmel Hwy, SR-9, is open year-round. Cold river temperatures and heavy current will deter most hikers in the winter months.

Off the Beaten Path: Yes.

Best Season: Mid-June to mid-September when the water is warmer.

> Do not hike if there is a chance of rain in East Zion or the SR-9 corridor, north of Mount Carmel Junction. Hiking in slot canyons present a danger from flash flooding. Remember a storm far off can trigger a flash flood. Weather information: http://www.weather.gov/

㉔ FAT MAN'S MISERY –> ELEPHANT BUTTE EXIT DETAILS

1 SHUTTLE SET UP - The Elephant Butte exit requires a 4WD shuttle. Begin by driving to Coral Pink Sand Dunes State Park. From the Chevron in Mount Carmel Junction, drive south a little over 3 miles to the signed entrance to the Coral Pink Sand Dunes State Park. Turn right here. Four miles past the State Park ranger station and tollbooth, turn right at the gravel pullout. Follow the sandy road. Ignore the offshoot roads, staying right (north-northeast). At 3.5 miles from the turn off from the Sand Dunes Road, turn left at signpost K1265. At 4.2 miles, at the junction, go to the right (there is a good view of Zion's West Temple from here). At 7.2 miles is another intersection. Turn left here. At 9 miles there is another junction and sign: K1290. Go right at this junction. The roads will begin to twist and turn sharply through the junipers. At 10 miles is another intersection, stay to the left. Soon you will see Parunuweap below. At 11.5 miles there should be a Wilderness Study Area sign. At 12 miles is a dirt parking area and the exit for Parunuweap Canyon. Leave a vehicle here, then drive the second vehicle to the Checkerboard Mesa trailhead.

2 TRAILHEAD - Park your vehicle at either the Checkerboard Mesa viewpoint parking area, just north of Checkerboard Mesa on the east side of Zion, or locate the pullout a half-mile to the west on the Zion-Mt. Carmel Highway, which accommodates four vehicles, maximum.

3 TRAIL - Locate the slickrock wash separating Checkerboard Mesa and, just west, Crazy Quilt Mountain. Follow this wash south, past several potholes. Soon the canyon closes in, creating a shady path to travel. Stay in the slot as the "trail" gradually ascends. There will be a seemingly impassable dryfall partway up the canyon—get around this by taking the slickrock "ramp" on the left, prior to the dryfall. Shortly after, a ridge divides the canyon. Ascend the ridge until the trail descends left and back into the wash below. Continue up the drainage trying not to take any "social trails" that lure you up and out of the wash. At 1.3 miles the path is no longer gradual in its ascent. It is now necessary to scramble to your right and ascend the dirt path as it rises toward the saddle 400 feet above. This part of the route is steep and sandy, but it is the last major uphill ascent before the trail begins the long descent to Parunuweap. At the top, stop and take in the fabulous, panoramic views of the East Rim of Zion, Parunuweap and the numerous plateaus. After taking a breather, descend to the south following the obvious path. The "trail" will follow the drainage below but eventually it will steer left and out of the wash onto the plateau at the south end of Checkerboard Mesa.

CHECKERBOARD ARCH - The path now bears southeast, with Checkerboard Arch visible to the north and some large, white sandstone ridges to the east. (For a shorter hike, Checkerboard Arch is a nice location from which to turn around and head back to the trailhead).

SLICKROCK RIB - The south end of the farthest white sandstone ridge will become the objective as you travel through several small washes en route. Sometimes the "trail" is very prominent where it has been worn into the sandy terrain, other times it is necessary to locate cairns marking the path across the sandstone. Once on top of the massive, white sandstone ridge, peer off to the east and down into the gorge far below. This gorge is the West Fork of Fat Man's Misery. It is easiest to head up (north) on top of the ridge and then look for the easiest descent into the wash far below.

Rappelling and excellent down-climbing skills are required to navigate through Fat Man's Misery. Remember, slot canyons can change dramatically in a short time due to flash floods and water levels in this canyon can change fast. These directions are only a general reference. Be prepared for variations.

FAT MAN'S MISERY SLOT CANYON (WEST FORK) DETAILS

OBSTACLE OR RAPPEL - Once at the bottom of Misery Wash follow it downstream for about 0.75 miles to where the canyon funnels to a narrow slot with an immediate 12-foot drop. This can be down-climbed or you can set up a hand- or rappel-line from a single bolt located on the left side of the wall. Don't be lured to slings that may be wrapped on a tree trunk above and to the left of the slot.

OBSTACLES - Continue down the slot canyon negotiating boulder down-climbs. The canyon will open up periodically then narrow down again presenting interesting boulder problems and slickrock slides.

OBSTACLE OR RAPPEL - Near an open area the canyon drops abruptly out from underneath, and there is a 70-foot rappel into potholes. Escape from these potholes may not be easy, but if you have good route-finding skills you can scramble up and to the left where you will find a steep descent into the sandy bottom of the wash.

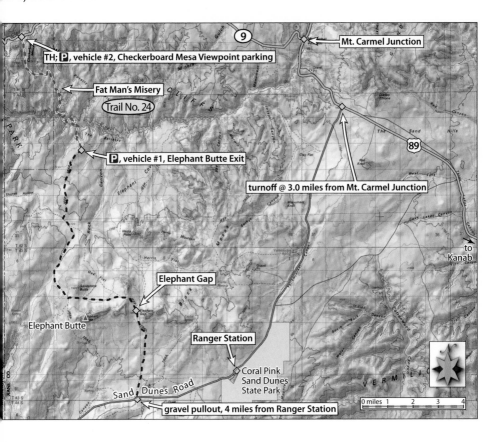

9 RAPPEL - The final narrow section requires a 35-foot rappel. The anchor is webbing that has been slung around some boulders on the left side of the head of the drop. This rappel has an awkward overhanging start and a free-hanging finish. Conditions may change and anchor-building skills may be required.

10 RAPPELS OR OBSTACLES - The spectacular final narrows reveals a dark room with a double natural arch (or, technically, a bridge). The final section, Sulfur Spring, has potholes fed with clear warm water spurting from a small tube in the rock. The roar of water in Parunuweap Canyon can now may be heard, and the East Fork of the Virgin River can be seen just around the next bend.

11 EAST FORK VIRGIN RIVER AND LABYRINTH FALLS - Towering canyon walls enclose the East Fork of the Virgin River in much the same manner as at the Zion Narrows, so, before leaving, it's worth exploring the magnificent slot canyon formed by the lower narrows section of Parunuweap. Hike 0.3 miles downstream to find the Powell Plaque and 0.4 miles farther to see Labyrinth Falls, just inside Zion National Park. There is a technical section before reaching Labyrinth Falls, requiring a rappel (see page 84 for more details). The canyon beyond Labyrinth Falls is officially off-limits.

12 POWELL PLAQUE - The plaque reads: "Major John Wesley Powell 1834-1902 explorer, scientist, Steven V. Jones 1840-1920 teacher, topographer, Joseph W. Young 1829-1873 Mormon pioneer leader, descended Labyrinth Falls 1/2 mile below Monday, September 30, 1872 during first Parunuweap Canyon traverse. Powell named this canyon from the Paiute Indian word 'Parunuweap' which means roaring water canyon. Dedicated September 30, 1972."

13 EXIT TO ELEPHANT BUTTE AND ELEPHANT GAP ROAD - From the bottom of Fat Man's Misery, go upstream on the East Fork of the Virgin River for 2.5 miles. At the 2-mile mark a major drainage, Poverty Wash enters from the north side. At 2.5 miles you will see a prominent wash entering from your right (south) side. This is the exit canyon that will lead to the Elephant Butte-Elephant Gap Road. Turn right into this canyon and hike upstream. Watch for poison ivy during the next 0.35 miles. The slot canyon ends at a seemingly impassable dryfall. Here, bear right up the steep, vegetated dirt slope until you are level with the top of the dryfall, then bear left and cross over the slickrock dryfall, aiming for the steep, vegetated rock/dirt hill in front. Continue northeast, up this slope, until you arrive at a cliffbase and a broken chute. Work your way (northward) up this chute and arrive atop a ridge. You have traveled approximately a half-mile since you left Parunuweap. Now follow the ridge south for 0.75 miles until it intersects with the Elephant Butte-Elephant Gap Road.

Parunuweap

GPS Coordinates
WGS84 Datum
Checkerboard Mesa Parking
37°13.620N, 112°52.911W

Misery Wash
37°12.076N, 112°51.788W

Exit from Parunuweap Canyon to
Elephant Butte Parking
37°10.521N, 112°50.672W

Elephant Butte Parking
37°09.838 N, 112°50.503 W

Turnoff from Coral Pink Sand Dunes Road
37°01.467 N, 112°48.180 W

OPTIONS

- To avoid the 4WD shuttle, descend Fat Man's Misery and exit near the Powell Plaque. Head back north to the Checkerboard Mesa parking. (See map below, also map and information on page 83).

- To enjoy a splendid, non-technical through-hike that visits Checkerboard Arch and Parunuweap Canyon but avoids the technical slot canyon of Fat Man's Misery, simply hike in from Checkerboard Mesa and out via Elephant Butte. Park at Checkerboard Mesa; enter Parunuweap Canyon at the Powell Plaque (as for Parunuweap Canyon, see map on page 83). Exit via Elephant Butte/Gap using a shuttle.

- Backpack in to Parunuweap Canyon from Mount Carmel Junction which is located 12 miles past the east side of Zion National Park.

Bo Beck enjoying the delights of Fat Man's Misery

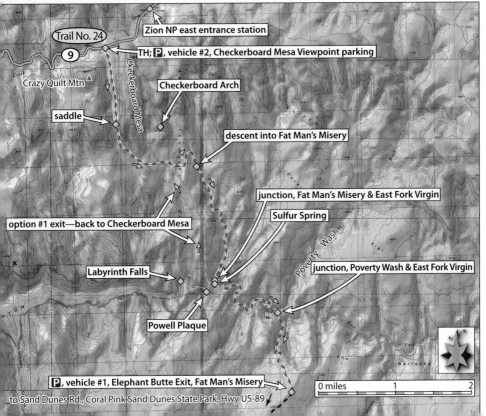

RED CANYON SLOT (PEEK-A-BOO) ㉕

Southern Utah has its share of unique desertscapes, but the land here offers something different too—slot canyons. These abundant yet hidden gems start out as small cracks in the sandstone. The tremendous force of runoff from occasional storms and floods, over time, etches and scours the cracks into deep and narrow slots, which are further sculpted by incessant winds.

The beauty of these dimly-lit chasms entices hikers into their mysterious depths. The price of admission into such a canyon often includes a long approach, the need for advanced skills in down-climbing, as well as possession of ropes and other technical equipment and a familiarity with advanced ropework.

Fortunately, there are some slot canyons that can be experienced without such a hefty price. Red Canyon, or as locals call it, Peek-a-Boo, does not require any hiking to get to, but instead is an adventure that has the thrill of four-wheeling in deep sand through a desert landscape of junipers, pinyons, yuccas and cacti. The trip culminates with an easy stroll through a slender passage that will tantalize photographer and hiker alike with a visual array of warm reds, cool browns, and hot oranges windswept into rippled and fluted sandstone walls. An ATV club has developed an optional trailhead and approach, which leaves the pavement at a different location and takes a more technical route to Red Canyon (for details, see map and note on facing page).

AT A GLANCE

Day Hike: Yes.
Hiking Distance: 0.7-mile round-trip.
Average Hiking Time: 1 hour exploring and 3 hours driving.
Difficulty: Easy hiking.
Equipment: 4WD.
Sun Exposure: Full sun.
Trailhead:: Best Friends Animal Sanctuary (Angel Canyon), between Kanab and Mt. Carmel Jct.

Trailend: Same as trailhead.
Trail Access: The trail begins right off SR-9.
Best Season: Year-round, when weather cooperates. Hiking in slot canyons presents a very real danger from flash flooding. Do not hike this trail if it is raining. Remember a storm far off can trigger a flash flood.
Elevation: 5,525 feet.
Off the Beaten Path: Yes.

㉕ RED CANYON (PEEK-A-BOO) SLOT DETAILS

1 **VEHICLE PREPARATIONS -** Load your 4WD vehicle with refreshments and gasoline. Bring an air compressor, so that if the need arises you can refill tires; you may need to release air pressure in order to "float" over the deep sandy road. Bring a trash bag to haul out any trash you might have accumulated.

2 **RECOMMENDED TRAILHEAD -** From the Chevron in Mt. Carmel Junction, drive 9.2 miles south on US-89. Look on the left side of the road for milepost 72 and the turnoff to the Coral Pink Sand Dunes on the right side. Just past these landmarks, make a left turn onto the next road, which will be a primary paved road heading east from US-89. This is an entrance into the Best Friends Animal Sanctuary and Angel Canyon. (If driving from Kanab, drive 6.6 miles north on US-89 and turn right onto the same primary paved road). After 0.25 miles on this primary road, just prior to the Best Friends Animal Sanctuary buildings, turn left off the paved road onto a sandy road. This deep sand, 4WD path is what you will navigate for the next 3 miles. Be sure to put the vehicle into 4WD and set your tripmeter. Pass the buildings to the right. After driving for a mile on 102M notice the cattle guard. After this the road will fork. Stay to the right on the main road, now 102. At 1.8 miles is another fork. Turn right at this fork to remain on 102 (The left fork is 102L, which has very deep sand and is not recommended). At almost 3 miles the road passes through an open fence; stay right and 30 yards farther the road intersects with a wide wash. Turn left and follow the dry creekbed for a mile to arrive at the mouth of Peek-a-boo slot canyon.

3 **PEEK-A-BOO –** From where you parked you can see the slot canyon to the west. The canyon is usually dry and is only about 0.35 miles long.

4 **THE SLOT -** As you explore, the slot twists and turns, opens and narrows and the canyon floor rises and falls throughout the short hike. Notice how some sections are warmer and others are flushed with chilly air, Stripped logs, twigs, and other debris wedged up high offer evidence of past violent flash floods that have raged through the waterway and forged the sandy chasm. The enclosed setting of a weathered canyon with towering walls, abstract designs and dramatic lighting combine for a photographer's cam-

era, as oils on a canvas do for an artist's brush, providing the ideal tools to create a perfect image. Most sections in this slot are well-lit, but a few places can only be captured with a steady hand or the use of a tripod. All too soon a large chockstone, 15 feet up, wedged between the walls ends exploration.

SHAMAN'S NEEDLE - Back at the slot's entrance, look for a small drainage that enters from the north. Taking a casual stroll just 100 yards up this sandy wash will reveal a "pencil-stick" stone structure. Exit the same way as you drove in.

ALTERNATIVE, ATV CLUB TRAILHEAD - An ATV club has provided an alternative trail-head which doubles as a camping area. Travel is more difficult on this route than on the recom-mended one, but this is probably a fun trip for those who love to ride ATVs. This entrance is 3.5 miles from the Chevron in Mt. Carmel Junc-tion and 7.5 miles from the Kanab city sign.

Summer Milligan in Peek-a-Boo

GPS Coordinates, WGS84 Datum
Turnoff from US-89: 37°08.698 N, 112°34.078 W
Turn onto K2605: 37°08.710 N, 112°33.885 W
First "Y" in road: 37°09.522 N, 112°33.597 W
Enter dry streambed: 37°10.643 N, 112°32.827 W
Red Canyon Slot: 37°10.765 N, 112°33.563 W

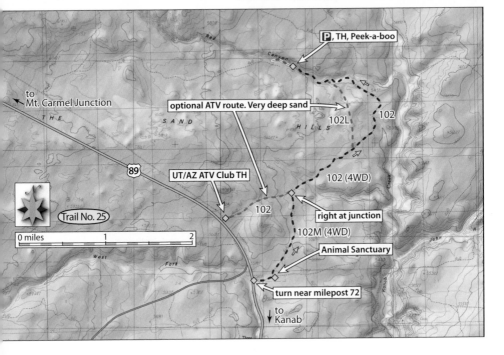

RED HOLLOW ㉖

This short but sweet slot canyon provides an unbelievably awesome canyoneering experience. Red Hollow requires no special equipment, but the very end is too tight and constricted for this to be treated as a simple hike; you can test basic canyoneering skills such as stemming and low-level bouldering. Plus, it is extremely easy to access—no 4WD needed. If you are lucky enough to visit when water is running through the narrow winding walls a beautifully sculpted, sandstone waterfall awaits at journey's end.

AT A GLANCE

Day Hike: Yes.
Trail Distance: 3.2 mile round-trip.
Average Hiking Time: 2 hours.
Equipment: Sticky-rubber hiking shoes, water, sun-protective clothing.
Difficulty: The hiking is easy to, and through the start of, the slot canyon. If water is running then stemming above it in the narrow canyon is difficult—a canyoneer's dream. Though, if you prefer, you can walk down in the water. Even when dry, it is difficult to get up and over a couple of the boulder obstacles near the end.
Sun Exposure: Full sun on the way to the canyon, then shady and cool inside.

Permits: Not required.
Trail Conditions: Unmaintained route.
Trailhead: Red Hollow Drive in Ordervillle, Utah, on the east side of Zion National Park.
Trailend: Same as trailhead.
Best Season: Year-round unless snow is present.
Trail Access: Within Orderville city limits.
Elevation: Trailhead: 5,550 feet; trailend: 5,850 feet.
Off the Beaten Path: Yes.
Restrooms: Orderville.

Bo Beck in Red Hollow

Tanya Milligan stemming in Red Hollow
Photo: Bo Beck

26 Red Hollow Details

INTRODUCTION - For slot canyon enthusiasts that thrive on stemming and bouldering in narrow passages, this is the ticket. There are no access issues and no permits needed. Just park your car and saunter through a beautiful hollow to a short but impressive bit of canyoneering paradise. Play in the slot and know it's just 15 minutes back to the car. The Elkheart Cliffs, rising on both sides of Red Hollow, provide a great scenic backdrop.

TRAILHEAD - From Mt. Carmel Junction drive 5 miles north on US-89 to the town of Orderville. Turn right on 100 East and drive to a T junction. Turn left and continue past the paved road and onto the dirt road. Park at the dirt parking area near the fence. Avoid the fenced area by dropping into the wash. Follow the cobblestone streambed into the hollow. Beautiful red cliffs rise to the southeast. About 300 yards ahead the canyon walls close in on both sides of the wash. Junipers and pines are the dominant trees. The wash is normally dry. When there is water it is usually from snowmelt, but be aware that this canyon can be very dangerous when it flash floods.

SLOT SECTION - This classic, though short slot canyon features vertical walls towering above the canyon floor. The watercourse has carved through the soft sandstone forming a narrow channel which is barely a body-width in some places. A person can place a foot on each wall, apply pressure, and carefully progress vertically—this is what canyoneers refer to as "stemming."

ORDERVILLE HISTORY - Orderville has a unique history. The town—with a current population under 600—successfully thrived as a United Order until support from the Mormon church waned in the 1880s. Today a model of the United Order and other tidbits of history are stored inside the Historic Rock Church in Mt. Carmel and Orderville's Daughters of Pioneers Museum.

GPS Coordinates
WGS84 Datum
Parking Area
37°16.252N, 112°37.620W
Trailend
37°15.957N, 112°37.244W

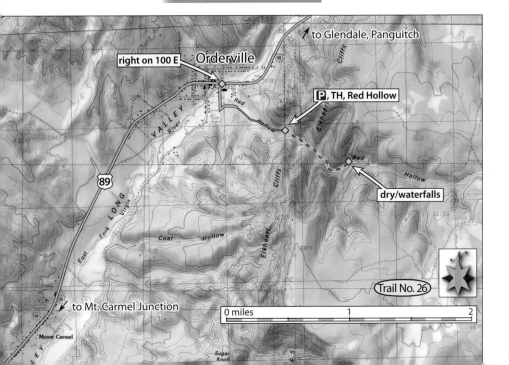

Meadow Creek to Mineral Gulch (27)

This long day-hike, just outside Zion National Park boundaries, provides an opportunity to explore isolated terrain that includes a photogenic slot section and some unique arches. It begins fairly close to the east entrance of the park, descends a generally wide, open wash, reaching the halfway point near the East Fork of the Virgin River. Meadow Creek offers an entry leading to the river and lots of territory that is worthy of exploration.

At a Glance

Day Hike: This is usually done as a day hike, but it's a rushed trip and might be impossible during the times of year when it gets dark early; therefore this does make a nice backpacking trip.

Distance: 14- to 16-mile round-trip, depending on the trailhead used. Our preference is the Meadow Gulch entry rather than the Mineral Gulch way.

Average Hiking Time: 8–12 hours.

Equipment: 50 feet of rope or webbing.

Sun Exposure: Full sun, except for inside the slot section.

Permit: Not required for camping since this route is outside Zion's boundaries, but be careful and do check the weather report before hiking this trail. Do not go if it looks like rain.

Difficulty: Strenuous hiking due to the length, but this route is lacking significant changes in elevation. The trip is mostly walking through washes, but there is some scrambling to get around a couple of obstacles.

Trailhead: Park just off SR-9, between Zion's east entrance and Mt. Carmel Jct. The easiest way to begin is to drop into Meadow Creek from SR-9, just west of where the creek passes under the highway, bypassing two downstream waterfalls. Another option is to park at Mineral Gulch, where it goes beneath the road, entering private property and skirting the southeastern rim until you find a weakness into the gulch, which will be several miles downstream.

Trailend: Same as trailhead.

Trail Access: SR-9 is open year-round. If the ground is dry then this is a good cold-weather hike, but once it gets wet it's a slippery mess, deterring most hikers in the winter.

Best Season: There is water in Meadow Creek, making the summer heat more tolerable, but the best time to do this route is early fall.

Descent/Ascent: 1,100 feet.

Off the Beaten Path: Yes. You should not see any other hikers.

(27) Meadow Creek to Mineral Gulch Details

1 TRAILHEAD – From Zion's east entrance drive 5.8 miles east. Look for a faint dirt road heading south, 7.3 miles west of Mt. Carmel Jct. Follow it 0.25 miles, through remnants of the original, and now broken, pavement of SR-9. Park and walk south down the pinyon and juniper blanketed ridge. Don't be lured into the depths of the deepening washes, instead stay on the fingers where it's easier travel into the bottom of Meadow Creek.

2 MEADOW CREEK – Once in Meadow Creek, head downstream, hiking through a mostly open wash that deepens the further south you travel. After a mile or so there is a 25-foot waterfall or dryfall, depending on recent weather. If a 50-foot rope is tied onto a pine tree on the left bank it can be used as a hand-line to navigate the obstacle. If no rope is available, go to the ridge on your left and traverse until a weakness is found to the bottom. It is loose shale and will be difficult to navigate. Continue downstream for a half-mile where you will encounter another dryfall or waterfall. Hike right; pass under an old barbed-wire fence, traverse 100 yards to a descent back into the creek. There should not be any formidable obstacles while hiking in the creek bottom for the next 5.5 miles. Keep watch for two unnamed arches. Look left to spot one perched high on the ridge and just below it at ground level is another arch.

3 MINERAL GULCH – Watch for the confluence with Mineral Gulch; this will appear on your left. Follow this wash downstream where after a mile or so it becomes a stunning slot canyon. At about the 7-mile mark look for a cave on the left, just above the canyon floor. This may have been used as a shelter by ancient civilizations. Across the wash and slightly upstream are some nice petroglyphs, providing more evidence that ancient people spent time here.

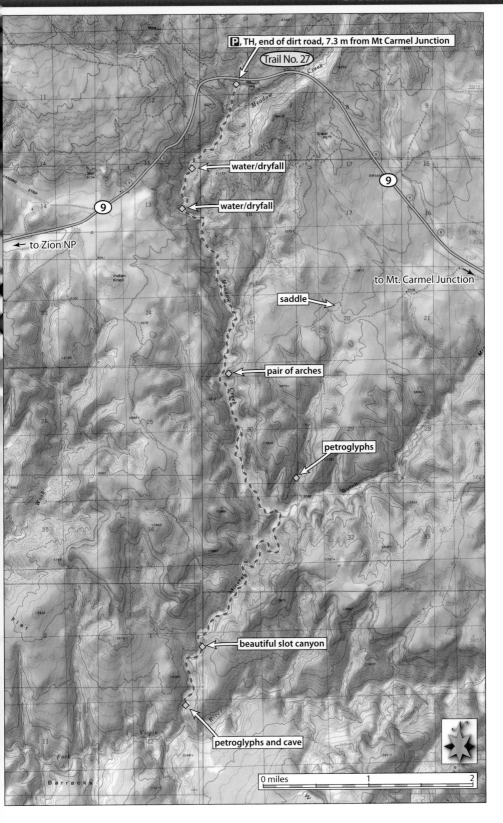

P, TH, end of dirt road, 7.3 m from Mt Carmel Junction

Trail No. 27

water/dryfall

water/dryfall

9

to Zion NP

to Mt. Carmel Junction

saddle

pair of arches

petroglyphs

beautiful slot canyon

petroglyphs and cave

0 miles   1   2

4 PARUNUWEAP - It is less than a half-mile downstream to the confluence of Mineral Gulch and the East Fork of the Virgin River. Farther down the East Fork of the Virgin River is a fascinating area known as Parunuweap which is discussed in a different trail report in this book. For this hike, remember that the trip out is still ahead so watch your time and energy.

5 "7" CANYON - On the hike out, if time and energy permits, just a short distance up Mineral Gulch from the confluence with Meadow Creek is another canyon called "7" Canyon, which enters from the left. It was given this name because an arch within the canyon looks like the number seven. A short hike up this canyon reveals some faded petroglyphs on the left, under a large blind arch. Another 0.75 miles up this same canyon is an abrupt ending at a headwall and the 7 Arch.

6 EXIT FROM "7" CANYON - If you stationed a vehicle at the Mineral Gulch parking area, it is possible to scramble up a ramp just before the headwall and then from the top follow the righthand wash until it meets a road and take that back to where the dirt road intersects with SR-9, just a short distance west of the Mineral Gulch parking area. Obviously if this is your plan, don't leave ropes at the waterfalls in Meadow Creek. If you choose to hike back out the way you entered, leave in plenty of time to finish in daylight as the exit up the hillside to the vehicle can be easily missed.

MINERAL GULCH EAST RIM - We do not recommend the hike down the eastern rim of Mineral Gulch as it crosses private lands and the ramp into Mineral Gulch is steep and exposed in places.

Mineral Gulch

GPS Coordinates
WGS84 Datum

Meadow Creek Parking
37°15.674 N
112°47.141 W

Mineral Gulch Parking
37°13.995 N
112°44.136 W

Twin Arches in Meadow Creek
37°13.364 N
112°47.175 W

Caves and petroglyphs in
Mineral Gulch
37°10.680 N
112°47.629 W

Bryce Canyon

Bryce Canyon National Park is home to the most unusual erosional forms on the planet. Few places on earth can boast of the stark first impression made when standing on the rim, or the bizarre uniqueness of the land. In the big geological picture, Bryce is the top riser of the formations of the Grand Staircase and the youngest of its layers; the Grand Canyon is the bottom and the oldest.

It's the smaller picture that draws the crowds; the multitude of hoodoos that decorate the series of 14 enormous amphitheaters cut into the Bryce plateau. The name Bryce Canyon implies that the park is a canyon, but real canyons, such as the Grand Canyon or Zion Canyon, are formed by flowing water. At Bryce, this is not the case: instead, craggy crevices and contorted pillars were created by frost wedging. Water, derived from rain and snow, is trapped in cracks in the rock. If the water freezes it expands, acting like a wedge, widening crevices and prying off flakes, year by year, century by century, slowly sculpting the land into the convoluted labyrinth we see today.

The park is open throughout the year, drawing over 2 million visitors annually from all around the globe. While exploring Bryce, expect to find peculiar twists of nature with quaint names such as Gulliver's Castle, Wall of Windows, The Poodle, Sinking Ship, Silent City, Mormon Temple, Chinese Wall, Fairy Castle, Thor's Hammer and the Great Cathedral. By contrast to the arid land below the rim, Bryce Canyon's higher elevations features a cool, green forest of ponderosa pines, fir, spruce trees and meadows of wildflowers that serve to remind us that we are standing at over 8,000 feet.

Routes in Bryce Canyon National Park

The boundaries only encompass 38,385 acres but tucked into that small space are 50 miles of superb hiking trails including the four trails described in this chapter: Fairyland Loop, Hat Shop, Queen's Garden-Navajo Loop and Mossy Cave. These are all day-hikes, requiring no technical equipment.

Getting There

From Zion, leave the park through the east entrance and follow SR-9 to the junction of SR-9 & US-89 at Mt. Carmel Junction. From there it is 60 miles to Bryce Canyon. Follow US-89 north, then turn east on SR-12. Follow SR-12 through scenic Red Canyon, a section of Dixie National Forest, then another 9 miles to SR-63. Turn south and you have arrived. See map facing page. Area map is on page 7.

Birds' eye view east from Bryce Canyon

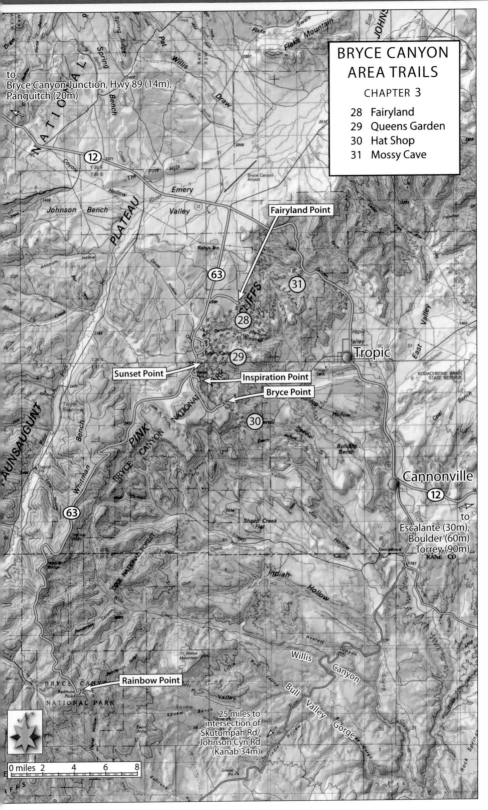

BRYCE CANYON
AREA TRAILS

CHAPTER 3

28 Fairyland
29 Queens Garden
30 Hat Shop
31 Mossy Cave

to
Bryce Canyon Junction, Hwy 89 (14m),
Panguitch (20m)

Fairyland Point

Tropic

Sunset Point
Inspiration Point
Bryce Point

Cannonville

to
Escalante (30m),
Boulder (60m),
Torrey (90m)

Rainbow Point

25 miles to
intersection of
Skutumpah Rd/
Johnson Cyn Rd
(Kanab 34m)

0 miles 2   4   6   8

FAIRYLAND LOOP AND TOWER BRIDGE TRAIL 28

Most visitors are content to look down from Bryce Canyon's rim, examining, from a distance, the jaw-dropping views of the vast array of misshapen hoodoos, but the true beauty of Bryce is found by venturing below the rim and hiking amidst the delicate structures and around the fabulously weird landscape.

Once under the rim you can wander through a labyrinth of erect spires positioned perfectly amid the sparse forest dotted with firs, juniper, ponderosa, and even ancient bristlecone pines. In the warmer months the contrast of multicolored limestone, shaded canyon walls, green vegetation and a deep blue sky makes for some amazing photo opportunities. If winter travel is on the agenda, you will be rewarded with special photographic opportunities—the park's landscape only gets better as this magnificent craggy desert becomes iced with a subtle white layer of snow.

AT A GLANCE

Day Hike: Yes.
Distance: 7.6 round-trip
Average Hiking Time: 4–8 hours.
Equipment: Wear rugged shoes, sun-protective clothing and bring emergency gear to include first aid supplies. Bring a minimum of 2–4 liters of water per person and high-energy food and snacks.
Difficulty: Strenuous, for Bryce.
Sun Exposure: Full sun in most places.
Permits: Not required.
Trail Conditions: Generally, the trail is quite gentle, but don't be lured into a false sense of security. Travel can be very hazardous if one becomes careless. The loose limestone scree on hard-packed surfaces can be unstable.

Trailhead: Fairyland Point Trailhead.
Trailend: You will arrive at the rim near the general store. From here you will walk north on the rim trail back to Fairyland Point.
Trail Access: The 1-mile road to Fairyland Point is generally open year-round; however it may be impassible due to heavy snowfall during winter months.
Best Season: Summer, fall and spring.
Elevation: Trailhead: 7,770 feet, Lowest Elevation: 7,170 feet at Tower Bridge. Highest Point: 8,150 feet at the Rim
Off the Beaten Path: No.

Bo Beck in Fairyland

㉘ FAIRYLAND LOOP DETAILS

TRAILHEAD - Begin at the Fairyland Point parking area, which is located just inside the Bryce Canyon National Park boundary.

TRAIL - The loop runs clockwise. Hike east from the Fairyland Point parking area, and drop down toward Fairyland Canyon. The descent is generally moderate, but keep in mind that after reaching the lowest elevation at Tower Bridge, one must ascend over 1,000 feet back to the rim. The sun can be intense and there is little shade on the trail so remember to bring plenty of water and sun-protective clothing.

WINDOWS - Along the way admire the odd formations and the many windows, as well as the delicately balanced spires that make Bryce such a special place. There are some short spur trails that offer fine platforms for photo opportunity along the entire path.

TOWER BRIDGE - Tower Bridge is roughly halfway through the hike. There is a shaded area at this structure making for an excellent picnic and rest area before beginning the ascent back up to the rim.

CHINESE WALL - Don't miss this feature; it can be seen by peering through the large window marked on the map. Be respectful and stay on the trail unless there is a well-established path to a viewpoint.

FAIRYLAND TRAIL OPTIONS:

1- This loop can be done counterclockwise: hike south along the rim toward Sunrise Point and then hike east off the rim toward Campbell Canyon.

2- You can start this trail from Sunrise Point, near the Bryce Canyon lodge.

GPS Coordinates WGS84 Datum	Trailhead 37°38.961N, 112°08.852W	Junction with Rim Trail 37°37.914N, 112°09.750W
	Tower Bridge Viewpoint 37°37.930N, 112°08.649W	Highest Point on Rim Trail 37°38.558N, 112°09.793W

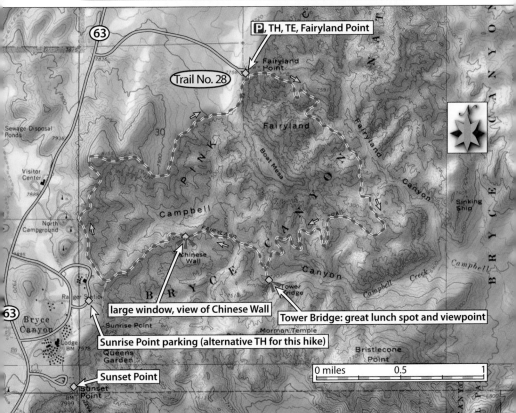

large window, view of Chinese Wall

Tower Bridge: great lunch spot and viewpoint

Sunrise Point parking (alternative TH for this hike)

Sunset Point

QUEENS GARDEN & NAVAJO LOOP TRAIL ㉙

The dramatic displays of craggy rock at Bryce Canyon are evidence of an incredible geological story. Wide, flat, vertical plates of rocks, called fins, are scoured by the wind, which sometimes erodes holes right through to the other side—these are then called windows. When these windows grow large enough, the rocks atop them collapse and the pillars left behind form hoodoos.

The Queens Garden Trail, probably the most popular hike in the park, descends steeply down into the Queens Garden and visits some of the most noteworthy formations of the entire park, including the Queen herself, standing on a backward-facing camel and seemingly calling out orders to far-off ships.

AT A GLANCE

Day Hike: Yes.

Distance: Queens Garden Loop Hike is a 3.5-mile hike beginning at Sunrise Point, connecting with the Under The Rim Trail and exiting up the Navajo Loop Trail to Sunset Point and finishing on the Rim Trail back to Sunrise Point.

Average Hiking Time: 2.5 hours.

Difficulty: Gradual descent on sometimes loose gravel and a steep ascent up Wall Street.

Sun Exposure: Full sun.

Permits: Not required.

Trail Conditions: This gravel and dirt path can be slippery and steep in areas.

Trailhead: Sunrise Point - Queens Garden Trailhead.

Trailend: Sunset Point (via Sunset Point and the Rim Trail).

Trail Access: Limited due to winter snow.

Best Season: April to October.

Elevation Gain: Sunrise Point: 7,950 feet, Queens Garden: 7,668 feet, Sunset Point: 8,017 feet.

Off the Beaten Path: No, this is one of the mos popular trails in the park.

Restrooms: Visitor Center, lodge, general store, Sunset Campground

Queens Garden Trail

29 QUEENS GARDEN EXITING VIA THE NAVAJO LOOP TRAIL DETAILS

TRAILHEAD - From the visitor center, drive 0.4 miles to the Sunrise Point turnoff. Follow the road to the parking area and walk up to Sunrise Point.

SUNRISE POINT - Glance to the northeast at the sloping group of hoodoos, which is a unique canted plateau called the Sinking Ship. Violent tectonic activity about 15 million years ago forced the Pausagunt plateau to rise and drag sections of rock along the faults. Also, in the distance is the Aquarius Plateau, the highest plateau in North America; an astounding 2,000 feet higher than the Pausagunt Plateau.

The Queen

THE HIKE - Follow the signed Queens Garden Trail, following it below the rim. You will encounter human-made tunnels bored into walls of hoodoos as well as some switchbacks. At the intersection take the signed Queens Garden Trail to the garden itself. Once there, sit in the shade of the trees and make out the shape of the queen's dress as it billows and caresses the rocks below.

NAVAJO LOOP EXIT - After enjoying the wonderful rock formations, continue southeast on the trail. Disregard the first intersection with the Navajo Loop Trail (that passes through Two Bridges) and follow the trail west around the end of the ridge. The trail eventually veers northwest toward Wall Street and then climbs to Sunset Point at the rim. Once at the rim follow the Rim Trail north for 0.5 miles back to Sunrise Point.

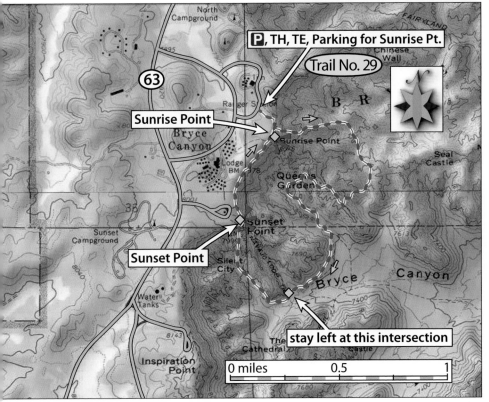

HAT SHOP TRAIL ③⓪

This small, southwestern Utah park is a 25-mile-long series of breaks, encompassing 36,000 acres, carved into huge amphitheaters. According to Paiute myth, people long ago angered the coyote so he turned them all to rock. When you visit, think of this tale while peering down into the amphitheaters—it's easy to spot faces and human likenesses in the tall, proud pillars. These 14 amphitheaters plummet 1,000 feet into a bizarre and colorful maze. Tall, free-standing, misshapen limestone formations crowd together to form magnificent castle-like scenes. These sedimentary formations are called hoodoos, and are common in Bryce.

Yet, even by local standards, the Hat Shop hoodoos have a peculiar personality all their own. These odd creations appear as though a child has been playing in a limestone-filled sandbox. Perhaps you can envision a child scooping up the limestone mixture, letting it drip down to form a cone-shaped structure and then placing a rock on top—the hat!—to protect the hoodoo from the vagaries of the weather. Such rock-crowned hoodoos are not common in the park, but the hike described here, the Hat Shop Trail, leads to a cluster of them.

The Hat Shop Trail is the first part of the 23-mile-long Under-the-Rim Trail. En route to the Hat Shop the path descends below the rim, winding its way through Douglas fir, ponderosa and limber pines, as well as past hoodoos with a more traditional appearance.

Hat Shop hoodoos

AT A GLANCE

Day Hike: Yes.
Distance: 3.8-mile round-trip.
Average Hiking Time: 4 hours.
Difficulty: Moderate hike with a steep descent and ascent upon return.
Sun Exposure: Full sun throughout the trail. In the summer begin early in the day.
Permits: Not required.
Trail Conditions: Rock and sand, which can be slippery. From the rim to the "hats" is a steep downhill hike, and since you return the way you came, the hike out is mostly steep and uphill.
Trailhead: Bryce Point.

Trailend: Same as trailhead.
Trail Access: There can be significant snow October through March, limiting trail access.
Best Season: April to October.
Elevation: Descent to trailend: 1436 feet, ascent back to trailhead: 1436 feet.
Water Availability: None, bring your own.
Off the Beaten Path: This is not one of the most-used trails in the park, but expect to see others along the path.
Restrooms: Visitor center, lodge and the general store.

Hat Shop hoodoo detail

30 HAT SHOP TRAIL DETAILS

TRAILHEAD - Begin at Bryce Point, located 2.0 miles south of the visitor center near the park entrance. Turn left at the sign for Inspiration and Bryce Point then follow the road to the parking area. Walk up toward the rim to locate the sign indicating the Bryce Point Trailhead, a popular place for squirrels and chipmunks as well as humans who gather here to enjoy the spectacular views. This is a great spot for early risers to watch the sunrise touch upon the jagged pink stone of the vast amphitheater below.

DESCENT - You will quickly come to a junction with the Peek-a-boo Trail. Here the Hat Shop Trail heads south, descending farther into the bowl. The trailend is not marked by an interpretive sign or marker, but once you see the balanced rock columns on the right (just where the trail begins to level out atop a ridge) you will know you are there.

HOODOOS- Although the dolomite toppers appear to be part of the original columns, they are not, but instead fell from cliffs above, creating an umbrella of sorts that serves to protect the softer rock below. In this area, stay away from edges and do not attempt to scramble down to where the top-heavy hoodoos stand.

RETURN - From here, return the same way you came. The hike out is steep and in full sun, so if you are doing this in the summer, it is wise to begin early in the day.

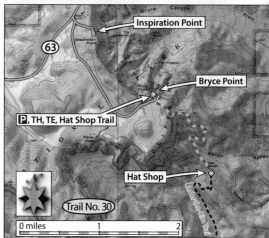

Mossy Cave Trail and Water Canyon ㉛

Mossy Cave is a family-friendly path, isolated from the mingled maze of trails that steeply descend into the bowels of the main Bryce Canyon amphitheaters. Expect great views, little elevation change, a refreshing stream, fairytale-like hoodoos, windows and a visit to the lush mossy alcove this trail was named for.

The area visited by this hike has an interesting history. Mormon pioneers Ebenezer and Mary Bryce were sent to settle this area. It came to be known first as Bryce's Canyon and now Bryce Canyon. The unique landscape is prone to flash flooding, drought and other hardships that eventually forced the last of the Paiute and many early pioneers (including the Bryces), to leave the area. In May of 1891, settlers i Tropic began a daunting 3-year-long task of digging the 10-mile "Tropic Ditch," rerouting water from the East Fork of the Sevier River, across the Paunsaugunt Plateau, through the park and eventually emptying into two ponds in Tropic Valley. The flow of water created a true canyon within the park called Water Canyon where the Mossy Cave Trail is found.

At a Glance

Day Hike: Yes.
Distance: 0.9-mile round-trip.
Average Hiking Time: 1 hour.
Difficulty: This is a great family hike, with little elevation change.
Sun Exposure: There is sparse shade along the trail and it can be hot in the summer at midday.
Permits: Not needed.
Trail Conditions: Wide, sandy trail.
Trailhead: This is located on Highway 12, just outside the main section of Bryce Canyon. You do not have to enter the park to access this trail.

Trailend: Same as trailhead.
Trail Access: Limited due to winter snow.
Best Season: April to October
Elevation Gain: 150 feet.
Off the Beaten Path: This is a classic, so it gets a lot of use, but far less than the trails in the main part of Bryce Canyon.
Restrooms: Nearby businesses (or enter the park).

The Mossy Cave Trail

Kyra Milligan, and Kelsey Shroeder-Milligan, enjoying the cool water on the Mossy Cave Trail

㉛ Mossy Cave - Water Canyon Details

1 **Trailhead -** Highway 12 in Utah was designated an "All American Highway" due to its dramatic beauty. If one had to choose the best part of this 123-mile road it would have to be the stretch around Bryce Canyon. To get to the Mossy Cave Trailhead, you do not enter the park. Instead drive 4.0 miles east from the junction of Highways 12 and 63. Look for a dirt pullout and the small, brown Mossy Cave sign on the right side of the road, between mile markers 17 and 18.

2 **Water Canyon -** From the parking area, walk along the easy-to-follow dirt path going up Water Canyon, past the footbridge and over the stream.

3 **Waterfall -** Soon you will come to a "T" intersection. The right fork leads to a small waterfall. Take care approaching the edge of the stream since the flow can be furious at times. Beneath the lip of the waterfall there is a layer of dolomite, a hard limestone that slowed erosion and allowed the waterfall to form (dolomite can also be seen capping the Hat Shop hoodoos). This 15-foot waterfall is a wonderful place to stop and view the isolated rock structures along the path. The large window above the falls is also quite interesting. From the waterfall, it is possible to take the path along the stream for a longer side trip hike if you desire.

4 **Mossy Cave -** When ready, go back down the trail to the intersection, taking the opposite fork to get to Mossy Cave itself. This large alcove has been created by seepage in the bedrock. In the colder month of winter the dripping creates impressive icicles. When done, simply follow the dirt trail back to the trailhead and your vehicle.

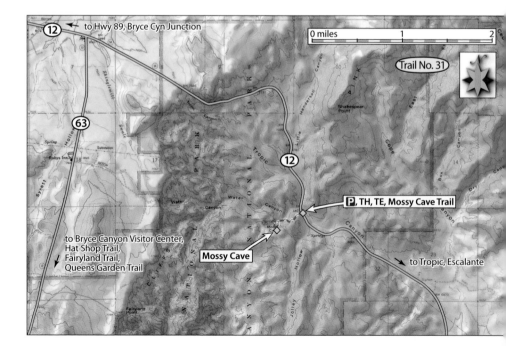

Toroweap, perhaps the most spectacular view in the Grand Canyon

Grand Canyon National Park

Nature has not rested in Arizona, but has spent millions of years excavating, sculpting, and polishing a masterpiece—the Grand Canyon. The Colorado River has created a vast canyon deep in the earth, layered with evidence of its handiwork. It has cut deep through rocks that are millions—sometimes billions—of years old, exposing a history rich in fossils and rocks for us to wonder at. The vast width of the canyon was made through weathering, erosion and tributary streams. Uplift, erosion, submergence and lithification has worked together to create a massive and impressive wilderness.

Another feature of the Grand Canyon is the isolation it creates; the canyon creates an impenetrable barrier between Arizona and Utah. The South Rim lies close to Flagstaff, AZ, and sees the huge majority of tourists. The North Rim is located far from cities, towns and highways, allowing the Kaibab Plateau to remain pristine and primitive. On its way to the North Rim, AZ-67 meanders through the forested lands of the Kaibab National Forest; here you will find the trailhead for Thunder River, one of the great hikes into the canyon. These desolate hinterlands in and near the North Rim are the setting for the other three trails described in this chapter.

The Grand Canyon Lodge and Grand Canyon Visitor Center generally close mid-October each year. If visiting after the lodge closes, be prepared for no services after Jacob Lake. The North Rim itself, and the trails, remain open until AZ-67 is officially closed—AZ-67 usually closes after the first heavy snow and does not open again until mid-May. From mid-October to mid-May, check first to see if roads are open. Even if the roads are open in winter, there will still usually be no services at the North Rim.

Getting There

The entrance to the North Rim of the Grand Canyon is 85 miles from Mount Carmel Junction, which is located 12 miles from the east entrance of Zion National Park. The two parks are conveniently close to each other. From Zion, travel SR-9 to Mount Carmel Junction, then turn south on US-89 to Kanab. In Kanab proceed through the second stop light; this is where US-89 changes to US-89A. Fredonia, Arizona is just a few miles away, across the Utah-Arizona border. Take US-89A for 36 miles to Jacob Lake and then travel US-67 through the Kaibab Forest to the North Rim park entrance (see map on facing page, also regional map on page 7).

The authors, Bo Beck and Tanya Milligan, deep in the Grand Canyon, on the Vaseys Paradise Trail

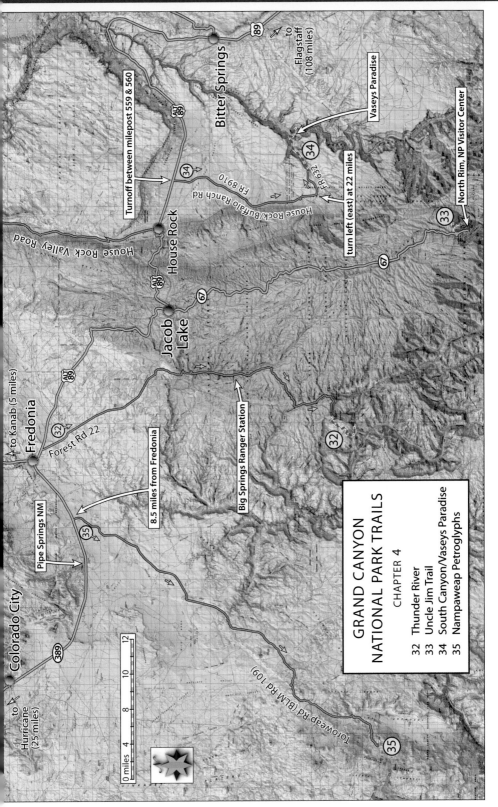

to Flagstaff (108 miles)

Vaseys Paradise

Turnoff between milepost 559 & 560

turn left (east) at 22 miles

North Rim, NP Visitor Center

House Rock/Buffalo Ranch Rd

FR 8910

FR 632

House Rock

House Rock Valley Road

Bitter Springs

Jacob Lake

to Kanab (5 miles)

Fredonia

Forest Rd 22

8.5 miles from Fredonia

Big Springs Ranger Station

Pipe Springs NM

Colorado City

to Hurricane (25 miles)

Toroweap Rd (BLM Rd 109)

GRAND CANYON
NATIONAL PARK TRAILS
CHAPTER 4

32   Thunder River
33   Uncle Jim Trail
34   South Canyon/Vaseys Paradise
35   Nampaweap Petroglyphs

0 miles   4   8   10   12

THUNDER RIVER BACKPACK ㉜

Autumn is an ideal time to hike trails, such as this, that cannot be accessed in the winter or are too hot to endure in summer. A day trip to the Esplanade and back, or a three-day backpack to Thunder River and down Tapeats Creek to the Colorado River, are perfect for the cool days of November.

If you enjoy scenic drives to remote places, be sure to visit Crazy Jug and Monument Points. These are little-known viewpoints in the Kaibab Forest that offer spectacular views of the Grand Canyon.

AT A GLANCE

Day Hike: This trail is best done as a 3-day hike. Do not attempt to walk down to Thunder River and back in 1 day.

Distance: 25-mile round-trip.

Average Hiking Time: 3 days. Expect 5 hours from Monument Point trailhead to the campsite on the Esplanade; 3 hours from the Esplanade to Thunder Spring; 2 hours from Thunder Spring to the Colorado River.

Equipment: Sleeping bag, pad, tent, rugged hiking shoes, extra socks, clothing, jacket, rain gear, hat, first-aid kit with ibuprofen, blister treatment, personal hygiene accessories, wag bags, stove and fuel, pot for heating water, freeze dried foods, electrolyte replacement powder, 1.5-gallon water containers for each person, water filter or purification treatment, map, compass, zip locks for trash and toilet paper carryout. Hiking poles can be useful. Keep your pack as light as possible.

Difficulty: Strenuous. Also, skills are needed for navigating remote, backcountry areas and for a brief scrambling section. The descent from the rim to Thunder River and the climb back up again is beyond what most backpackers are comfortable with.

Sun Exposure: You will mostly be in full sun.

Permits: Yes, for camping. Log onto the NPS website: <www.nps.gov/grca/index.htm>; go to the Grand Canyon directory and look for backcountry permit procedures. You will need to complete a downloadable, faxable permit registration; include the dates you anticipate camping, where you will be entering the Grand Canyon and where you plan to camp. There is no guarantee that you will get the requested dates that are submitted, so if there is some flexibility in your schedule then you may wish to submit second date choices.

Trail Conditions: This trail is hot in the summer.

Trailhead: Bill Hall Trailhead, at Monument Point, Grand Canyon North Rim.

Trailend: Same as trailhead.

Trail Access: Roads in the Kaibab National Forest are good, but they are dirt roads and can be impassible if they are wet, have fresh snow on them, or if there is melting snow nearby. In summer, the roads dry out fast even after a heavy storm and can usually be traveled the next day.

Best Season: Spring and fall.

Elevation: Highest elevation near Monument Point – 7,166 feet.

Elevation: Rim of the Esplanade – 5,000 feet.

Elevation: Thunder River – 3,850 feet.

Elevation: Colorado River – 2,000 feet.

Total Descent: 5,250 feet.

Total Ascent: 5,250 feet.

Off the Beaten Path: Yes.

Water Availability: Thunder River - purify before use.

Restrooms: None. Pack it in, pack it out—including toilet paper. Use 6-inch-deep cat holes and stay away from any water source.

Thunder River: Photo: Bo Beck

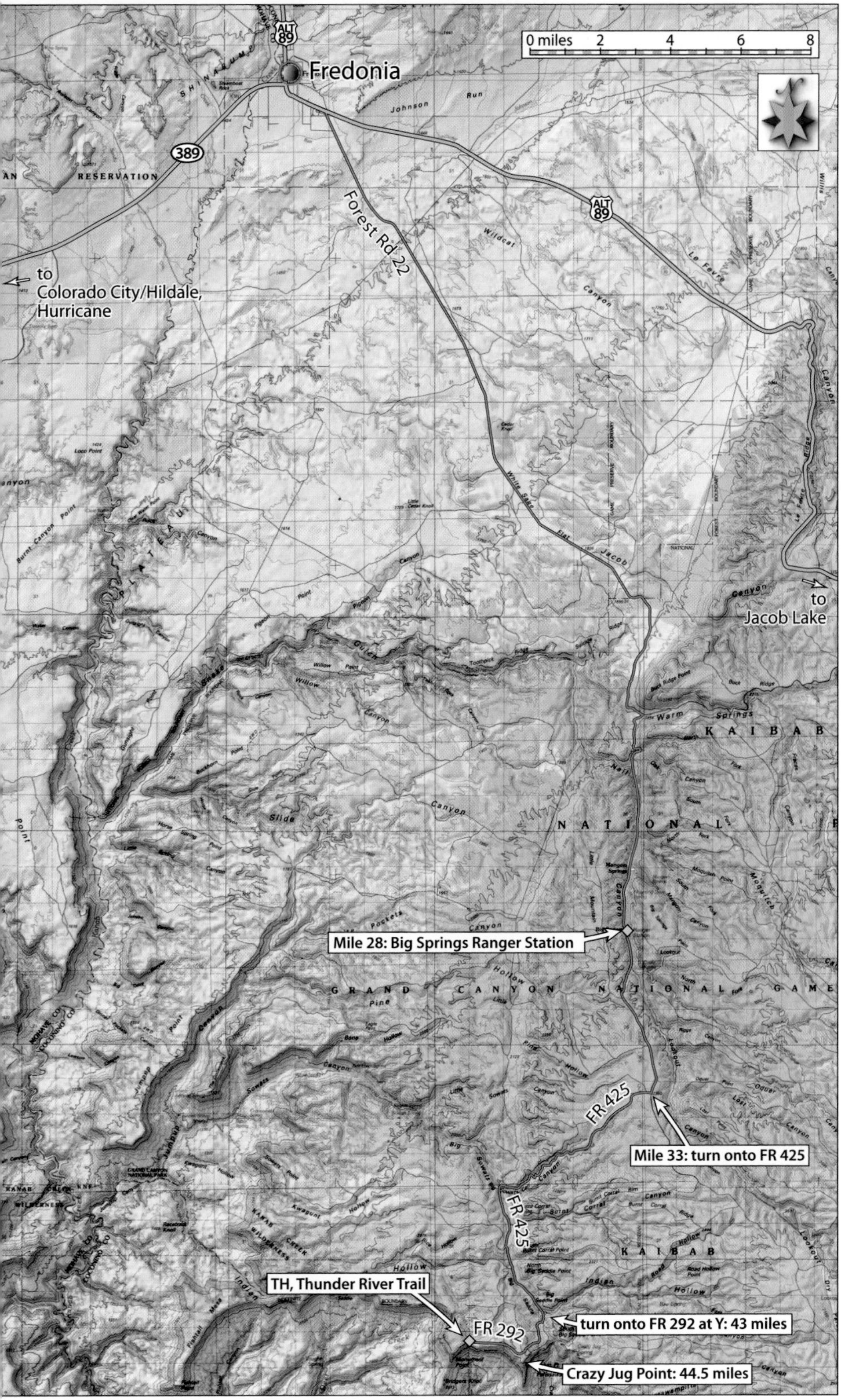

0 miles   2   4   6   8

Fredonia

ALT 89

389

Forest Rd 22

ALT 89

Johnson Run

Wildcat

to
Colorado City/Hildale,
Hurricane

RESERVATION

to
Jacob Lake

KAIBAB

NATIONAL

Mile 28: Big Springs Ranger Station

GRAND   CANYON   NATIONAL   GAME

FR 425

Mile 33: turn onto FR 425

FR 425

KAIBAB

TH, Thunder River Trail

FR 292

turn onto FR 292 at Y: 43 miles

Crazy Jug Point: 44.5 miles

(32) THUNDER RIVER BACKPACK DETAILS

1 **TRAILHEAD -** From Fredonia, Arizona, drive south on AZ-89A toward Jacob Lake for 1.5 miles and look for Forest Road 22 on the right. Set your odometer here at the junction of AZ-89A and FR-22. Turn onto paved FR-22 and follow the road, driving past several intersections and signs that indicate various vistas. The pavement ends after about 20 miles and changes to a maintained dirt and gravel road. At mile 28, notice the Big Springs Field Ranger Station. At 33 miles, turn right onto Forest Road 425, headed toward Monument Point. Watch for signage leading to Monument Point. Do not follow signs to the "Thunder River Trailhead"—you are headed to the Bill Hall Trailhead. There is another intersection at mile 41 but continue straight on FR-425. Look for remnants of a corral on the right side of the road and a "Y" in the road at mile 43, where you will turn right on Forest Road 292. The road will narrow and climb. Continue for 0.3 miles to the next "Y" staying on the same road as it changes now to FS-292G. At mile 43.5 a sign indicates the way to Monument Point; follow it, taking FS-292A toward Monument Point. There is one more intersection at 44.5 miles; continue straight through it and drive 2 more miles to the Bill Hall Trailhead and Monument Point.

2 **DAY 1: MONUMENT POINT TO THE ESPLANADE -** Start early in the morning to take advantage of cooler temperatures for this 5.4-mile hike. At Monument Point, locate the sign for the Bill Hall Trailhead and begin the hike. The descent is steep and in full sunlight. Initially, the trail descends but then it begins a gradual climb up the ridge to the west. The path will eventually bring you to the southern slopes of the point. Looking south are views of Bridgers Knoll, the Colorado River and the Esplanade. The rock formations of the Esplanade are absolutely stunning, showcasing expanses of slickrock, large smatterings of hoodoos, and an ample display of weather-cut canyons. Far below and to the southeast is Tapeats Creek and to the west is a glimpse of Deer Creek Canyon. After traversing to the west for 0.5 miles, you will find a weakness in the limestone cliff where a steep descent begins. A short section in this area might require the use of a rope to assist unsure hikers or to lower packs. Many switchbacks later, the trail dives into a final descent to the slickrock below. After passing the Indian Hollow Trail the dirt path changes into slickrock strewn with cairns. Hike across the rock for the next 3.0 miles, heading toward the descent trail into Surprise Valley. Cairns will generally mark the path across the Esplanade. Be sure to carry enough water for the first day of hiking, cooking at camp and the strenuous downhill trip to Thunder Spring the following day.

3 **CAMPING ON THE ESPLANADE -** Choose a previously used campsite. Try not to disturb the ground, and avoid all cryptobiotic soil. Keep in mind that campfires are not permitted.

4 **DAY 2: THUNDER SPRING -** Hiking from the Esplanade to Thunder Spring promises a full day of adventure and exploring. Descend the steep path into Surprise Valley carefully since the trail is loose in places. The path is in full sun so carry plenty of water, and, of course, take all empty containers to refill at the spring. After descending 1,600 feet and doing a little over a mile of hiking you will arrive at upper Surprise Valley and the upper intersection to Deer Creek. A little farther down the trail is the lower intersection and trail to Thunder River. Once on top of the ridge, the scenery is amazing and Thunder Spring appears far below. The next half-mile and 400-foot descent is rough and steep, but the terrain is quickly forgotten once you see the rush of water cascading hundreds of feet through the rugged limestone.

5 **THUNDER RIVER & TAPEATS CREEK -** Continue a half-mile past the spring, contouring above Thunder River. This river eventually flows into Tapeats Creek. From the junction of Tapeats Creek and Thunder River it is 2.5 miles to the Colorado River and the Tapeats Rapid. From here, you might spot a river trip as it runs this exciting section of the river. You have now hiked half of the 25-mile round-trip, and you have dropped 5,250 feet since leaving the Bill Hall Trailhead. Allow lots of time to head back to the spring, fill containers and hike the 3.0 miles from Thunder Spring (2,100 feet ascent) back to camp on the Esplanade.

6 **DAY 3: ESPLANADE TO THE BILL HALL TRAILHEAD -** Again, leave camp early in the morning so the long, steep ascent to Monument Point is done during the cool part of the day. Hiking up through the slickrock of the Esplanade gives a totally new perspective from the hike coming down 2 days previously.

GPS Coordinates WGS84 Datum	Monument Point Trailhead 36°26.080N, 112°25.791W	Descent from Esplanade into Surprise Valley Begins 36°24.524N, 112°28.376W
	Bill Hall Trail Begins Descent 36°25.854N, 112°26.392W	Thunder River Spring 36°23.725N, 112°27.491W

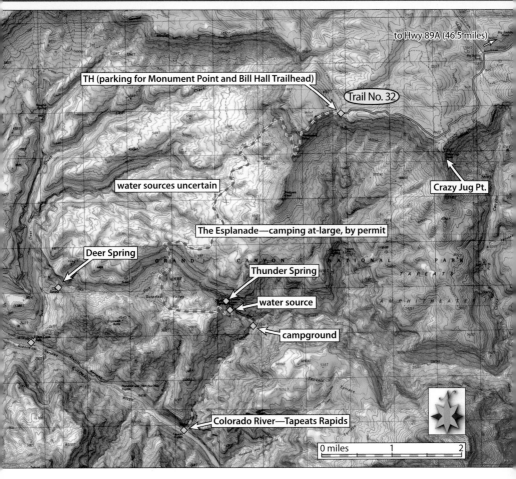

to Hwy 89A (46.5 miles)

TH (parking for Monument Point and Bill Hall Trailhead)

Trail No. 32

Crazy Jug Pt.

water sources uncertain

The Esplanade—camping at-large, by permit

Deer Spring

Thunder Spring

water source

campground

Colorado River—Tapeats Rapids

0 miles   1   2

Tanya Milligan looks down to the Esplanade and across to the South Rim of the Grand Canyon. Photo: Bo Beck

UNCLE JIM TRAIL �33

Many think that when the Grand Canyon Lodge closes its doors in winter, entry to the North Rim is halted. The truth is that this is the best time to visit the park if you enjoy National Parks but want to escape the crowds. Highway 67, the road to the North Rim, is under the management of ADOT and they keep the road open until the first heavy snow. This means the road is almost always open in late November, and for many years it has stayed open until mid-December. If you do visit this time of year, be prepared for the high elevation cold and lack of services.

A wonderful trail to take when the temperature dips is the Uncle Jim Trail. This is a moderate hike with a few minor elevation changes. Most of the trail is located within the wooded areas of the North Rim Plateau, but travel along the rim affords beautiful views of Roaring Springs Canyon and Bright Angel Canyon far below.

AT A GLANCE

Day Hike: For those looking for a longer day-hike that does not go below the rim, this trail is ideal.

Distance: 5-mile round-trip.

Average Hiking Time: Allow 4 hours.

Equipment: Sturdy hiking shoes and appropriate clothing for the season are suggested. During late spring, summer and early fall, the bugs may be a nuisance, so insect repellent may be desirable. There is no water available on this hike. Shade can be found under the forest trees, but much of the hike will be done in direct sunlight. It is always a good idea to have a full gas tank, a cooler of food, drinks and extra water when going to a remote place like the North Rim, especially in the late fall or winter.

Difficulty: This 5-mile trail has some moderate, uphill hiking.

Sun Exposure: Most of the trail is in full sun.

Permits: Not required unless camping.

Camping: Camping is "at large" along this path which means you can camp just about anywhere, but be sure to camp out of site of the trail and obtain a permit from the NPS.

Trailhead: Ken Patrick Trailhead at the North Kaibab/Ken Patrick parking lot.

Trailend: Same as trailhead.

Trail Access: Easy access unless there is snow. Note the possible road closure of AZ-67 in the winter.

Best Season: The Uncle Jim Trail is good to hike year-round, but if the mule dung and the heat of the sun get to you then opt to hike this trail after the services at the North Rim close in mid-October.

Elevation: Trailhead 8,180 feet.

Elevation: Highest Point 8,427 feet.

Off the Beaten Path: No, this is a busy trail.

Water Availability: None.

Restrooms: The trailhead has portable potties.

�33 UNCLE JIM TRAIL DETAILS

1 TRAILHEAD - The trail begins at the North Kaibab/Ken Patrick parking lot located just over 2 miles north of the Grand Canyon Lodge. The parking lot is large (it's also the beginning point for the North Kaibab Trail that leads to the Colorado River and Phantom Ranch). To begin your hike, locate the sign at the end of the parking lot that indicates the start of the Ken Patrick Trail and provides a brief history of Ken Patrick. The trail heads east; the first part has wonderful rim views. After 0.75 miles you will reach the intersection of the Ken Patrick Trail and the Uncle Jim Trail. Turn right at the sign and follow the path downhill. The trail will gradually descend into a wooded wash and then climb east out of this hollow. Soon, another intersection is met. Go right and continue ascending to the southeast through a gently undulating forest landscape. The trail veers southwest and the rim comes into view.

2 UNCLE JIM POINT - Here, beneath soaring ponderosa pine trees, you will discover cables for tethering pack mules and some charming, wooden-wheel stools. Mixed zones of spruce, fir and aspen are seen along the trail at various points. This area is a popular viewpoint and picnic area shared with pack mule trips operating during the summer months. Continue past this area. Ahead, you will see a prominent headland of Kaibab limestone; this is Uncle Jim Point. This point has impressive views of Roaring Springs Canyon, portions of the Grand Canyon Lodge, Walhalla Plateau, as well as Deva, Brahma and Zoroaster Temples. Looking upcanyon (to the right) the switchbacks of the North Kaibab Trail can be seen, descending the cliff faces far below.

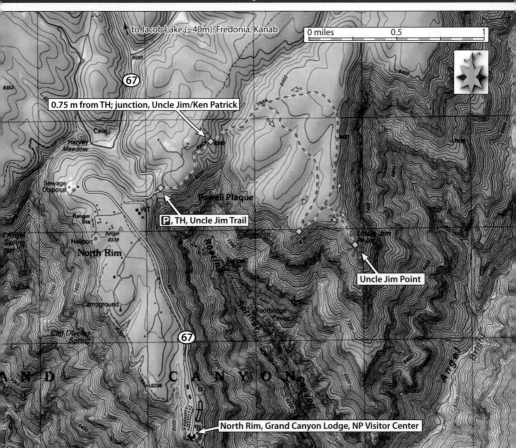

The Uncle Jim Trail has spectacular views into the Grand Canyon

LOOPING - Just back from Uncle Jim Point, a trail continues northeast along the rim for a short distance, then ducks into the woods, and then once again continues along the rim. Glimpses of Bright Angel Canyon appear to the east, far below. After about 0.75 miles the trail leaves the rim and winds its way through the woods then once again arrives at the loop intersection. The path then continues back to the intersection with the Ken Patrick Trail and the 0.75 mile walk back to the North Kaibab/Ken Patrick parking lot.

Overall, this hike is a wonderful reprieve from the busy rim trails located near the lodge. The views are certainly worth the moderate walk through the beautiful forest rimming the north edge of the Grand Canyon. Be on the lookout for the elusive Kaibab squirrel. This unique squirrel is found only in the ponderosa pine forests of the North Rim. The Albert squirrel, found on the South Rim and Kaibab squirrel share the same ancestor, but after separation for thousands of years the Kaibab squirrel developed different characteristics, including its bushy white tail.

TRAIL HISTORY - James T. Owens, known as Uncle Jim, was awarded the position as the Grand Canyon Game Reserve's first warden from 1906 until the park was established. Over a period of 12 years he killed several hundred mountain lions on the North Rim. The deer population exploded and many died from lack of food. The aftermath of this dramatic reduction of mountain lions led to the knowledge that killing predators is damaging to the delicate balance of nature.

The start of the Bright Angel Trail, viewed from Uncle Jim Trail

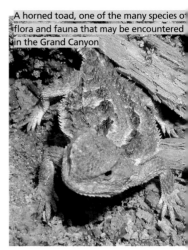

A horned toad, one of the many species of flora and fauna that may be encountered in the Grand Canyon

GPS Coordinates
WGS84 Datum

Ken Patrick Trailhead
36°13.052 N, 112°03.346 W

Ken Patrick Trail and
Uncle Jim Trail Intersection
36°13.594 N, 112°02.962 W

Uncle Jim Loop Trail Intersection
36°13.536 N, 112°02.680 W

Uncle Jim Point
36°12.826 N, 112°02.517 W

SOUTH CANYON & VASEYS PARADISE 34

This is a visit to paradise! Follow a remote canyon of the Grand Canyon down to the Colorado River and camp on a beach. Near the beach is a unique, thundering waterfall: Vaseys Paradise. This cascading fall is a spectacular display of water spurting from at least two caves in the cliffside. In addition, seeing the Colorado River up close, in these rocky depths, is a special sight. This tiny piece of the Grand Canyon is a magical oasis.

AT A GLANCE

Day Hike: Possible, but not recommended. The route is usually done as a 3-day backpack.

Distance: 16-mile round-trip. It's 6 miles from the rim to the Colorado River and 2 more miles to Redwall Cavern.

Average Hiking Time: 8 hours, one way, to the river. Add 1 hour to get to Redwall Cavern.

Equipment: For backpacking: Standard backpacking equipment to include: food, shelter, clothing adequate for the season, cooking supplies and emergency supplies. Other equipment for dayhiking and backpacking: Sticky, supportive hiking footwear, at least 3 quarts of water per person, water purification or filtration means.

Difficulty: Strenuous, with some boulder hopping and scrambling. Navigation skills are required.

Sun Exposure: Mostly full sun.

Permits: Required for camping.

Trail Conditions: The route follows dirt paths during much of the hike, with occasional boulder hopping. There are a couple of narrow ledges.

Trailhead: South Canyon, located 20 miles east of Jacob Lake on AZ-89A, then 22 miles south on a dirt road.

Trailend: Same as trailhead.

Trail Access: Year-round, but the dirt road to the trailhead may be impassible when wet.

Best Season: Spring, fall and winter, when weather cooperates.

Start Elevation: 5,576 feet at the South Canyon Rim.

River Elevation: 2,920 feet.

Restrooms: None. You will need to dig a 6-inch-deep cat-hole for human waste and pack out toilet paper.

Off the Beaten Path: Yes.

Water Availability: Vaseys Paradise is a reliable spring but water must be filtered.

Bo Beck at Vaseys Paradise

The river, close up. Great Blue Herons are not uncommon

㉝ SOUTH CANYON–>VASEYS PARADISE DETAILS

HOUSE ROCK BUFFALO RANCH ROAD - From Fredonia, Arizona, drive southeast on AZ-89A. In Jacob Lake, don't take AZ-67 to the North Rim; stay on AZ-89A. Turn right (south), between mileposts 559 and 560, onto House Rock Buffalo Ranch Road. The graded dirt road is 22 miles long. Follow this road for 19 miles to the junction with USFS road 632. Turn left on Road 632. This road is usually passable with a 2WD but, after rain or snow, the road can become impassible even with a 4WD. The flat strip of land to the left is a primitive airstrip. Turn right at the end of the airstrip and follow the rough road for 1.0 mile to the rim of South Canyon.

TRAILHEAD - Locate the sign for the trailhead and begin the descent. The first mile requires a descent of 1,140 feet to the canyon floor below. Do not stray from the cairn-defined route. The start of the hike is a chute, followed by a series of steep switchbacks and a few short down-climbs over and between fallen boulders. Be careful: down-climbing in this section can be difficult with a large backpack. A flat outcropping of limestone forms a large shelf about two-thirds of the way down. A well-beaten dirt path traverses the outcropping of limestone leading to a slickrock break. Follow the cairns and footpath down the cliffside to the final set of switchbacks, descending to the canyon floor.

SOUTH CANYON - South Canyon is usually dry but, if hiking after heavy rain or when snow is present, water may flow through the creekbed. The mileage to the river from the canyon bottom is 6 miles, but with all the maneuvering around obstacles the route is much longer, and quite time consuming. Carrying a large pack through much of this hike can be difficult. Locating cairns is not always easy as the path goes over boulders and through bushes, into the wash, crisscrossing to both side of the canyon, and sometimes up high on ledges to avoid pour-offs. However, try to follow the cairns and the well-traveled

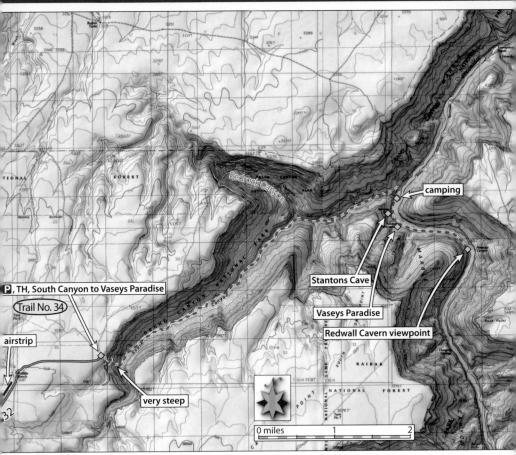

footpaths. Note the limestone alcove on the left. The sandy bottom changes to hard rock, and about 2 hours into the hike, you will find yourself on a carpet of stone. The scenery is particularly beautiful in this section, especially if water is trickling over the stone. Soon the hike gets into more boulder hopping and navigating around dryfalls. To get around the first two large (15- to 20-foot) dryfalls, locate a path on the ledge to the right. At the third dryfall, follow a path on the left. The largest obstacle is about 3 hours into the hike: a 40-foot drop-off. Find a path on the right to get around this. This path ends at a junction with an unnamed canyon. Past the unnamed canyon, on the left side of the creek, is Bedrock Canyon. This intersection is 4.3 miles from the trailhead. Somewhere in this section, you should begin to hear the the Colorado River flowing roughly past the junction with South Canyon.

GRAY REDWALL LIMESTONE FORMATION - About 1 mile past the Bedrock Canyon junction is an area which is difficult to navigate. The trail here veers left out of the watercourse onto the boulders, talus, and ledge systems in order to avoid dropping into the deepening slot canyon. You will notice that the Redwall limestone in this area, despite its name, is gray; you may also notice glimpses of the river from atop the Redwall. Stay on the cairned trail to the junction of South Canyon and the Colorado River.

DESCENT TO THE COLORADO RIVER - Downriver is Vaseys Paradise and Marble Canyon. Follow the cairned path left, then back right to a rockslide ravine of boulders. Look for the remains of Anasazi pit-houses in this area. The final descent to the river is steep, and hard on the knees after a full day's hike with a heavy pack.

COLORADO RIVER - The descent ends at a small, quiet beach. Choose your campsite. Be prepared, during the warmer months, to encounter groups of river runners, especially at the larger beach down-river.

7 CAMPING ON THE RIVER - There are two nice beaches for camping. When descending to the Colorado River, the first beach is farther from the rough water and thus quieter. Water can cover this beach depending on water release from the Glen Canyon Dam. The larger beach slopes towards the back making the front area by the trees the best tent area. The rocks near the back of the site are ideal for hanging food. Just knot the rope in the food bag and slide it in the crack of the rock. This is the area where the Stantons Cave Trail is accessed.

8 LANDMARKS - Now you can explore the treasures that await downriver: Stantons Cave, Vaseys Paradise, the proposed Marble Gorge Dam remnants, and Redwall Cavern. Vaseys Paradise is 0.25 miles downriver from South Canyon. This verdant garden is the place to go and filter water, but watch for poison ivy lurking amid the monkey flowers, columbines, and watercress.

9 STANTONS CAVE TRAIL - Rather than traversing the slippery slope along the river, go to the rear of the large beach and climb up the rockslide gully. There is a nice trail on top leading to Stantons Cave.

10 STANTONS CAVE - Stantons Cave, a large solution-cave about 160 feet above the river, is barred to protect the amazing historic artifacts inside. Remains from 10,000-year-old giant condors and mountain goats have been discovered in this cave; along with shells, beads, and scores of 4,000-year-old split-twig figurines. The survivors of the 1889 Brown-Stanton expedition stashed gear inside, and hence the name Stantons Cave. Today, Townsend's big-eared bats find protection, behind the bars, from humans.

11 VASEYS PARADISE - Vaseys Paradise (mile 33 on the river) as described by John Wesley Powell: "On coming nearer we find fountains bursting from the rock high overhead, and the spray in the sunshine forms the gems which bedeck the wall. The rocks below the fountain are covered with moss and ferns and many beautiful flowering plants. We name it Vaseys Paradise, in honor of the botanist who traveled with us last year."

12 MARBLE GORGE DAM SITE - These "human-made caves"—test holes, drilled in 1964 for the proposed Marble Gorge Dam—can be explored. Neither the Marble Gorge Dam nor Bridge Canyon Dam were built, due to political pressure which came mainly from the Sierra Club, but in 1966 the Glen Canyon Dam was completed, creating Lake Powell.

13 REDWALL CAVERN - The Redwall Cavern, an enormous, erosive river cave (mile 34 on the river), was first seen by John Wesley Powell. He estimated that the cave would hold "50,000 men." It takes an hour to bushwhack, boulder hop, and scramble from Vaseys Paradise to a spot directly across the river from the colossal Redwall Cavern.

BACKCOUNTRY OVERNIGHT USE PERMITS - Obtain and submit forms by mail or fax to the **Backcountry Information Center, Grand Canyon National Park, P.O. Box 129, Grand Canyon, AZ 86023**. Submit permits at least 3 weeks in advance of proposed hiking date, but no sooner than 4 months before your hiking date. Permit applications can be obtained, in person, at the Backcountry Information Centers at the North and South Rims. Same-day permits may be possible at these locations. The Vaseys Paradise "Use Area Code" is AC9.

REMOTE SITE PERMITS - Pipe Springs National Monument near Fredonia, Arizona, BLM Interagency office in St George Utah, BLM office in Kanab Utah, and rangers on duty at Toroweap, Meadview, and Lees Ferry Ranger Station. With a valid credit card, last-minute permits may sometimes be obtainable. These permits will not be issued more than one week in advance of proposed start date.

GPS Coordinates WGS84 Datum	Parking for South Canyon Route 36°28.453 N, 111° 55.684 W
Turnoff from 89A onto Buffalo Ranch Road: 36°42.291 N, 111° 56.815 W	Camping on River 36°30.159 N, 111°51.467 W
Turn to Buffalo Ranch after 19 Miles on Dirt Road: 36°27.485 N, 111°58.646 W	Vaseys Paradise 36°29.884 N, 111°51.464 W
Turn from Buffalo Ranch to Trailhead 36°28.262 N, 111°56.921 W	Redwall Cavern Viewpoint 36°29.581 N, 111° 50.468 W

NAMPAWEAP PETROGLYPHS 35

The hectic world seems to vanish as the sun peeks over the Colorado Plateau, lighting and warming the ancient rocks. Limestone sparkles as sunlight dances off its surface. Nature, unwilling to rest, has spent millions of years tirelessly changing and reshaping the canyon.

Exploration of the great gorge fosters an interest not only in the geology, but of the people who, in the distant past, roamed—and even made their homes in—this harsh land. Hints to their lives are scattered here and there—pieces of a puzzle with clues dating back thousands of years and now spread far and wide.

Seemingly random, but strikingly sophisticated designs have been discovered engraved in rock: human figures, animals, and odd, geometric designs. These may be messages, written in an ancient, forgotten tongue, a form of communication that we may never unravel.

The large display of rock art visited by the trail described here is found in the Grand Canyon-Parashant National Monument. Nampaweap petroglyphs, created thousands of years ago, were chiseled into the rock; a stone was used to hit another stone, pecking away flakes from the dark-skinned surface of the local basalt, exposing the lighter color beneath.

The two types of ancient rock art, petroglyphs and pictographs, are created differently. Petroglyphs are chiseled from the rock surface, pictographs are painted, using natural pigments, onto rock. Both types are irreplaceable cultural resources. Our public lands allow you to visit these treasures, while at the same time strong federal laws try to ensure protection and preservation for these ancient etchings and paintings.

Protecting Rock Art - Please educate yourself and help to teach others how to protect ancient forms of communication such as pictographs and petroglyphs:

Rock Art is Fragile!

Don't forget —The greatest danger to rock art is people!

Don't touch rock art—Never make rubbings or touch the art, however lightly, even with your fingertips. Oil from our bodies can discolor and damage fragile pigments; and modern human contact degrades the site for possible future archeological research.

Don't make a fire anywhere near a rock-art site. Smoke can cause enormous damage, even from some distance away. Report any sign of fires you see near rock art.

Don't camp near any rock-art site.

Don't dig near, or climb above rock art. Please respect the outdoor museums of our public lands in the same way that you would an indoor museum. If you know of any vandalism to rock art, call the Archaeological Resources Protection hot line at 1.800.227.7286.

Nampaweap

㉟ NAMPAWEAP PETROGLYPHS DETAILS

1 DRIVING INSTRUCTIONS - From Fredonia, drive 8.5 miles west on SR-389 to the junction with the Toroweap road (BLM Road 109). Turn here, and head south for 46 miles (see roadmap page 111). Turn right at the signed road to Mount Trumbull and drive 4 miles as the rocky path climbs toward the summit. Look for the sign indicating the "Nampaweap Rock Art Site." Turn left and go 1 mile to the parking area.

2 TOROWEAP ROAD HAZARDS - No services are available: bring food, plenty of water, a good spare tire, and fill up with gasoline. This dirt road is notorious: long, rocky, washboarded, and difficult when wet. Bring the proper equipment and be prepared to change a tire if needed.

3 NAMPAWEAP TRAIL - An information kiosk describes the 0.75-mile trek to the petroglyphs. Thousands of defined etchings can be found on the boulders that sit above the floor of the dry streambed. This canyon is called Billy Goat Canyon by the locals due to the numerous "billy goat" petroglyphs found on the rock. It is considered to be the largest rock-art site on the Arizona Strip. Do not climb on the rocks. Don't touch or otherwise damage the petroglyphs. Watch out for rattlesnakes among the rocks. Stay in the wash below, where the drawings can easily be seen.

TOROWEAP OVERLOOK - Spectacular views of the Grand Canyon and a small campground (free, no permit needed, first-come first-serve) are located about 12 miles farther south on BLM Road 109.

GPS Coordinates WGS84 Datum	Turnoff from Toroweap Rd onto Mt. Trumbull Rd 36°23.894 W, 113°03.409 W	Nampaweap Parking and TH 36°21.340 N, 113°07.189 W
	Turnoff from Mt. Trumbull Rd to Nampaweap 36°21.980 N, 113°06.370 W	Nampaweap Petroglyphs 36°21.295 N, 113°06.602 W

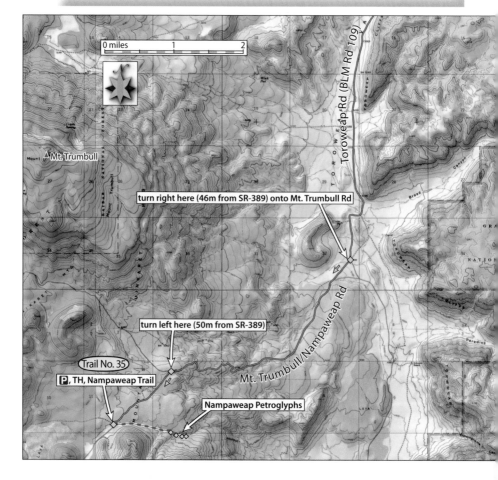

Trey Milligan and Cobe Reck at Cedar Breaks

CEDAR BREAKS NATIONAL MONUMENT

Cedar Breaks is perhaps the most rapidly-eroding place in North America. The monument is small compared to nearby National Parks, but it is not lacking in either scenery or adventure. The impressive, craggy, rock display of the Cedar Breaks amphitheater formed long ago and has never stopped sculpting and molding itself, putting on a magical show for all to see. This show is far from static; rare but powerful summer thunderstorms and winter blizzards pummel the rocky landscape, deepening old gullies, carving new ones, creating more change. Frigid winter ice pries flakes away from soft limestone hoodoos and gravity also lends a hand, pulling boulders down from undercut cliffs.

This chapter takes hikers to a remote National Monument that rivals many National Parks in beauty. Cedar Breaks showcases the tremendous contrast between the surrounding high-elevation forest (the monument lies at around 11,000 feet) and the colorful desert scenery of the amphitheater under the rim. We will visit two classic trails, Spectra Point and Wasatch Ramparts, and an interesting extension of the latter called the Shooting Star/Bartizan Trail, which explores a waterfall and a double arch. A much longer hike, also described here, is the Rattlesnake Creek-Ashdown Gorge, which winds its way from a high-elevation forest into the boulder-strewn slot canyon of Ashdown Gorge.

Note: Cedar Breaks National Monument borders Dixie National Forest and some trails overlap. The Beneath-the-Rim route (page 143) starts just outside the monument but ventures deep inside and explores the bottom of the Cedar Breaks amphitheater, a place where where few ever go and amazing hoodoos can be seen close up.

There is a plan to designate Cedar Breaks as a National Park. It certainly deserves that status.

GETTING THERE

From Cedar City or US-89, take SR-14 to the turnoff to SR-148 and follow it to the monument. If approaching from the north, on I-15, exit at Parowan then take SR-143 to Cedar Breaks. Check for road closures in the winter, early spring and late fall (see map on facing page; regional map is on page 7).

Bo Beck looking down into Rattlesnake Creek-Ashdown Gorge

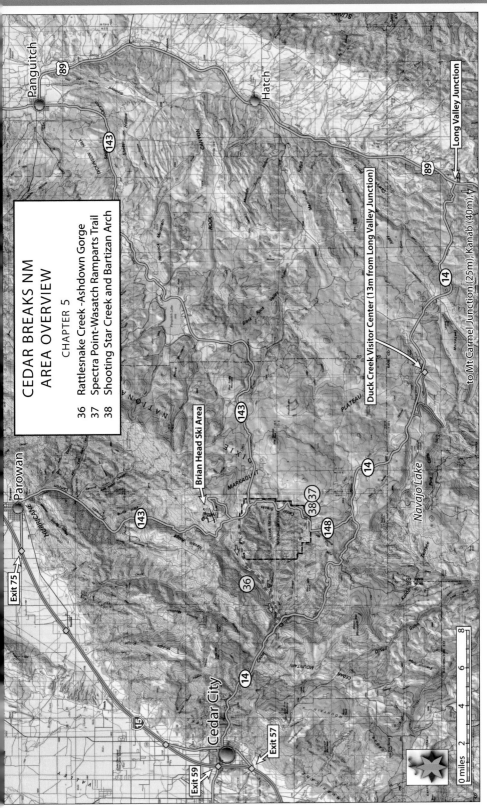

CEDAR BREAKS NM AREA OVERVIEW

CHAPTER 5

36 Rattlesnake Creek - Ashdown Gorge
37 Spectra Point - Wasatch Ramparts Trail
38 Shooting Star Creek and Bartizan Arch

Panguitch

Hatch

Long Valley Junction

Duck Creek Visitor Center (13m from Long Valley Junction)

to Mt Carmel Junction (25m), Kanab (40m),

Parowan

Brian Head Ski Area

Navajo Lake

Cedar City

Exit 75

Exit 59

Exit 57

0 miles 2 4 6 8

Rattlesnake Creek - Ashdown Gorge

When summer brings hot temperatures to the arid deserts of the Southwest, this hike comes into its own. It starts at the northern boundary of Cedar Breaks National Monument, then descends deep into the Ashdown Gorge Wilderness Area, exploring an impressive variety of ecozones.

The trail begins amidst high-alpine meadows and a surprising selection of evergreens—including bristlecone pine, the earth's oldest living tree. The initial section of the hike has wonderful views of the monument.

As you take the trail farther, you will wind your way into the Ashdown Creek wilderness area, where you will find yourself following crystalline mountain streams that have cut narrow passages through porous limestone. As a bonus, there is an arch and a brief side-trip to a pair of seldom-visited waterfalls.

This trek is mostly downhill. It's also a one-way journey, so it does require a shuttle.

Ashdown Creek originates in Cedar Breaks, makes its way through Ashdown Gorge and empties into the head of Coal Creek. The gorge is named after George Ashdown and family, who, in the 1890s, owned a ranch and two sawmills.

At a Glance

Day Hike: Yes, but it is often done as a backpack.

Distance: The route is 10 miles. It's another 1.5 miles to do the side-trip to the waterfalls.

Average Hiking Time: About 8 hours during normal conditions and water levels

Difficulty: Moderate; most of the hiking is downhill. The creek can be strenuous and slippery.

Equipment: Sticky-rubber canyoneering shoes are a must, as well as trekking poles. Bring energy snacks, at least 2–3 quarts of water for each person, and filtration or purification means—the first water source is several miles into the hike. The best map for this route is the "Cedar Mountain-Pine Valley Mountain" National Geographic-Trails Illustrated.

Sun Exposure: There is some shade from trees and canyon walls but be prepared for quite a bit of direct sunlight.

Permits: Not required.

Trailhead: Just north of the Cedar Breaks boundary on SR-148 at the trailhead sign for the Ashdown Creek Route (about 12 miles east of Cedar City).

Trailend: SR-14 in Cedar Canyon, 10.2 miles west of the intersection of SR-14 and SR-148 (at time of writing, 2012, rerouting around a large landslide area may change the mileage).

Trail Access: SR-148 to Cedar Breaks closes in the winter, due to snow.

Best Season: Summer, after mid-June, when the snowpack runoff subsides. Any earlier and the snowmelt causes high water making hiking difficult or even impossible.

Elevation at Trailhead: 10,400 feet.

Elevation at Trailend: 7,000 feet.

Total Descent: 3,400 feet.

Off the Beaten Path: Yes.

36 Rattlesnake Creek - Ashdown Gorge Details

1 SHUTTLE SET UP - Park the first vehicle just off SR-14, 7 miles east of Cedar City, near the mouth of Ashdown Gorge. If driving from the west, this is 10.2 miles west of the intersection with SR-148.

2 TRAILHEAD - Arrange a drop-off or drive a second vehicle to Cedar Breaks. Park at the Ashdown Creek trailhead, at the north entrance to Cedar Breaks National Monument, approximately 8.5 miles from the SR-14 and SR-148 intersection and 5 miles north of the visitor center on SR-148. Notice the trailhead sign for the Ashdown Creek trail.

3 ROUTE - Begin the hike by following the north boundary line of the monument, heading west, entering a spruce forest. After a short 0.6 miles, a spur trail to the left (50 yards long) affords open views of Cedar Breaks to the south and the valley and mountains to the south and west. Continue another 0.2 miles to another spur trail, again to the left, which gives even better glimpses and is graced with several healthy, green bristlecone pines.

4 STUD FLAT - For the next mile the trail descends a bit more steeply and winds down into fir and aspen trees. Soon the route leads to the open meadow of Stud Flat, nestled above Rattlesnake Creek. Cairns help mark the path through Stud Flat as the grass and wildflowers sometimes obscure the beaten path. On the west end of Stud Flat, the trail begins to bear north with several long switchbacks and drops toward Rattlesnake Creek.

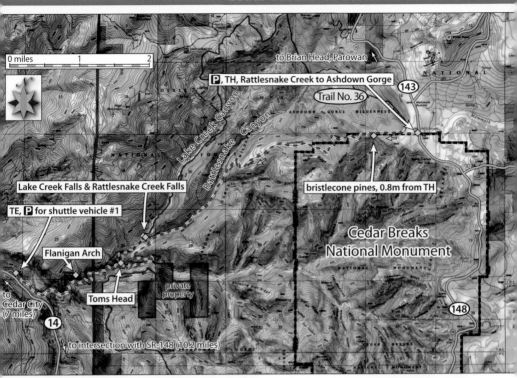

to Brian Head, Parowan

P, TH, Rattlesnake Creek to Ashdown Gorge

Trail No. 36

143

bristlecone pines, 0.8m from TH

Lake Creek Falls & Rattlesnake Creek Falls

TE, P for shuttle vehicle #1

Cedar Breaks National Monument

Flanigan Arch

Toms Head

private property

to Cedar City (7 miles)

14

148

to intersection with SR-148 (10.2 miles)

Bo Beck hikes the Rattlesnake Creek-Ashdown Gorge Trail

5 **RATTLESNAKE CREEK -** Soon the path parallels just above Rattlesnake Creek for a short time then descends into the creekbed. This is a good spot to take a lunch break and refill water in the shade of the fir trees. Be sure to filter or purify water. The trail now crosses over to the northwest bank of Rattlesnake Creek and continues southwest following the creekbed for the next mile then arrives at the intersection with the High Mountain Trail. Once again, cross Rattlesnake Creek, rejoining the southeast bank, and gradually ascend the ridge that separates Rattlesnake Creek from Ashdown Gorge. The route soon doubles back to the east and arrives at the beginning of Ashdown Gorge.

6 **ASHDOWN CREEK -** If you are not already wearing your canyoneering shoes, put them on now and prepare your hiking poles. The next 3 miles will be in the creekbed, with numerous crossings on sometimes slippery boulders. The farther west you go, the deeper and more beautiful the slot canyon becomes. At 0.75 miles down the creek, Toms Head towers on the right, indicating the upcoming confluence of Ashdown Creek with Rattlesnake Creek/Lake Creek, entering from the right.

7 **RATTLESNAKE AND LAKE CREEK WATERFALLS -** Don't miss the opportunity to make a relatively easy jaunt up Rattlesnake Creek to the intersection of two creeks at 0.6 miles. The creek entering from the left is Lake Creek and the one from the right is Rattlesnake Creek. A 100- to 200-yard-long walk up either of these slots will end at wonderful waterfalls.

8 **FLANIGAN ARCH -** Hike back to Ashdown Creek and continue downstream. After a mile, as the cliffs on the right begin to elevate, start looking at the skyline to the north. Stay on the left (south) bank whenever possible and you will arrive at a house-sized, black boulder which is also on the left side of the creek. From here you can view Flanigan Arch. In fact, the arch can only be seen from the large plateau upon which the boulder sits. This flat area is expansive (maybe 2 acres) but could change with future floods. From the arch it is about 1.3 miles down Ashdown Gorge to the awaiting shuttle vehicle. Farther downstream, particularly on the right bank, up high, are some long-abandoned 1940s vehicles that were used in construction and mining. Coal Creek enters from the left and the walls open up shortly before reaching the parked shuttle vehicle.

GPS Coordinates WGS84 Datum	Trailhead	Trailend
	37°39.762 N	37°38.124 N
	112°50.273 W	112°56.798 W

Flanigan Arch

Ashdown Gorge

THE SPECTRA POINT-RAMPARTS TRAIL

Cedar Breaks National Monument is without a doubt one of the most unusual and spectacular places in the natural world. However, it lies near three famous National Parks: Zion, Bryce Canyon and Grand Canyon, so has something of an under-the-radar status. Over 600,000 people make it to this monument each year, yet its visitation pales compared with the three powerhouse parks of the Southwest. Its off-the-beaten-path status makes Cedar Breaks an absolute gem. The fact that the monument has not been commercialized further enhances its beauty and appeal.

Another big plus is that Cedar Breaks sits at nearly 11,000 feet, offering summer temperatures no higher than 80 degrees in the day and nights getting down to a chilly 40 degrees. When temperatures soar in Zion or the Grand Canyon it's time to migrate to the mountains for a reprieve from the heat.

The high-altitude forest of Cedar Mountain is a haven of flora dominated by tall fir, pine, some dwindling spruce and of course the lanky quaking aspen. It's interesting that this tree competes with the bristlecone pine, also common on the mountain, for title of world's oldest living organism. Among these trees, on the soft-lit forest floor, is an odd selection of mushrooms and other fungi. Away from the shadows of towering leafage, in the sunlit meadows, there is such a mélange of flowers that each year a wildflower festival is held celebrating the diverse show of colors on the mountain.

A 5-mile rim drive provides easy access to four viewpoints: Sunset View, Point Supreme, Chessman Ridge and North View. Each features a different perspective of the glowing hoodoos in the great amphitheater. If you can go early or late in the season when there is a sprinkling of snow on the rocks, the views are all the more spectacular.

Top off your visit to Cedar Breaks with the fun hike described here. The Spectra Point Trail takes you to a great viewpoint with a sweeping panorama into the amphitheater. From here continue west on the Ramparts Trail, which winds its way to a yet grander promontory with amazing views.

The Spectra Point-Ramparts Trail features spectacular views across southern Utah

AT A GLANCE

Day Hike: Yes.

Distance:
Spectra Point: 1.75-mile round-trip.
Ramparts Trail: 3.2-mile round-trip.

Average Hiking Time:
Spectra Point: 45 minutes one way.
Ramparts Trail: Add another 45 minutes to the end of the Ramparts Trail. You need 3 hours to do the entire route.

Equipment: Be sure to take plenty of water, energy snacks, a hat, sun-protection and comfortable, closed-toe hiking shoes.

Difficulty: The monument rates this trail as moderately strenuous. It is 10,000 feet above sea level and includes a lot of elevation changes, but on the other hand it is on an established and maintained trail with traffic—so *we* rate this one as moderate. This is a good hike for the entire family, but there are nearby drop-offs, so watch children carefully.

Sun Exposure: You will be in the sun most of the hike, but even in the summer the temperature rarely exceed 80 degrees. This is a wonderful place to escape the summer heat.

Trail Conditions: Well-maintained, dirt path.

Trailhead: Cedar Breaks Visitor Center parking lot. The trail can be accessed either directly on the west side of the parking lot, or immediately from the visitor center itself.

Trailend: Same as trailhead.

Trail Access: Unless it's summer, check road conditions before heading to the monument. SR-148 is not plowed after the first large snowfall, which often occurs as early as October. The road usually reopens in May. During road closure, the monument remains open to cross-country skiers and snowmobiles (snowmobiles are limited to the roads).

Elevation: The ascent is 125 feet to the water towers, then the trail descends 240 feet to Spectra Point. From there to the end of the Ramparts Trail you descend 335 feet. The total elevation change from trailhead to trailend is 700 feet.

Best Season: It's best to plan a visit to the monument in the summer or early fall before winter storms close the road. The best times of day to see the amphitheater are sunrise and sunset.

Off the Beaten Path: No, this is one of only three trails advertised at Cedar Breaks, so expect a lot of foot traffic.

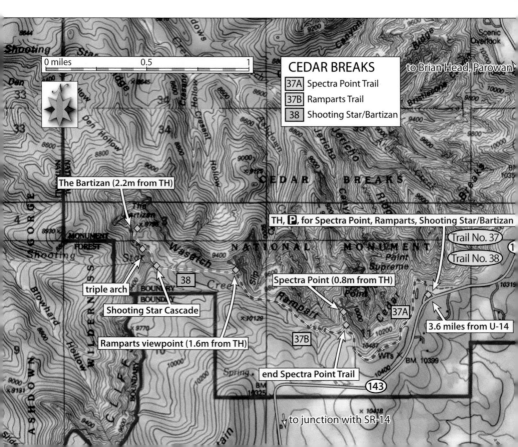

③⑦ THE SPECTRA POINT-RAMPARTS TRAIL DETAILS

TRAILHEAD - From Cedar City, drive about 15 miles east on SR-14 to Cedar Mountain. Turn left onto SR-148, drive 3.6 miles, then pull into the parking area. The Spectra Point-Ramparts Trail can be accessed either directly on the west side of the parking lot, or immediately from the visitor center. This rustic building was constructed in 1937 by the Civilian Conservation Corps (CCC). Consider taking a moment to go inside and look around. Ranger talks and walks are posted there as well as campfire and star programs.

SPECTRA POINT - From the fenced viewpoint locate the trailhead sign for the Spectra Point Trail. From the parking area the path ascends a short distance north, leading to the rim. It then skirts the edge of the canyon to the southwest as it approaches some water tanks, then descends toward Spectra Point. There is a meadow to your left with evergreen trees mixed among a multitude of wildflowers. For those that love the simple beauty of flowers, Cedar Breaks is the place to go. One of the floral showstoppers is the delicate columbine which can be seen along this trail. Views to the right of the path will vie for your attention: equally delicate rock spires of peculiar sizes and shapes are on display, the result of millions of years of erosion. Depending on the time of day, these hoodoos are fiery orange, tangerine, or sometimes the lightest of pinks. The array of colors showcased in the large bowl contrasts delightfully with the clear blue sky and billowy, white clouds. Head up the hill toward the water tank, where the route immediately begins a descent to Spectra Point. You will reach Specta Point after 0.8 miles. Here a 270-degree view reveals a fantasy-land of geological formations, including a few natural windows. See if you can find the oldest tree at Cedar Breaks; it's over 1,600 years old and it is found along this trail.

RAMPARTS TRAIL - Once at Spectra Point, you have the option to turn around and retrace the trail you just hiked or continue to the end of the Ramparts Trail, which will make the total hike about a 3-mile round-trip. If you choose to continue, follow the beaten path to the west, a little less than a mile, as it descends 335 feet. There are many new perspectives of the magnificent amphitheater below and at the end of the trail is a particularly amazing viewpoint. The dirt path periodically skirts the rim as it descends the hillside through the ever-more-numerous bristlecone pine trees. These ancient beauties delight the senses—then, at the end of the trail, fresh views of the expansive chasm below, filled with rugged rock sculptures rising from pink earth, provide a sensory overload. Return the same way you came.

The improbable geometry of Bartizan Arch (see next page). Two arches are visible here, a third is hidden behind. Photo: Bo Beck

GPS Coordinates
WGS84 Datum
Trailhead in Cedar Breaks
37°36.716 N, 112°50.260 W

Spectra Point
37°36.652 N, 112°50.699 W

Ramparts Viewpoint
37°36.825 N, 112°51.256 W

SHOOTING STAR CREEK AND BARTIZAN ARCH ③⑧

Most of the trails and viewpoints at Cedar Breaks congregate around the amphitheater, but this route, an extension of Trail No. 37, will take you off the beaten path to see a small-but-unique triple arch called Bartizan Arch. Along the way hikers will also get a glimpse of the stair-stepped cascade of Shooting Star Creek as it splashes down a vertical rimrock sending water on its way into the riparian void far below. For map, see Spectra-Ramparts Trail map on preceding page.

AT A GLANCE

Day Hike: Yes.

Distance: 4.5-mile round-trip.

Average Hiking Time: 4-hour round-trip.

Equipment: Bring 2–3 liters of water per person, sunscreen, supportive hiking shoes, sun-protective clothing and emergency supplies.

Difficulty: Strenuous off-trail hike.

Sun Exposure: Full sun most of the hike.

Permits: Not required.

Trail Conditions: The long, dirt path has several elevation changes, and you will be required to do some route-finding in a forested area.

Trailhead: Cedar Breaks Visitor Center parking lot.

Trailend: Same as trailhead.

Trail Access: Check road conditions before heading to the monument in spring, fall and winter. SR-148 closes due to snowfall, but the monument remains open to cross-country skiers and snowmobiles. Snowmobiles are limited to roads. Highways are not plowed after the first large snowfall, which may occur as early as October. Normally the roads open again in May.

Best Season: This is best done in the summer or fall before any winter storms. Snow makes hiking hazardous near the creek and arch.

Elevation Loss and Gain: 900 feet.

Off the Beaten Path: Well-traveled to the end of the Ramparts Trail. Few venture beyond, so the rest of the trek is more of a route-finding adventure.

③⑧ SHOOTING STAR CREEK AND BARTIZAN ARCH

1 TRAILHEAD - Begin as for Spectra Point and the Ramparts Trail. From the parking area the path ascends a short distance north, leading to the rim. It skirts the edge of the canyon to the southwest and approaches some water tanks, then descends to Spectra Point. Do a quick jaunt to Spectra Point for an amazing view into the depths of Cedar Breaks and then backtrack a short distance to the Ramparts Trail and walk westerly as the path continues to descend until its end.

2 SHOOTING STAR CREEK - From the end of the Rampart Trail, continue west, staying near the rim for about 0.25 miles. When the terrain steepens, bear left, leaving the rim and heading into the vegetation. The creek will be on your left. Head downward, southwest, choosing the clearest path through the foliage and toward the creek. Do not go all the way into the bottom of Shooting Star Creek; instead bear right and contour above the drainage bottom. Choose the easiest path to follow downstream as you approach the rim and arrive at the 40-foot-high spillover. You will have hiked almost 2 miles at this point. Be cautious near the edge; the limestone is unstable. Whenever rock is wet it is more apt to break but, wet or dry, avoid getting too close to the rim. Walk to the north side of the cascade for a good place to see the multi-stepped waterfall. Water is usually running, but it may dry up in late summer or fall.

3 BARTIZAN ARCH - From the cascade, scan for a game trail that leads west-northwest. This path will drop into and climb out of several small drainages. The Bartizan is the peak at the end of the ridge that resembles a turret, visible about 0.2 miles from the cascade. From here you can see the southern side of the structure and a short distance to the south or left of the high point, poised on the rim edge, you should be able to identify two arches. There is a small, third arch but it is only visible from the backside. The best area to get photos is near the Shooting Star Cascade; however, all three arches cannot be seen from there. Scramble toward the arches, being careful while traversing the loose limestone scree slopes. From the arch, bear north to arrive atop the Bartizan. There are flat areas there offering shade, making an ideal spot to eat lunch and relax as well as to take unique photographs of the amphitheater. Return the same way you came; this will be mostly uphill.

**GPS Coordinates
WGS84 Datum**

Trailhead
37°36.716 N, 112°50.260 W

Spectra Point
37°36.652 N, 112°50.699 W

Rampart Viewpoint
37°36.825 N, 112°51.256 W

Shooting Star Creek Cascade
37°36.842 N, 112°51.703 W

Bartizan Arch:
37°36.951 N, 112 51.799 W

Bartizan Summit:
37°37.018 N, 112°51.769 W

6 Cedar Mountain/Dixie National Forest

Surrounded by deserts, Dixie National Forest is an oasis of green, here viewed from the Cascade Falls Trail

CEDAR MOUNTAIN AND DIXIE NATIONAL FOREST

The Markagunt High Plateau Scenic Byway, SR-14, is well named. Markagunt is an Indian word meaning "highland of trees," which well describes this area since the Markagunt Plateau is one of the largest and highest plateaus in southern Utah. And as for the "scenic" part, this 40-mile-long road is lined with crowded groves of aspens, towering evergreens, ancient lava rock and a diverse display of wildflowers.

Fall arrives early at this high elevation, chasing green from the aspens in October. In the forest, clean, bright blue skies can be seen high above an almost endless sea of autumn leaves stretching as far as the eye can see. It's a treat to drive this scenic byway in September as air grows brisk and green leaves transform to red and yellow. There is absolutely no mistaking why this area is known as "color country."

The hiking opportunities in this huge area, simply known as Cedar Mountain by the locals, are endless and a welcome change of pace when lower elevations are broiling. In this chapter we describe two short, fun trails and one much longer route; each highlights the beauty and variety of this area.

First we take you on a nice stroll along the Cascade Falls Trail to the headwaters of the Zion Narrows via a short, scenic walk. Groves of bristlecone pines grow along the Markagunt High Plateau Scenic Byway and we have included a short jaunt that begins right off the highway to a stand of gorgeous specimens. The third route ventures in amongst the seldom-visited hoodoos below the Cedar Breaks rim.

GETTING THERE

From St. George, drive north on I-15 to Cedar City. From Cedar City, head east on SR-14. If you are approaching from the north on I-15 exit at Parowan, then take SR-143 past Brian Head Ski Resort and Cedar Breaks National Monument to SR-14. From Zion National Park, take US-89 north to Long Valley Junction and the eastern terminus of SR-14. Check for road closures in the winter, early spring, and late fall. See map on facing page; also area map on page 7.

Navajo Lake in winter. Photo: NIkki Milligan

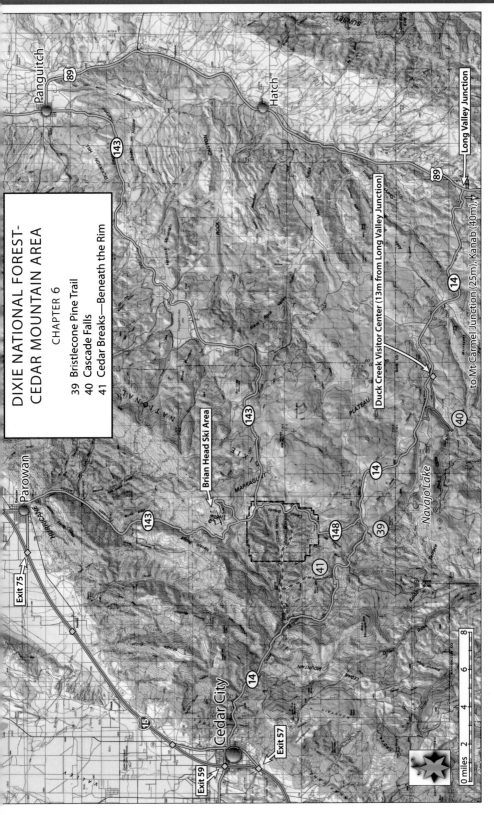

DIXIE NATIONAL FOREST – CEDAR MOUNTAIN AREA

CHAPTER 6

39 Bristlecone Pine Trail
40 Cascade Falls
41 Cedar Breaks—Beneath the Rim

BRISTLECONE PINE TRAIL 39

The easy, half-mile Bristlecone Pine Trail is a great hike for families; you can see Zion National Park in the distance as you meander among a grove of young bristlecone pines.

Scientists have long considered the bristlecone to be the oldest living thing (some specimens are over 4,700 years old). However, some researchers have proposed that recently-sprouted plants that emerge from single, large roots and form clonal colonies, such as aspen and creosote, may be even older, since their root systems go back many tens of thousands of years. Under this new definition, these plants make even the oldest of all known bristlecones seem like youngsters—but it is all about how "oldest living thing" is defined. If you are talking about a single, independent trunk or stem, then the bristlecone is probably the oldest single living organism.

The bristlecones along this trail are not quite the oldest in the world, but some have been dated to 4,500 years old. These trees have adapted to living on barren slopes and cliffs. If unsure which are the ancient pines, look for needles in groups of five. The leaves will be 1 to 1.5 inches long. Bristlecone trees have a thin, smooth bark which is grayish white on young stems, but as the stems age, the color becomes a reddish brown and the trunks begin to twist. The pinecones are tipped with long bristle seeds.

Surrounding this quiet place, high on the mountain, a lush, sub-alpine forest of quaking aspens thrives.

Kyra Milligan at the end of the Bristlecone Pine Trail

—— AT A GLANCE ——

Day Hike: Yes.

Distance: Half-mile round-trip.

Average Hiking Time: 30 to 60 minutes.

Equipment: Comfortable hiking shoes, water, hat and other sun protection.

Difficulty: Expect an easy hike on a well maintained, although uneven, forest trail. Kids will enjoy this short path, but hold young children's hands because they can, and sometimes do, stumble on uneven hiking surfaces, littered with occasional rocks and other natural debris.

Sun Exposure: Full sun except under the shade of the trees.

Permits: Not required.

Trail Conditions: Dirt, forest path lined with trees and wildflowers.

Trailhead: Just off SR-14 near the SR-14 and SR-148 junction. Look for the large pullout immediately west of the turnoff to Cedar Breaks.

Trailend: Same as trailhead.

Trail Access: Summer is best, but you can usually get to the trail early in the fall or late in the spring. Snow levels will limit access in the winter.

Best Season: Anytime the road allows travel.

Elevation Change: 25 feet of undulating terrain.

Off the Beaten Path: Yes; low to moderate usage.

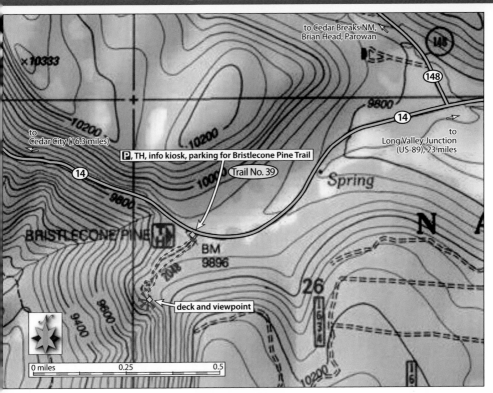

To Cedar Breaks NM,
Brian Head, Parowan

148

14

to
Long Valley Junction
(US-89), 23 miles

to
Cedar City (16.3 miles)

P, TH, info kiosk, parking for Bristlecone Pine Trail

Trail No. 39

Spring

14

BRISTLECONE PINE

BM
9896

26

deck and viewpoint

0 miles   0.25   0.5

39 BRISTLECONE PINE TRAIL DETAILS

TRAILHEAD - From Cedar City - Set your odometer at the mileage sign on SR-14 seen as you are leaving Cedar City. Drive 16.3 miles to the Zion Overlook pullout and another half-mile to the Bristlecone Pine Trailhead, both of which are on the right. It is 17.8 miles to the junction of SR-14 and SR-148, so if you see that, then you've gone too far.

From Jct. SR-14 and US-89 - If you are coming from Long Valley Junction (the intersection of SR-14 and US-89), it is about 23 miles to the SR-14 and SR-148 intersection, and then another half-mile past that on the left is the Bristlecone Pine Trailhead. This is 23.5 miles from Long Valley Junction. Watch for the asphalt pullout on the south side of SR-14. This pullout is large enough to accommodate 6–8 vehicles and houses the wooden kiosk describing the bristlecone pine trees and a sign for the trailhead.

BRISTLECONES - This dirt path is surrounded by fields of wildflowers and trees and allows you to enjoy a serene, lazy stroll through the coniferous woodlands. This culminates at a wooden deck overlook that provides a panoramic view of Zion National Park in the distance—a view enhanced by the crystal clear air and the fresh floral aroma. Colorful lichens, symbiotic plants that grow in areas with good air quality, are found in abundance. At the end of the trail the bristlecone pines have taken over the space. There are young and old, but all seem to be green and thriving. Pinecones and needles litter the forest floor and wildflowers add a hue of color all around. Rare in most of the rest of the state, bristlecones thrive on Cedar Mountain.

GPS Coordinates
WGS84 Datum

Bristlecone Pine Trailhead:
37 34.043 N, 112 50.951 W

Bristlecone Pine Trailend
37 33.890 N, 112 51.053 W

CASCADE FALLS (40)

The Markagunt High Plateau Scenic Byway, SR-14, which winds from Cedar City to a junction at US-89, is a popular recreation area known by most locals simply as Cedar Mountain.

Near the summit of this road lies picturesque Navajo Lake, which sits at an elevation of 9,200 feet. A quick stop at the nearest pullout is a must, to let visitors feast their eyes on this tree-rimmed, crystal-blue body of water. Sink holes in Navajo Lake are an important conduit in providing the source of water that flows to the highlight of the trail described here: Cascade Falls. The water flows from here into the North Fork of the Virgin River and the Zion Narrows, the area's most famous "trail" (see page 24 for details of the Narrows). These flowing waters have helped carve the deep gorges of Zion National Park.

AT A GLANCE

Day Hike: Yes.

Distance: 0.45 miles one way, or a 0.9-mile round-trip.

Average Hiking Time: Allow about an hour for a casual walk and time to enjoy the waterfall at the end of the trail.

Equipment: Comfortable hiking shoes, hat, sun-protection and water.

Difficulty: This is an easy hike on a maintained trail that's ideal for kids. For younger children, holding a hand is suggested because of the steep terrain; kids can, and sometimes do, stumble on uneven hiking paths, such as this one, that are intermittently covered with loose rocks and other tripping hazards.

Sun Exposure: Full sun.

Permits: Not required.

Trail Conditions: This is a dirt path with slippery, loose scree in sections; there are some wood bridges and steps on the short, steeper parts. The path should be easy for most people to walk on; however, there have been injuries here.

Trailhead: Turn off SR-14 onto Forest Road 053 at Navajo Lake or turn at the Duck Creek Visitor Center, 2.5 miles east of the Navajo Lake Road. Follow the signs to Cascade Falls.

Trailend: Same as trailhead.

Trail Access: In winter, early spring and late fall check to see that SR-14 is open before attempting to drive to this trailhead. Snowy, wet conditions may render dirt roads impassable. The trail to Cascade Falls is located on the southwest end of Cow Lake near the back of the large parking lot.

Best Season: Summer.

Elevation Change: 100 feet.

Off the Beaten Path: Yes.

Tanya Milligan and Bo Beck at Cascade Falls

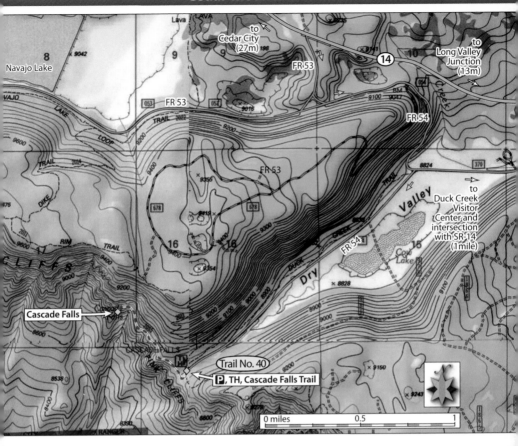

Cascade Falls

④⓪ CASCADE FALLS DETAILS

1 DRIVING APPROACH - From Cedar City drive east on SR-14 for approximately 25 miles to Navajo Lake. Turn right and follow signs to Cascade Falls or continue to Duck Creek Visitor Center and follow Forest Service Road 54 to Cascade Falls.

From US-89: Coming from Long Valley Junction (the intersection of US-89 and SR-14), drive west 13 miles on SR-14, then turn left at the Duck Creek Visitor Center onto Forest Service Road 54.

2 DUCK CREEK VISITOR CENTER - Pass the visitor center, driving southwest on the dirt and gravel road. At 1.8 miles, Road 54 comes to a "Y" intersection. Go left and travel alongside the normally dry Cow Lake for 1.6 miles to the Cascade Falls Trailhead.

The Cascade Falls Trailhead can also be accessed from Navajo Lake by turning south onto Navajo Lake Road, then traveling 0.3 miles to an intersection, steering left at the "Y" and looping around the ridge to arrive at the intersection at Cow Lake. Follow the road alongside Cow Lake to the Cascade Falls Trailhead.

3 CASCADE FALLS - This friendly, fun round-trip hike is a little under a mile long and is pretty flat. The route overlooks the southern edge of the Markagunt Plateau and ends at a rocky ledge with water tumbling down from a limestone cave. There is a wooden deck at the end to stand on and view the stream of water as it pours downward. It's not safe to get in the stream; it is slippery and the rocks are sharp.

GPS Coordinates WGS84 Datum	Cascade Falls Trailhead 37°29.838 N, 112°45.105 W
Duck Creek Visitor Center and Road to Cow Lake 37°30.947 N, 112°41.944 W	Cascade Falls Trailend 37°30.149 N, 112°45.429 W

Spectacular scenery under the Cedar Breaks rim, on the "Beneath the Rim" hike (No.41)

BENEATH THE RIM AT CEDAR BREAKS

Cedar Breaks appears as a magical world where sculpted hoodoos, fins and windows shine in vivid colors. Due to the extreme erosion at the monument the formations have no equal in color or composition. The amphitheater formed long ago, but today the molding and sculpting still continues as water runs down the maze of rock pillars, carving gullies along the way, making this one of the most beautiful places in North America.

The Beneath-the-Rim Trail highlights the absolute best of this magical world, taking you deep into the labyrinth of gullies and hoodoos that are are usually only glimpsed from afar.

AT A GLANCE

Day Hike: Yes, but often done as a backpack.

Camping: Backcountry camping is not allowed within the monument boundaries, but you can set up camp in the wilderness area.

Distance: 14–18 miles depending on side trips.

Average Hiking Time: 10 hours.

Equipment: Comfortable, supportive hiking shoes are a must. Trekking poles if the creeks are running high. At least 2–3 quarts of water. Emergency equipment and plenty of energy snacks. The best map is the "Cedar Mountain - Pine Valley Mountain" National Geographic-Trails Illustrated.

Difficulty: Strenuous route, plus stream crossings.

Sun Exposure: Full sun during most of the hike.

Permits: Not required.

Trail Conditions: Forested, downhill path and river hiking. The water can be too high if done early in the season.

Trailhead: Crystal Springs Trailhead.

Trailend: Same as Trailhead.

Trail Access: SR-14 is open year-round.

Elevation at Trailhead: 8,900 feet.

Highest Elevation: 9,100 feet.

Off the Beaten Path: Yes.

Best Season: The best time of the year is June through October when the snowpack has melted and water levels are lowest.

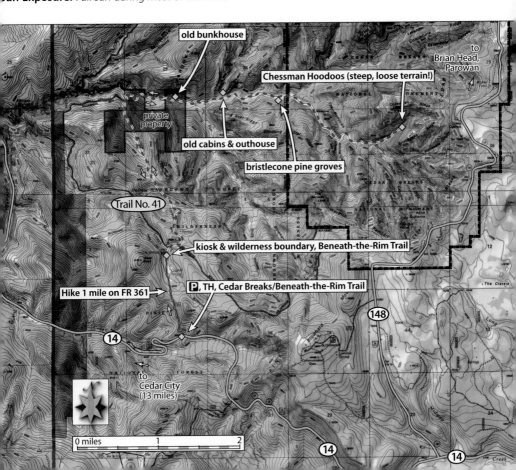

㊶ BENEATH THE RIM DETAILS

1 **PARKING -** Crystal Springs Trailhead - From Cedar City, drive about 13 miles east on SR-14 through Cedar Canyon; drive past the campground and navigate the tight "S" curves. Just past the bend, look on the north side of the highway for a gate and the unpaved Forest Road 361. Park without blocking the gate.

2 **TRAILHEAD -** Walk around the gate and up the road for 0.25 miles, passing through a spruce and fir forest. The road begins a gradual descent for the next 0.75 miles, passing the Blowhard Trail and Crystal Spring, then ends at the Ashdown Gorge Wilderness Boundary. From the boundary follow the beaten path along the creek for a short distance, first north-northeast then east. Climb a small ridge to the north, then continue down the back side of the ridge into a draw. Locate the cairn at the end of the small meadow. The "trail" once again ascends 200 feet, leading to the top of the ridge overlooking Ashdown Creek to the north and Cedar Breaks to the east. Head downhill to the creek and Potato Hollow.

3 **POTATO HOLLOW -** Once at Potato Hollow the path is faint. Hike north-northwest along the wash for the next 0.75 miles, staying on whichever side has a visible beaten path.

4 **OLD ROAD -** Soon the path meets an old road above the creek. Turn right and follow the road. You will come to an area posted private property. Turn left, following the property boundary until you get to Ashdown Creek. Cross the creek, then head upstream to the old bunkhouse. From the bunkhouse follow another road bearing east through the forest, toward Cedar Breaks.

5 **ASHDOWN CREEK AND ARCH CREEK-** The next 3 miles are in Ashdown Gorge, crossing back and forth, walking along the banks. Look for the dilapidated sawmill, about 0.75 miles north of the bunkhouse, at the confluence of Spring Creek and Ashdown Creek. At 1.6 miles from the confluence of Spring Creek and Ashdown Creek, the usually dry Adams Canyon Wash enters from the north. You will see groves of both young and old bristlecone pines along Ashdown creek. Continue upstream, passing Meadow Hill on its southern flank, until you reach the confluence of Ashdown Creek and Arch Creek.

6 **CHESSMAN WASH AND CHESSMAN RIDGE -** At this confluence, head left, up Arch Creek. Almost immediately there is a half-mile scramble up Chessman Wash. This leads to the base of Chessman Ridge and its amazing hoodoos. These formations are particularly photogenic close up— they are usually viewed only from a long distance away, from above the rim. If you have the time and energy, head back to the confluence of Chessman Canyon and Arch Creek, then hike up Arch Creek where you will find yet more hoodoos.

7 **EXIT -** Retrace the route back to Crystal Springs Trailhead.

Looking up the Ashdown Creek drainage toward a stormy Cedar Breaks—beware of possible flash floods if the weather looks like this

GPS Coordinates WGS84 Datum	
Crystal Springs Trailhead 37°35.620 N 112°53.629 W	Bunkhouse at Sawmill 37°38.080 N
Ashdown Gorge Wilderness Boundary at Crystal Springs 37°36.543 N 112°53.788 W	Sawmill Structures at Spring Creek 37°38.100 N 112°53.127 W
Trail Intersection with Road at Ashdown Creek 37°38.062 N 112°54.364 W	Arch Creek meets Ashdown Creek 37°37.617 N 112°51.267 W
	End of hike up Chessman Cyn 37°37.875 N 112°50.548 W

Bo Beck in Bull Valley Gorge, GSENM

to Panguitch (15m)
Hatch

0 miles 2 4 6 8

63

Bryce
Canyon
National
Park

14

to
Cedar City

Long Valley Junction

Rainbow Point

Lick Wash

turn east at 300 North

Glendale

Bench Road

Skutumpah Road

Orderville

89

Johnson Canyon Road

9

Mt. Carmel Junction

to
Zion
NP

89

89

Kanab

89

8.5 miles east of Kanab

UTAH
ARIZONA

ALT
89

to
Big Water (57m)
Page (74m)

to Fredonia (1m)

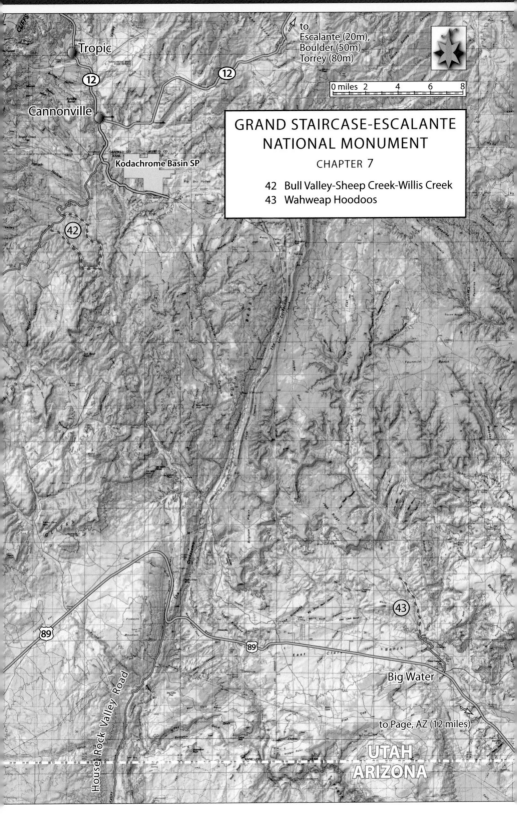

Tropic

to
Escalante (20m),
Boulder (50m),
Torrey (80m)

0 miles 2   4   6   8

12

Cannonville

Kodachrome Basin SP

**GRAND STAIRCASE-ESCALANTE
NATIONAL MONUMENT**
CHAPTER 7

42 Bull Valley-Sheep Creek-Willis Creek
43 Wahweap Hoodoos

42

Fourmile Ranch

89

43

89

Big Water

House Rock Valley Road

to Page, AZ (12 miles)

**UTAH
ARIZONA**

Grand Staircase-Escalante National Monument

The Grand Staircase-Escalante National Monument is an enormous expanse of colorful country filled with canyons, buttes, terraces and wilderness. This arid landscape features some of the most photogenic slot canyons anywhere. Pristine and remote are appropriate words to describe the terrain within the Grand Staircase-Escalante National Monument (GSENM).

Access to, and within GSENM is via just a couple of highways. US-89 defines the southern border and SR-12 accesses the northern side. Glendale, Utah, located on US-89, northeast of Zion National Park, connects the east side of Zion to Bryce Canyon via the Glendale Bench Road and the scenic backroad, Skutumpah Road. To the north, SR-12, designated as an "All American Highway," connects Tropic and Boulder, winding north all the way to Torrey and Capitol Reef National Park. In addition to these highways there are 959 miles of open road in the Staircase. At the southern end of the monument, roads connect Kanab, Utah and Page, Arizona. See map on previous pages, also area map on page 7.

US-89 travels through spectacular scenery. From the turnoff with SR-12 (which heads toward Bryce Canyon) all the way south to the Utah-Arizona state line, US-89 presents an amazing trip through the geologically defined steps of the Grand Staircase. The top riser creates the Pink Cliffs, exposed around Bryce Canyon; a layer below is the White Cliffs formation, extending east from Mt. Carmel Junction. US-89 is the main artery connecting the best of the Southwest's parks and monuments: Zion National Park, Grand Staircase-Escalante National Monument, Cedar Breaks National Monument, Bryce Canyon National Park, Paria Canyon Wilderness, The Vermilion Cliffs National Monument and the north rim of The Grand Canyon National Park. We call this area "Canyon Country."

We particularly like the Skutumpah Road area. It is accessed either by the Glendale Bench Road (starting in Glendale) or the paved Johnson Canyon Road, near Kanab. Skutumpah Road leads to Kodachrome Basin State Park, near Bryce Canyon. Along the way you pass the wonderful slot-canyon/trail combination of Bull Valley Gorge to Sheep Creek to Willis Creek. In another part of the Staircase, near the town of Big Water is one of the most unusual hiking destinations, the giant, white Wahweap Hoodoos.

All interior roads, except for portions of the Burr Trail and Johnson Canyon Road, are unpaved, and may be impassable if wet. The boundaries of Utah's Kane County and Garfield County enclose the monument lands. Kane County claims 68 percent of the monument and Garfield County holds 32 percent.

Wahweap Hoodoos

BULL VALLEY GORGE –> SHEEP CREEK
-> WILLIS CREEK ④②

Bull Valley Gorge is a dimly-lit canyon cut into the rugged and wild land of the Grand Staircase-Escalante National Monument. Some distance into this trip, canyon walls begin to spread out, allowing rays of sunlight to bathe the sandy ground as you leave the tight confines of the slot. The next leg of the journey takes you through Sheep Creek where the sound of flowing water eventually lures you on toward an eerie canyon with a yellow glow. This is Willis Creek, a delightfully bright assemblage of sculpted rock embracing a gentle, cobblestone stream that meanders through the serene passage.

This is a long, all-day route that may require a 50-foot length of rope. For a shorter hike that samples the delights of Willis Creek but avoids technical obstacles, simply do this route backwards, starting at the trailend, Willis Creek; go as far as you are comfortable with then turn around and go back to your vehicle.

The nearest town is Cannonville, located on SR-12 (see area map on page 147).

Summer and Kyra Milligan in Willis Creek

AT A GLANCE

Day Hike: Long day-hike or a casual backpack.

Distance: 15 trail miles, and 2 more miles hiking the road back to the trailhead: Total 17 miles.

Average Hiking Time: 10 hours.

Difficulty: Moderate hiking with bouldering and down-climbing required inside Bull Valley Gorge. The gorge can be difficult if there is water or if the weather is cold. As with all slot canyons, conditions can change and this canyon may require technical skills and equipment.

Equipment: Emergency gear, sun-protective clothing, extra socks, sticky-rubber shoes that drain well, at least 3 quarts of water per person, energy snacks, map and 50 feet of rope or webbing.

Sun Exposure: Full sun in the last section of Bull Valley Gorge and in Sheep Creek.

Permits: A permit is required for overnight camping. Permits are free and easy to obtain. Just fill out the form at the trailhead or at any Grand Staircase Escalante National Monument visitor center.

Trail Conditions: Bull Valley Gorge is often dry in the summer. After rain expect to navigate wet conditions which may include slick mud and pools. If there is water in the slot it will be cold.

Trailhead: Bull Valley Gorge at Skutumpah.

Trailend: Same as trailhead.

Trail Access: It's best to do this route in the early summer. In the winter and spring snowmelt on Skutumpah Road can leave the road impassable In the winter Bull Valley Gorge can contain very cold water.

Best Season: Early summer.

Off the Beaten Path: Yes. Few venture into Bull Valley Gorge and Sheep Creek. Willis Creek gets more travel.

Water: Willis Creek runs year-round but it is best not to use it since cattle graze in the area and horses walk right down the waterway. Sheep Creek will often have runoff from Willis Creek. Willis Creek flows west-to-east until the confluence with Sheep Creek, Sheep Creek flows north-to-south.

Summer Milligan in Willis Creek

42 BULL VALLEY GORGE –> SHEEP CREEK –> WILLIS CREEK DETAILS

APPROACH: GETTING TO SKUTUMPAH ROAD - if you are driving from St. George there are two options for reaching Skutumpah Road (see local map pages 146–147; also area road map page 7):

1. Go through Zion National Park and then take US-89 north to Glendale. Turn right on 300 N. (Bench Road) and follow the graded dirt road to where it intersects with Johnson Canyon Road and Skutumpah Road. There is an information kiosk at this junction.

2. Alternatively take UT-389 out of Hurricane to Fredonia, Arizona, then continue east on US-89 toward Page. Locate Johnson Canyon Road, which will be on the left side of the highway about 8.5 miles east of Kanab. Turn north and travel the paved road until it intersects Skutumpah Road at the information kiosk.

If you are approaching from north of the Grand Staircase (SR-12), drive south out of Cannonville for 4 miles, then turn right onto the northern end of Skutumpah Road. Drive about 7 miles southwest to Bull Valley Gorge.

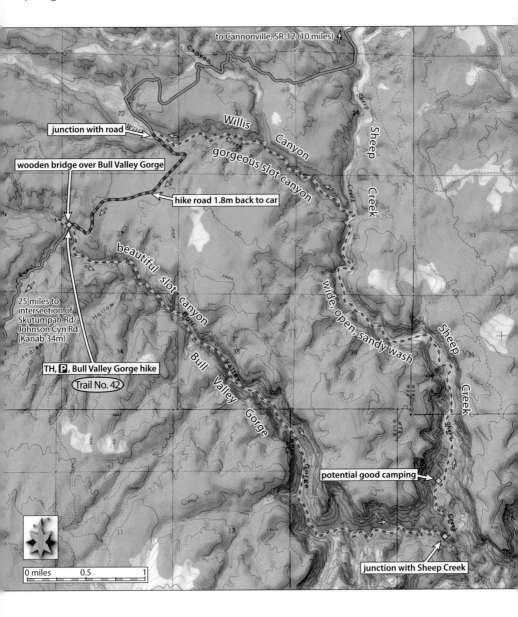

2 APPROACH: SKUTUMPAH ROAD TO BULL VALLEY GORGE - Take Skutumpah Road at the intersection and continue 25 miles northeast to Bull Valley Gorge. You will pass Lick Wash on the right at 15 miles. There may not be a sign, but look for the narrow wooden bridge that stretches over the gorge. If you continue another 1.8 miles you will be at Willis Creek where your hike will end.

Flash floods dramatically rearrange obstacles in this gorge, so be aware that deep pools of cold water, waterfalls or dryfalls may be present. Wear sticky-soled shoes and bring a 50-foot section of rope or 1" tubular webbing.

3 TRAILHEAD - Park by the bridge then hike upcanyon, staying on the right side of the drainage to locate the registration box. Stay along the edge until you find a shallow place to climb down into the canyon. Don't drop in too soon or you will miss a spectacular section of narrows. Most of the down-climbs should be fairly easy, but it's always safer to have a climber or experienced canyoneer in the group.

4 BULL VALLEY GORGE - The walls of this dimly-lit earthen crevice are tall, fluted and spectacular. If you are lucky there might be a stream of water forming puddles as it flows down the wash. A short distance downstream, note a 1954 pickup truck, wedged into the slot, making up a portion of the bridge. Not far past the bridge are a couple of tributaries, one on the right and another on the left. At about the 2-mile mark there are large juniper and fir trees growing on the sides of the canyon and soon two more side-washes enter the gorge. After about 3 miles walls widen to about 400 yards and the rocky bottom gives way to clay and sand.

5 SHEEP CREEK - At 3.5 miles look for a large fin of rock, up high and on the left side of the canyon and notice an arch or small window. The gorge will bend around this large buttress making a dogleg turn to the east (left) and steer toward the confluence with the north-to-south-running wash of Sheep Creek. A narrow slot will come into the gorge at about the 6-mile mark, where you will turn left and travel north into Sheep Creek. Follow the fairly level terrain for about 4 miles. It may be hot in this section and there is little to no shade. About midway through, a gentle flow of water trickles through the sandy wash.

6 WILLIS CREEK - 10 miles into the hike there should be a wilderness sign where another canyon intersects with Sheep Creek from the west. Follow the stream of water that has been present through Sheep Creek by turning left and you will begin the Willis Creek narrows. Horses and cows visit here, so treat water before drinking. You pass Averett Creek, on the right, 1.3 miles from the Sheep Creek-Willis Creek confluence. The constricted walls of Willis Creek capture the afternoon sun and at the right time of day, sunlit rock in this 2.5-mile-long passage puts on a grand show for photographers. There are a couple of fun little waterfalls near the end of the trail.

7 SKUTUMPAH ROAD BACK TO THE TRAILHEAD - Once at Skutumpah Road, turn left and walk 2 miles back to the Bull Valley Gorge trailhead and your vehicle.

HOW A TRUCK CAME TO BE PART OF THE BULL VALLEY GORGE BRIDGE - An interesting story about the vehicle wedged under the bridge is often told around campfires. The truck slid off the bridge and rolled into the gorge. Two men fell out and the body of a third was removed. The truck is difficult to see from above, as it is camouflaged by tightly packed dirt and rocks. Although wedged in 1954, the truck remains to this day, making up part of the narrow bridge. Be assured that as narrow as the bridge is today, it's wider than when this truck drove over it.

HOW BULL VALLEY GORGE GOT ITS NAME - The odd name, Bull Valley Gorge, was given when the area was used to raise cattle and bulls. The two genders were kept apart by the gorge. The gorge drains southeast into the Paria River.

AVERETT CANYON - Pioneers residing in what is now the town of Glendale, one of the entrances into the Grand Staircase, were in conflict with Indian raiders in 1866. Elijah Averett was killed by Indians.

GPS Coordinates: WGS84 Datum	Bull Valley Gorge & Sheep Creek confluence
Bull Valley Trailhead	37°26.050N, 112°03.067W
37°28.317N, 112°06.600W	Willis Creek and Sheep Creek confluence
Drop down into Bull Valley Gorge	37°28.400N, 112°03.917W
37°28.383N, 112°06.733W	Willis Creek Exit at Skutumpah Road
	37°28.967N, 112°05.783W

WAHWEAP HOODOOS

The sun-scorched lands of the Southwest are host to many bizarre things. Wahweap can claim some of the strangest: white stone spires, often called goblins, ghosts and toadstools.

Groves of stone-capped, white columns are located near Big Water, Utah, at the edge of the Grand Staircase-Escalante National Monument. The caps on these hoodoos are formed from 100-million-year-old Dakota sandstone. The posts of the hoodoos are molded from much softer Entrada sandstone that is 160 million years old. In between, 60-million-years-worth of intermediate rock layers is missing, notably sandstone of the Morrison formation. This is a fine example of what geologists call an unconformity.

AT A GLANCE

Day Hike: Yes.

Distance: 9.2 mile round-trip.

Average Hiking Time: 6 hours.

Equipment: 3 liters of water per person, energy snacks, emergency overnight supplies, sun-protective clothing, sunscreen and extra socks.

Difficulty: This is a relatively easy hike, lacking significant elevation change.

Sun Exposure: Full sun.

Permits: Not required.

Trail Conditions: This hike is through a wash that can be slippery if wet. When it's dry and hot there is little reprieve from the sun. There is a flash flood danger.

Trailhead: Wahweap Creek just outside of Big Water, Utah.

Trailend: Same as trailhead.

Trail Access: Year-round.

Best Season: Spring or fall. This trail is in full sun and it is generally too hot in summer.

Elevation Gain: 229 feet.

Starting Elevation: 4,042 feet.

Highest Elevation: 4,271feet at the peak.

Off the Beaten Path: Yes.

Wahweap Hoodoos

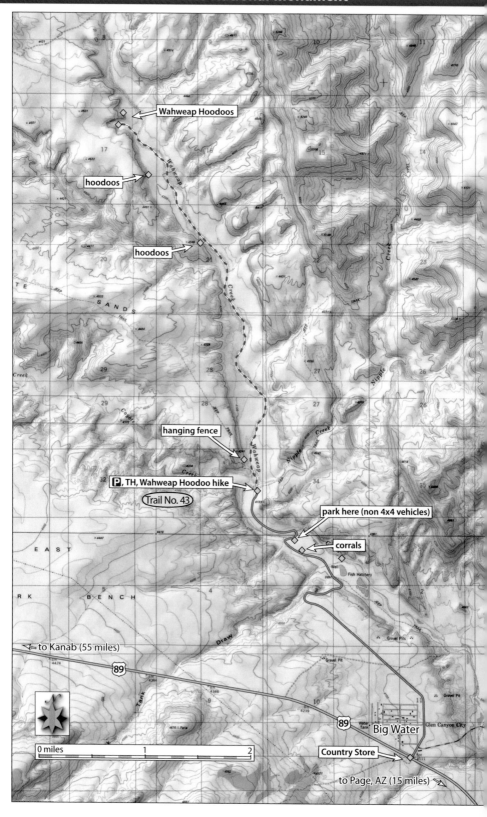

Wahweap Hoodoos

hoodoos

hoodoos

hanging fence

P, TH, Wahweap Hoodoo hike

Trail No. 43

park here (non 4x4 vehicles)

corrals

Fish Hatchery

to Kanab (55 miles)

89

89

Big Water

0 miles　　　1　　　2

Country Store

to Page, AZ (15 miles)

43 WAHWEAP HOODOOS DETAILS

TRAILHEAD - From Kanab, drive east on US-89 toward Lake Powell for approximately 55 miles, until reaching the small town of Big Water, Utah. At Big Water, turn left on the Ethan Allen Road, which is between mile markers 6 and 7, directly across the highway from the Big Water Grand Staircase-Escalante Visitor Center. Follow Ethan Allen past several streets to a "T" junction. Turn left here and pass the old softball field on the left side of the now gravel road. Follow this wide, graded road past two fish hatcheries. Continue north past a corral which is located 3 miles from US-89. If driving a 2WD, park on the right side of the road just before crossing the creek and then begin the hike up Wahweap Creek. High clearance 4WD vehicles can go past the corral, cross Wahweap Creek, and continue for 0.3 miles. The trail begins in Wahweap Creek just below the 4WD parking area.

Wahweap Hoodoo

2 WAHWEAP CREEK - Start at the confluence of Coyote Creek, Nipple Creek and Wahweap Creek. The trip through Wahweap Wash is a leisurely hike that is easily navigated. Be aware that if the clay at the edge of the creek is wet it can be extremely slippery. Hike north, up Wahweap Wash. Avoid damaging the environment by staying in the watercourse whenever possible. At about a half-mile, a dilapidated "hanging fence" is suspended over the creekbed. Continue past the fence, hiking in the wide open wash of Wahweap Creek. Spectacular views of the gentle sloping fields of "pocketed" white Entrada sandstone are seen to the north. Continue north, heading for the large "red buttress"on the east side of the creek. At the 2-mile mark, stop and hike toward the obvious white hoodoos located on the west (left) side of the wash. Continue toward these first teasers of brown-capped, tall, white hoodoos. At 2.3 miles, you should be up against the white, slickrock band on the western side of the wash. At 3 miles, more delicate, white, hoodoos become apparent. At 3.6 miles, you'll reach the first of the large, white, towering hoodoos.

3 SECOND COVE OF WHITE HOODOOS - To get to the next cove of hoodoos, also referred to as "Hoodoo Central" at 4 miles, stay close to the edge of the white rock and avoid as much of the dense tamarisk as possible. This path winds around into a deep grotto with more hoodoos. There is a beaten path close to the white columns, but staying at a distance is beneficial to the fragile rock and the surrounding cryptobiotic soil. The spectacular, pale hoodoos are formed by rapid erosion of soft Entrada sandstone and are easily damaged, so respect them by taking pictures from a distance and do not try to climb on or around them.

4 THIRD COVE OF WHITE HOODOOS - This cluster of pillars is known as the "Towers of Silence." A "famous photographed white hoodoo" is found at the 4.3-mile mark. Upon arrival at this bizarre and beautiful rock, one would almost sense that the formations have lives of their own, as they seem to be sprouting from the earth—these soft sandstone spires set the imagination free. This is the end of the coves. Relax in the shade, have lunch and prepare for the picturesque hike back down Wahweap Wash to exit.

OPTIONAL DESTINATION: TOADSTOOLS ROUTE - If time and energy permits, after hiking to the Wahweap Hoodoos, the short side-trip to the Toadstools will top off the day of hoodoo viewing. This wonderful and easily accessed cove contains darker versions of the white hoodoos, as well as magnificent pearly white columns. Nature's handiwork is mingled with whimsical peculiarities and nonsense in this arid land of sand and stone. To get there from Big Water, drive 12 miles west on US-89. Look for a small parking area and trailhead kiosk on the right (north) side of the road. There will be a register box and a hikers' gate to pass through.

After following the trail north for 0.6 miles, weaving alongside the wash and then dropping into the watercourse, you will see hoodoos up ahead. The trail branches either left to red-rock hoodoos, or up the righthand wash to the hoodoos formed in the white rock.

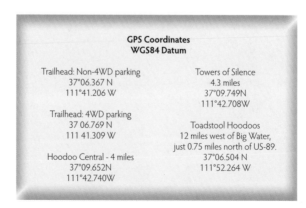

GPS Coordinates
WGS84 Datum

Trailhead: Non-4WD parking	Towers of Silence
37°06.367 N	4.3 miles
111°41.206 W	37°09.749N
	111°42.708W
Trailhead: 4WD parking	
37 06.769 N	Toadstool Hoodoos
111 41.309 W	12 miles west of Big Water,
	just 0.75 miles north of US-89.
Hoodoo Central - 4 miles	37°06.504 N
37°09.652N	111°52.264 W
111°42.740W	

Bo Beck at Water Canyon

CANAAN MOUNTAIN

The pristine, BLM-designated Canaan Mountain Wilderness is a unique masterpiece of visual imagery and mountain paths. Two trails that explore this area are described here, Canaan Mountain and Squirrel Canyon. On both routes, you will go through chasms with delightful waterfalls, travel over windswept stone, hike past volcanic rock and white hoodoos, step over moki marbles, meander through massive, slickrock bowls, catch glimpses into the depths of a narrow slot canyon and wander on ponderosa-dotted dunes. Stand in awe of the parade of magnificent white domes, hoodoos and the cornucopia of stepped rock. Stunning vistas unfold, one after another, entrancing and utterly absorbing—the best of the Southwest.

The unpaved and scenic Smithsonian Butte Back Country Byway stretches 9 miles, traveling south from Rockville, past Smithsonian Butte and terminating at Big Plain Junction on UT-59 just 8 miles northwest of Hildale, Utah. This drive has great views of Canaan Mountain, the Vermilion Cliffs and Zion National Park.

GETTING THERE

Both hikes described in this chapter start from Hildale. Hildale is located on UT-59 between Fredonia, Arizona and Hurricane, Utah. Hildale sits below the south end of Canaan Mountain and next to Colorado City, Arizona. The two towns appear as one, bisected by the state line.

From St. George: If traveling on I-15 from St. George, turn on SR-9 to Hurricane, Utah, then from Hurricane take UT-59. Travel approximately 22 miles east to Hildale.

From Zion's South Entrance: Travel to Rockville and turn on Bridge Road. Follow the Smithsonian Butte Back Country Byway for 9 miles to UT-59. Turn left on UT-59 and drive 8 miles to Hildale, UT.

From Zion's east side: If you are traveling from Zion National Park, leave the park through the east entrance, drive 12 miles to Mt. Carmel Junction (the intersection of SR-9 and US-89), then travel south on US-89 for 25 miles to Fredonia, Arizona. Turn west on AZ-389, travel approximately 25 miles, crossing the Utah-Arizona border, to Hildale, Utah (AZ-389 becomes UT-59 at the border towns of Colorado City, Arizona and Hildale, Utah). See map on facing page. Other relevant maps are on pages 17 and 73. Area map is on page 7.

Bo Beck, approaching Lower Mountain on the Water Canyon to Eagle Crags route, looking north toward Zion

to I-15 (2m)

Toquerville

Zion Lodge

Zion NP West Entrance

(9)

Virgin

(9)

Springdale

La Verkin

(9)

Hurricane

Rockville

to I-15
(10m)

(59)

Gooseberry

Smithsonian Butte Backway

Eagle Crags

(44)

Smithsonian Butte

(45)

Beehive
Mtn

(44)

(59)

(45)

UTAH
ARIZONA

Hildale

UTAH
ARIZONA

Colorado City

(389)

to
Pipe Spring NM,
Fredonia (25m)

0 miles   2   4   6   8

(9)

Rockville

Grafton Ghost Town

4WD

Smithsonian Butte Backway

Smithsonian Butte

(59)

SMITHSONIAN
SCENIC BACKWAY
(DETAIL)

0 miles   1   2   3   4

CANAAN MOUNTAIN
CHAPTER 8

44 Water Canyon to Eagle Crags (red)
45 Squirrel Cyn/Water Cyn Arch (blue)

Water Canyon –> Canaan Mtn –> Eagle Crags

This dramatic mountain path will take you to a historic site where lumber was once lowered, by windlass and steel cables, hundreds of feet down to the valley. The effort was long ago abandoned, but some of the hardware can still be seen. On the way, you will wander over a showcase of slickrock fields, and enjoy one of the most dazzling views of Zion National Park to be had anywhere.

The trail described here is a superb 2-day backpack that traverses some truly pristine wilderness. This trip is arduous, with 14 miles of hiking, 3,200 feet of ascent, and 4,000 feet of descent, but also very rewarding, exploring wondrous topography and beauty.

At a Glance

Day Hike: This is a 2-day backpack, but we include a shorter, day-hike option.

Distance:
Backpack: 14 miles, one way, with shuttle.
Day Hike to the Windlass: 12-mile round-trip.

Average Hiking Time: 9 hours to the windlass, or 2 full days for the backpack.

Equipment:
Day Hike: Clothing to protect from sun exposure, comfortable, sturdy hiking shoes or boots, high-energy food, emergency supplies and at least 4 quarts of water per person.

Overnight trip to Eagle Crags: In addition to the above, be sure to bring water purification or filtration means. Sawmill Spring may or may not have seepage. Be prepared with enough water for the remainder of the trip just in case the spring is dry. The USGS 7.5' Hildale, Utah, Smithsonian Butte, and Springdale West maps will be very useful, along with a compass.

Difficulty: This is a strenuous route. Good route-finding skills and a topo map are required if hiking beyond Water Canyon.

Sun Exposure: Full sun during most of the route.

Permits: Not required.

Trail Conditions: The start of the route is a dirt path littered with natural debris, but it is a well-worn path and easy to follow. The later part of the trail is mostly hiking on slickrock and sandy, long-abandoned, defunct roads.

Trailhead: You will drive through Hildale, Utah and the trailhead is just north of town.

Trailend:
Backpack Option: Eagle Crags near Rockville, Utah.
Day Hike Options: Water Canyon, same as the trailhead.

Trail Access: Limited by snowpack at least December through March.

Best Season: The trail to Water Canyon is a wonderful year-round hike. Winter hiking is rewarded with impressive water flow following a snowstorm. Keep in mind that the route to the windlass is usually impassable from December to March due to high snow levels, If the road to the trailhead is wet from snow, a 4WD will be required to get to the trailhead. In the summer direct sun on Canaan Mountain makes hiking uncomfortable, so the best times to hike are spring and fall.

Elevation: Trailhead: 5,200 feet, Highest Point: 7,200 feet, Trailend: 4,400 feet.

Off the Beaten Path: The route through Water Canyon is popular. Few venture past this, onto Canaan Mountain and beyond.

Water: Water Canyon generally has water flow or potholes with water that can be filtered or purified. However, after leaving this area and heading up to Canaan Mountain, water is scarce or non-existent except possibly in potholes. The camping area at Sawmill Springs usually has water but not always; the flow is intermittent.

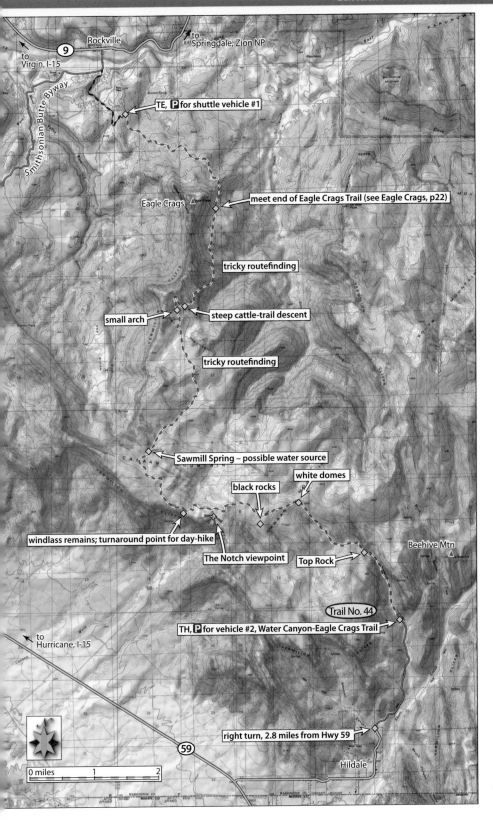

to
Virgin, I-15

Rockville

to
Springdale, Zion NP

TE, P for shuttle vehicle #1

meet end of Eagle Crags Trail (see Eagle Crags, p22)

Eagle Crags

tricky routefinding

small arch

steep cattle-trail descent

tricky routefinding

Sawmill Spring – possible water source

white domes

black rocks

windlass remains; turnaround point for day-hike

The Notch viewpoint

Top Rock

Beehive Mtn

Trail No. 44

TH, P for vehicle #2, Water Canyon-Eagle Crags Trail

to
Hurricane, I-15

right turn, 2.8 miles from Hwy 59

Hildale

0 miles   1   2

④ WATER CANYON –> CANAAN MTN –> EAGLE CRAGS DETAILS

1 PARKING - If you are doing the day-hike to the windlass and back you don't need to use a shuttle; simply park at the Water Canyon Trailhead in Hildale (see below). If you intend going from Hildale to Rockville, you will need to station two separate vehicles, one at Eagle Crags trailhead and the other at the Water Canyon Trailhead.

2 SHUTTLE SETUP, VEHICLE 1, EAGLE CRAGS TRAILHEAD - A high clearance 4WD vehicle is recommended, but even with one, the road may still be impassible when wet. Make your way to Rockville, just south of Springdale and the south entrance to Zion National Park. Once in Rockville, turn south on Bridge Road, set your odometer and drive south across the old bridge spanning the Virgin River. It is only a short distance before the paved road makes a hard right turn. Don't turn; go straight and follow a dirt road. Climb a steep grade before traversing up to the head of a large bowl. At 1.25 miles there is a three-way intersection. Continue through it, passing dwellings on both the right and left as you begin the short, rocky, uphill climb to yet another junction. Turn left and pass over the wash and drive up the hillside, bearing northeast. At 1.9 miles there is a small pullout on the right and a narrow ATV path doubling back to it. This is where you will leave your first vehicle. On the southeast edge of the parking area should be a BLM trailhead sign. It is often vandalized and missing, so don't count on it being there.

3 SMITHSONIAN BUTTE BACK COUNTRY BYWAY - Drive a second vehicle back down to the intersection of the paved road and dirt road just south of the bridge. Turn left (west) on the paved road, heading toward Grafton ghost town. This road will pass several residences, veer left and climb a hill, then drop back down. After about 1.3 miles, and before arriving at Grafton, there will be an intersection with a prominent dirt road on the left. This dirt road is the historic Smithsonian Butte Back Country Byway. Turn left (south) and follow this road as it winds around Smithsonian Butte. After about 8 miles you will join UT-59 at Big Plain Junction. Turn left on UT-59 headed toward Colorado City and Hildale. Drive for about 8 miles.

Old windlass relics atop Canaan Mountain

HILDALE - Hildale, Utah is located on UT-59 between Hurricane, Utah and Fredonia, Arizona. At Hildale, turn left (east) off UT-59 onto Utah Avenue. Follow the paved Utah Avenue east past a stop sign and continue on the road as it bends north. At 2.8 miles there are two dirt road intersections on the right. Take the second right onto Water Canyon Road. If you see Hildale's city park then you have missed the road to Water Canyon—backtrack a half-mile. A little more than a half-mile up Water Canyon Road is an intersection, stay left. About 2 miles up the road there is a small reservoir; the Water Canyon Trailhead is located at the north end of the reservoir at the large parking area.

WATER CANYON TRAIL - The trail begins by skirting the west side of Water Canyon and gradually ascends through junipers on a well-traveled sandy path. After a mile or so the walls begin to enclose. Search the skyline to the right to get a peek at Water Canyon Arch which sits 1,000 feet above the canyon floor (photo on page 167). Farther north, canyon walls narrow and travel is in the waterway and up a stepped waterfall. The trail scales up and to the left above the waterway and contours above the ever-restricting slot canyon. The sculpted slot below has become a popular destination for instructors leading guided canyoneering trips. Soon the trail begins a steeper ascent as it leaves the canyon bottom and leads farther north before ascending to the rim above Water Canyon. After several switchbacks, the steep trail leads to "Top Rock." This is the end of the Water Canyon Trail. To the east and north there is a showcase of slickrock fields and a watershed that carved the narrow passage through the soft sandstone below.

Canaan Mountain - The path now becomes a route rather than a trail. A map and route-finding skills are required to hike past Top Rock. Descend northwest through the forest and drop into the wash below. Once in the drainage, the beaten-path evaporates. Make your way by going upstream for about 0.25 miles. Another drainage enters from the north (right). Turn right into this wash and you should find easy travel. After about 0.5 miles in this wash, begin ascending the slabby and generally easy slickrock on the right. Hike in a general northerly direction toward the white domes and hoodoos at the top of Canaan Mountain.

Dean Kurtz on Canaan Mountain

From this area be sure to soak in the views of Zion National Park, Bryce Canyon, Cedar Breaks and the White Cliffs that rim the Grand Staircase-Escalante National Monument.

On top, behind the white domes, there is an old dirt road. The next part of the route follows this road west as it heads through the ponderosa dunes and periodically skirts the slickrock rim. Views unfold both north toward Zion and south to the Canaan Mountain ridges and valleys.

Notch - Travel west about 2 miles, past the white domes, toward a prominent notch at the rim's edge where there are wonderful views of Canaan Ranch and the valley to the south.

The Notch

Historic Windlass - Just beyond the notch, to the west, are remnants of the cable system that was used to lower timber to the valley below via an elaborate guiding cable. Now is the time to break for lunch, shake the sand from your shoes and socks, and prepare for the trek back to Water Canyon and your awaiting vehicle. Unless, of course, you are planning to continue this route as a two-day hike all the way to Rockville—if so, see the **Backpacking Option Details** below.

Backpacking Option Details

Sawmill Springs - From the windlass, follow the dirt road northwest for 1.4 miles to where you will find, nestled in a pine and aspen grove, Sawmill Springs. This is roughly halfway through the 14-mile backpack trip. This area provides ample space in the thick-forested area for camping and may be the only source of water available during the hike since leaving Water Canyon. (Even though the water seeps down Sawmill Springs Wash to the north, this cannot be counted on as a reliable water source). Be sure to leave your camp clean. Fires are not allowed in the Canaan Mountain Wilderness.

White hoodoos on Canaan Mountain

Lower Mountain - Follow Sawmill Springs Wash northeast and downhill toward Lower Mountain. There will be several slickrock bowls to navigate and dryfalls to skirt but nothing very difficult. The bowls that lead to the lower plateau afford views that are absolutely stunning. This area is untouched by ATVs and absolutely pristine. Follow the wash for 1.3 miles (do not go to its end) then begin to ascend, northwest, out of the wash and pass to the south of the rock outcropping of Lower Mountain. Once on top of the plateau continue northwest and soon the trail descends into a large basin/drainage. Look due north, across the drainage, to another rock outcropping of Lower Mountain and notice that on the farthest right side is a red dome.

Red Dome—descend gully just right of this

9 RED DOME - This dome is a useful landmark to help locate the Stock Trail, which descends from atop the plateau. Continue traveling out of the basin toward the Red Dome and as you approach the right base of the dome locate the cairn, a pile of rocks, that marks the beginning of the Stock Trail.

10 STOCK TRAIL - First of all understand that no modern-day cow is going up or down this trail. It was made, long ago, to move cattle from Springdale to the mountain. How they did this seems impossible when looking at what's left of the trail. It's rugged and steep. The trail begins with a descent through the cliffband, in a slot. Look for the needle-shaped hoodoo, several hundred feet below and in front, as the descent begins. This 200-foot-tall hoodoo lets you know that you are on course. The trail will skirt along ledges in the cliffband as it descends and then eventually begins tight switchbacks down the ridge. Keep eyes peeled for cairns, as

Stock Trail. The white hoodoo is center-right

the trail is old and not well beaten. After multiple switch-backs the trail dissolves and it will be necessary to begin traveling in a northerly direction. There are probably more cairns that mark the route as it makes its way to the Eagle Crags. For the next 1.3 miles there isn't a formal trail but cairns should mark the path as 10–12 drainages are passed through, bypassed or contoured. The going is somewhat tedious and difficult, but the light at the end of this short tunnel is knowing that the 2.5-mile-long Eagle Crags Trail is not far away.

Canaan Mtn exit views

11 EAGLE CRAGS - Once at the base of the first large spire within Eagle Crags, named Aunt Jemima, contour around to the right side. A trail now becomes apparent and easy to follow to your waiting vehicle. After 14 miles of hiking, 3,200 feet of climbing, and 4,000 feet of descending you should have had a good couple of days of exercise.

GPS Coordinates, WGS84 Datum

Parking in Water Canyon 37°02.240 N, 112°57.264 W	Historic Windlass 37°03.655 N, 113°00.882 W
Top Rock 37°03.126 N, 112°57.896 W	Sawmill Spring 37°04.438 N, 113°01.514 W
Turn right at wash intersection toward white domes. 37 03.212 N, 112 58.284 W	Exit Sawmill Spring Wash to the north 37°05.260 N, 113°00.577 W
White Domes 37°03.784 N, 112°58.993 W	Stock Trail Exit Down 37°06.677 N, 113°00.753 W
Black Rock Formations (Manganese-Oxide/Sandstone) 37°03.525 N, 112°59.664 W	Join Eagle Crags Footpath 37°07.642 N, 113°00.385 W
Notch 37°03.621 N, 113°00.406 W	Parking for Eagle Crags Trailhead 37°08.860 N, 113°01.877 W

SQUIRREL CANYON TO WATER CANYON ARCH 45

You will enjoy non-stop beauty along this trek. Expect cottonwood-speckled desert floors, ponderosa pine-forests, manzanita-carpeted sand dunes, a narrow slot canyon, and to cap it all, a walk across a magnificent arch suspended 1,000 feet above the canyon floor. Throw into the mix some interesting route-finding and an eclectic display of hoodoos dotting the sandstone fields of Canaan Mountain—hoodos that just beg to be explored—and you have an outstanding adventure.

AT A GLANCE

Distance: 11 miles, plus any extra added by exploring.

Average Hiking Time: 12 hours.

Equipment: Clothing to protect from sun exposure, comfortable, sturdy hiking shoes, high-energy food and emergency gear and supplies. Unless water has accumulated in potholes from a recent rain, there is no water available along this route after leaving Short Creek. Take at least 4 liters or more per person.

Difficulty: This is a strenuous 11-mile hike which climbs 1,800 feet and descends an equal amount.

Sun Exposure: Full sun during most of the route.

Permits: Permits are not required.

Trail Conditions: Uneven rocky terrain, slickrock scrambling, deep sand.

Trailhead: Hildale - Short Creek - Squirrel Canyon Trailhead.

Trailend: Hildale - Water Canyon Trailhead.

Trail Access: Access to the dirt road leading to the trailhead is easiest in the summer, spring and early fall and using a high-clearance vehicle. If this road is wet it may be impassible,

because the clay content in the dirt makes this road extremely slick and hazardous when wet. In winter, if there is melting snow on the road it should not be traveled, but you can park in town and walk to where the hike begins. Most likely, once on top of Canaan Mountain, you will find too much snow to proceed.

Best Season: The optimal time to do this loop hike is in the spring, after the snow has melted; or in the fall before snow has fallen. Hot summer months can be unpleasant unless you get an early start. Snow and ice in the winter months may make hiking hazardous.

Elevation: Trailhead: 5,100 feet, Highest Elevation: 6,900 feet, Trailend: 5,240 feet.

Off the Beaten Path: Yes. Few other hikers will be seen on most of the trail, though there may be some near the end of the hike, in Water Canyon. This is a popular destination for families taking the short hike to the Water Canyon waterfalls and for canyoneers navigating the slot-canyon section of Water Canyon.

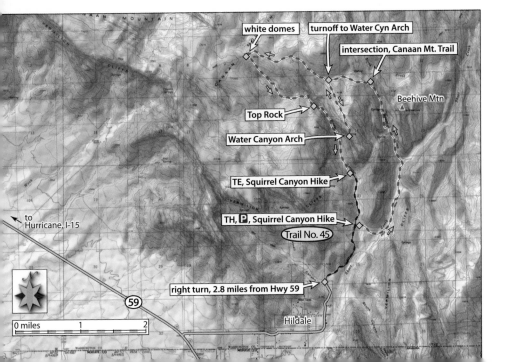

④ SQUIRREL CANYON TO WATER CANYON ARCH DETAILS

1 **HILDALE** - At Hildale, turn north onto Utah Drive. Set your odometer. After 1.8 miles Utah Drive comes to a stop sign. Continue straight. The road now steers north, meandering past homes and barns. At 2.8 miles there are two dirt-road intersections on the right. Take the second right, named Water Canyon Road. At about 0.5 miles you will pass the intersection of Water Canyon Road and a 4WD road into Short Creek. Continue left (north), and stay on the main road another 0.5 miles until you arrive at a clearing on the right.

2 **SQUIRREL CANYON TRAILHEAD** - At the clearing turn right on the faint road toward the wash below and drive 50 yards where you will find ample parking at the fence. This is where this hike will begin.

3 **WATER CANYON TRAILEND** - If driving two cars, drive both 1 mile past the Squirrel Canyon Trailhead to where the road ends at a reservoir and parking area for Water Canyon. Leave one vehicle here, then drive your second car back to the Squirrel Canyon Trailhead, park, and begin the hike.

4 **SQUIRREL CANYON** - Look east from the parking area across the wash and locate the trail leading up Short Creek and Squirrel Creek. Drop into Water Canyon wash just below and east of the parking area and follow the track up and out of the drainage onto the ridge on the opposite side. Follow this path back into Short Creek and continue northeast along the creek for 1.4 miles to an intersection of ATV roads. Beehive Mountain, towering above, will be almost due north. At this intersection, cross the creek to the left and walk north up Squirrel Creek. Initially the trail climbs onto a ridge to the west of Squirrel Creek, but it eventually drops into and crosses over the creek below. The trail is well-used and should be easy to follow. At 2.5 miles the path is now on the east side of the creek. Begin a steep ascent up rocky ledge systems gaining the top of a ridge that separates two drainages near the head of Squirrel Creek. Travel north, following a steep ridge. From this ridgetop, there are great views of Beehive Mountain to the east and the spectacular scenery to the south. About 3.75 miles into the hike, at the top of the ridge, you will meet the Canaan Mountain Trail. Turn left (west) onto this trail, traveling toward a large slickrock ridge towering above and to the north of the trail. The path drops into a slickrock wash at the base of this large slickrock ridge and then continues west.

5 **WATER CANYON ARCH** - After traveling west for about a mile from the intersection of the Squirrel Creek Trail and the Canaan Mountain Trail, look left and there should be a beaten path, or paths, leading south along the ridge. Follow this. As you continue southeast along the ridge, stay as high as possible while still keeping Water Canyon below and in view. At times it will be necessary to stray from the rim above the canyon, but return to the edge whenever possible. In the next mile you will pass a large sandy bowl on your right with several rock outcrops at the bottom which will hide the view of Water Canyon. Walk around the right side of a small rock outcrop just south of the bowl and drop down a sandy hill where you arrive at Water Canyon Arch. From the arch, look north-northeast and locate the large white domes. The domes are landmarks to be used to identify the exit from the Canaan Mountain Trail and the route that leads to Water Canyon.

One of the incredible white domes along this route

Bo Beck standing atop Water Canyon Arch

6 **WHITE DOMES AND ZION VIEWPOINT -** Enjoy lunch at the arch, dump the sand out of your shoes, rehydrate and prepare for the second leg of the trip. Follow your footsteps northward to the Canaan Mountain Trail. Turn left (west) on the Canaan Mountain Trail. The path is a wide slickrock wash for the next quarter-mile, then it bears left and out of the wash. Travel upward along a rocky ridge 0.25 miles before winding up the sandy Canaan Mountain Trail. Follow the Canaan Mountain Trail west, for another 0.65 miles, until arriving at the White Domes. These domes, with Zion National Park in the background, are quite photogenic.

7 **EXIT CANAAN MOUNTAIN -** At the White Domes the hike leaves the Canaan Mountain Trail and travel is now downhill for most of the remainder of the trip. Descend the massive slickrock field to the southeast. Do not try to walk through the slot canyon on the right; instead stay left and bear toward the small, multicolored domes to the left of the slot. Travel down the slickrock is somewhat steep in sections but it is not difficult. After 0.5 miles you will arrive at the bottom of the wash. Walk down the pleasant, sandy drainage for 0.5 miles to the intersection with another wash entering from the right. Turn left, following the wash downstream. A quarter-mile downstream from the intersection of the two washes, look for a path of travel to the right and up the ridge above. If a path cannot be located, start climbing southeast up the ridge and traverse, looking for a beaten path. Once located, this route will eventually arrive at Top Rock.

8 **WATER CANYON -** From Top Rock there are great views back to the White Domes and into Water Canyon below. The Water Canyon Trail becomes more visible as it drops down from Top Rock, to the east, and begins its steep descent into Water Canyon. The Water Canyon Trailhead is now 1.5 miles away. The well-used trail will follow ledges and wind its way down, eventually arriving at the bottom of the slot canyon. Soon the path leaves the confinement of the slot and follows the hillside above the creek. Be sure to look high up on the left to see how Water Canyon Arch, that you just visited, looks from below. Before you know it, the parking area at the Water Canyon Trailhead comes into view. If a shuttle was stationed here you are done hiking. If not, then it's an easy 1-mile walk back down the road to your waiting vehicle at the Short Creek-Squirrel Creek Trailhead.

GPS Coordinates
WGS84 Datum

Trailhead, Parking for Short Creek and Squirrel Canyon
37°01.530 N, 112°57.172 W

Parking Lot at Trailend at Water Canyon
37°02.235 N, 112°57.266 W (10 miles) End: 11 miles

Intersection of Squirrel Creek Trail with Short Creek Trail
37°02.388 N, 112°56.455 W at 1.5 miles.

Intersection of Canaan Mtn. Trail and Squirrel Creek Trail
37°03.441 N, 112°56.969 W at 3 miles.

Intersection, Trail to Water Canyon Arch
and Canaan Mountain Trail
37°03.482 N, 112°57.745 W at 3.75 miles.

Water Canyon Arch
37°02.739 N, 112°57.311 W at 4.75 miles.

White Hoodoos and Descent down Slickrock
toward top of Water Canyon
37°03.773 N, 112°58.953 W at 7.2 miles.

Top Rock and Trailhead to descend Water Canyon
37°03.126 N, 112 57.896 W at 8.5 miles

The Squirrel Canyon route traverses Canaan Mountain, a vast plateau of slickrock

Bo Beck in spectacular Buckskin Gulch

PARIA CANYON-VERMILION CLIFFS WILDERNESS AREA

To the east of Kanab, Utah, sprawls a huge expanse of colorful, desolate, alluring desert. Over 112,000 acres of this seldom-visited land was recognized as a special place and made into a federally-protected wilderness—the Paria Canyon-Vermilion Cliffs Wilderness Area. The beautiful Paria Canyon Wilderness is in Utah and the Vermilion Cliffs National Monument is in Arizona.

Paria Canyon contains the spectacular Coyote Buttes Special Management Area, visited by hikes described in this chapter. We will take you to remote places such as The Wave, Cobra Arch, White Pocket, Cottonwood Teepees, Paw Hole, and into one of the world's longest slot canyons, Buckskin Gulch.

GETTING THERE

The Paria Canyon-Vermilion Cliffs Wildernesss Area straddles the Utah-Arizona boundary. Access to this remote land is via a pair of east-west highways, US-89 to the north and and US-89A to the south, in Arizona.

The routes in this chapter are accessed either from US-89 or from House Rock Valley Road, a north-south road that connects the two highways. The north end of House Rock Valley Road intersects US-89 about 40 miles east of Kanab and 35 miles west of Page. The south end of House Rock Valley Road meets US-89A about 10 miles east of Jacob Lake. See maps: facing page, and also pages 7, 111 and 147.

The Wave, North Coyote Buttes

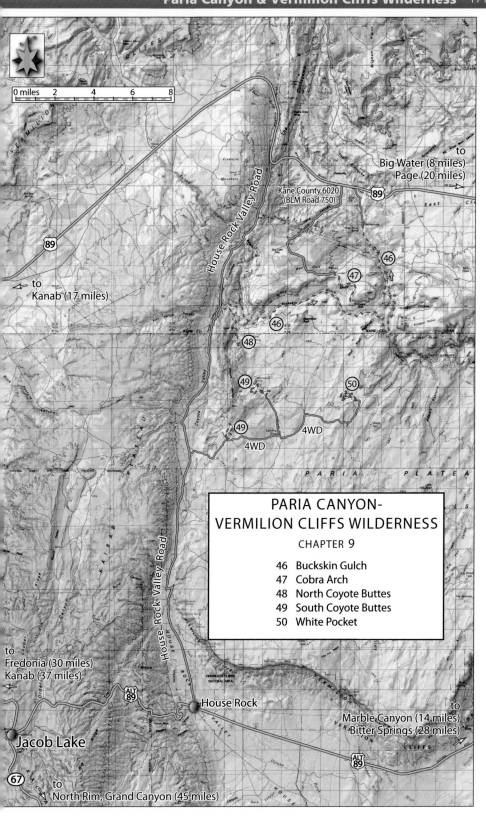

0 miles   2   4   6   8

to
Big Water (8 miles)
Page (20 miles)

Kane County 6020
(BLM Road 750)

89

89

46

47

← to
Kanab (17 miles)

46

48

49

50

49

4WD

4WD

P A R I A   P L A T E A

to
Fredonia (30 miles)
Kanab (37 miles)

ALT
89

House Rock

to
Marble Canyon (14 miles)
Bitter Springs (28 miles)

Jacob Lake

ALT
89

67

to
North Rim, Grand Canyon (45 miles)

PARIA CANYON-
VERMILION CLIFFS WILDERNESS
CHAPTER 9

46 Buckskin Gulch
47 Cobra Arch
48 North Coyote Buttes
49 South Coyote Buttes
50 White Pocket

BUCKSKIN GULCH

Buckskin Gulch is an exceptionally spectacular slot canyon. Touted as one of the longest in the world, Buckskin Gulch is 13 miles from start to finish. The extreme, narrow passage twists like a long snake. This deep slot opens up here and there, letting sunlight bake the canyon floor—then constricts and darkens again. The light, the rock texture, and colors shift and change with twists and turns in this magical place.

Buckskin is, in short, a great introduction to the relatively new and adrenaline-pumping pursuit of canyoneering. Aspiring canyoneers can head out for an overnight backpack, hike the complete route in a day, or just partake in a peek-and-retreat from the Wire Pass Trailhead to the confluence of Buckskin Gulch.

AT A GLANCE

Day Hike: Yes, but this slot canyon is usually done as a backpack.

Distance: The complete route is 21 miles. There is 13 miles of slot canyon and the rest is the exit through Paria Canyon.

Optional Day Hike: Wire Pass Trailhead to the confluence of Buckskin and return is 3.5 miles

Average Hiking Time: The Wire Pass Trailhead to the Whitehouse Campground Trailhead will take about 14 hours. Hiking from the Wire Pass Trailhead to the confluence of Buckskin Gulch and back should take you about 3 hours.

Mysterious, entrancing Buckskin Gulch

Difficulty: Strenuous. When the authors last hiked this canyon there was one obstacle that required 40 feet of rope to negotiate. Depending on the time of year and how wet the season has been, wading and swimming in very cold water might be necessary.

Equipment: Canyoneering shoes, sun-protective clothing, extra socks, emergency supplies including bivy gear, dry bags, plenty of water, water-purification or filtration method, 50 feet of rope, and a harness and rappel device.

Sun Exposure: You will get some sun at the start and end of the route, but while in the slot there is a lot of shade provided by the canyon walls.

Permits: A permit is required. Day-hiking permits can be obtained at the trailhead. For more information about overnight permits contact the Arizona Strip Field Office at 435.688.3200 or the Kanab Field Office at 435.688.3200.

Trail Conditions: This slot canyon has flash-flood potential. The canyon floor is often very sandy, making walking difficult. There is a possibility of wading or swimming in frigid water and at least one boulder obstacle will necessitate the use of a rope as a handline or rappel.

Trailhead: Wire Pass Trailhead.

Trailend: Whitehouse Trailhead—this requires that you set up a shuttle. Or just hike as far as you wish from Wire Pass Trailhead and turn around and end back where you began.

Trail Access: Year-round but, if the road is wet or there is melting snow, it can be dangerous or even impassable. A high-clearance vehicle or 4WD is suggested.

Best Season: Early to late spring is nice, but due to the shade this is also a good summer "trail."

Off the Beaten Path: This is a famous hike, yet still it is off the beaten path.

arch/bridge

confluence Buckskin/Paria River

good camping

boulder problem

Cobra Arch Hike (page xxx)

petroglyphs

to Hwy 89

TE, P for shuttle vehicle #1, (at the Whitehouse Trailhead, 2.25m south of Hwy 89)

Middle Exit, Buckskin

WEST CLARK BENCH

Steamboat Rock

0 miles   1   2

confluence Wire Pass/Buckskin Gulch

to Hwy 89

House Rock Valley Road

Wire Pass (8.3 miles south of Hwy 89)

N. Coyote Bluffs Hike (pxxx)

TH, P for Buckskin Gulch

Trail No. 46

to House Rock, AZ Hwy 89A

㊻ BUCKSKIN WASH DETAILS

VEHICLE SHUTTLE SETUP - From Kanab, drive 44 miles east on US-89. A little less than a half-mile after crossing the Paria River, turn right, heading toward the BLM Paria River Contact Station. Follow this dirt road 2.25 miles to the Whitehouse Campground and parking area. Leave a vehicle and return to US-89. Drive 4.5 miles back toward Kanab, and at a sweeping, righthand curve, protected by a guardrail, on the south side of the highway, look for the House Rock Valley Road turnoff, which is after the long curve. Turn left onto the dirt road and drive 8.5 miles to the Wire Pass Trailhead.

WIRE PASS - Walk east, across the road, and follow the "trail" to the register. The beaten path continues east, following the wash. Head east, ignoring the sign directing hikers toward the "Wave." At 1.3 miles, sandstone walls enclose dramatically, then open up again as travel continues toward the confluence with Buckskin. Soon the canyon constricts enough that hikers can barely slip through before the confining stone opens once again, exposing the sky above. At the confluence with Buckskin Gulch (1.75 miles) look for the Wire Pass petroglyphs at the base of the large alcove on the right.

BUCKSKIN GULCH - When you enter Buckskin, dramatic lighting haunts the slender crevice of this wind- and water-carved slot canyon, allowing spectacular photography during the next 12 miles. Almost 8 miles from the start of the hike (and a bit over 6 miles into Buckskin Gulch), there is an escape on the left side (north) known as the Middle Exit Trail. Walk up the steep, sandy ramp a short distance to see two sheep petroglyphs etched on a small panel. Return to the canyon floor where, 50 feet downcanyon, there are more weathered petroglyphs on the left wall. To see yet another, walk 100 feet downstream from the Middle Exit, look upstream and 100 feet vertically above the faded petroglyphs. There is a single human figure deeply etched into the darker stone. Around the corner, to the left, are several more drawings.

This is a good place to turn around and return to the Wire Pass Trailhead if you do not plan on hiking through to the Whitehouse Trailhead. Beyond this point there is a major obstacle that usually requires a rope to navigate. Depending on the condition of the canyon, you may be required to wade or swim.

THE THROUGH HIKE - If you are doing the through-hike, continue downcanyon where, roughly 4 miles from the Middle Exit, a large group of boulders make a formidable obstacle. To the left side is a 20-foot vertical drop, and "moki steps" carved into the rock. In the middle of the boulder pile is a 15-foot downclimb, where a rope can be threaded as a hand-line or rappel-line. Remember: floods have formed this canyon and the nature of the path can change quickly and dramatically. Be prepared for circumstances not described. About a mile past the obstacle, water usually seeps from the canyon floor and you can refill water bottles. However, don't count on the water always being there. Just before reaching the river you will see campsites above the floodplain, on both the left and right sides of the somewhat open wash. If you are spending the night, this is where you will make camp.

Bo Beck getting wet in Buckskin Gulch

EXIT - The Paria River enters from the left. Once there, turn upstream (left) at which point it is 7 miles to the Whitehouse Trailhead and your waiting vehicle. Tall sandstone cliffs line the path and a towering arch is dead ahead. The farther north you travel, the wider the canyon becomes until the walls finally disappear. Soft sand in the wash at the end of the route can really punish tired legs, especially if doing this as a one-day hike. Only those in excellent condition should attempt to do this in one day.

Flash flooding is a very real danger in this canyon. Contact the BLM for weather conditions before attempting this route.

STATELINE CAMPGROUND

This is on the House Rock Valley Road, 10 miles south of US-89. There are only 4 spots, so if you want to camp, get a spot early. It's first come first use. Two of the campsites are in Utah and two are in Arizona. There are vault toilets.

COYOTE BUTTES SPECIAL PERMIT OFFICES

Arizona Strip Field Office: 345 East Riverside Drive St. George, Utah 84790, Ph: 435.688.3200

GSENM Visitor Center: 745 E. & US 89, Kanab, Utah, 84741. Ph: 435-688-3200.

Paria Contact Station: Located south of US-89 between mile post 21 and 22.

GPS Coordinates
WGS84 Datum

Wire Pass Trailhead:
37°01.162 N
112°01.465 W

Wire Pass/ Buckskin Gulch Confluence:
37°00.193 N
112°00.167 W

Middle Trail Buckskin Exit:
37°01.872 N
111°55.302 W

Buckskin Gulch/ Paria River Confluence:
37°00.090 N
111°51.949 W

Arch In Paria River:
37°00.653 N
111 51.969 W

Whitehouse Trailhead:
37°04.731 N
111°53.423 W

Bo Beck in the depths of Buckskin Gulch

COBRA ARCH ㊼

Stunning Cobra Arch is nestled in a quiet corner of the Paria Canyon Wilderness, just north of Buckskin Gulch. The uniquely shaped structure rises up 30 feet from the ground and spans 35 feet. From the hood at the crest of the rock formation to the serpent-like striations down the length of the arch, this formation looks like a hooded cobra—a well-named arch.

En route to the destination, the path passes a marvelous display of crossbedded sandstone slickrock slabs, peculiar beehive-shaped domes, as well as a smattering of precariously stacked rocks. From the arch, the views to the south, east and west encompass the splendor of the Paria Canyon-Vermilion Cliffs Wilderness, including North and South Coyote Buttes special permit areas, Steamboat Rock and White Pocket.

AT A GLANCE

Day Hike: Yes.
Distance: 6.7-mile round-trip.
Average Hiking Time: 5 hours.
Equipment: Sticky-rubber hiking shoes, 3 quarts of water per person, sun-protective clothing, map, compass, energy food and emergency gear.
Difficulty: Moderately strenuous hiking, some route-finding skills are required.
Sun Exposure: Full sun during most of the hike.
Permits: Not required.

Trail Conditions: The trail is well-worn and easy to follow along the rim; beyond the rim there is some 3rd-class slickrock scrambling and some deep-sand travel.
Trailhead: A dirt road located 8 miles south of US-89 between Page, AZ and Kanab, UT.
Trailend: Same as the trailhead.
Trail Access: Year-round, but if the road is wet or there is melting snow it could be impassable. A 4WD is suggested, a high-clearance vehicle is required.

Best Season: It's best to hike this route in the winter or early spring when it is not as hot, but this is a year-round trail as long as the road is drivable. When it's hot out, hike early in the morning.
Total Descent–Ascent: 350 feet.
Off the Beaten Path: Yes.

Colorful Cobra Arch

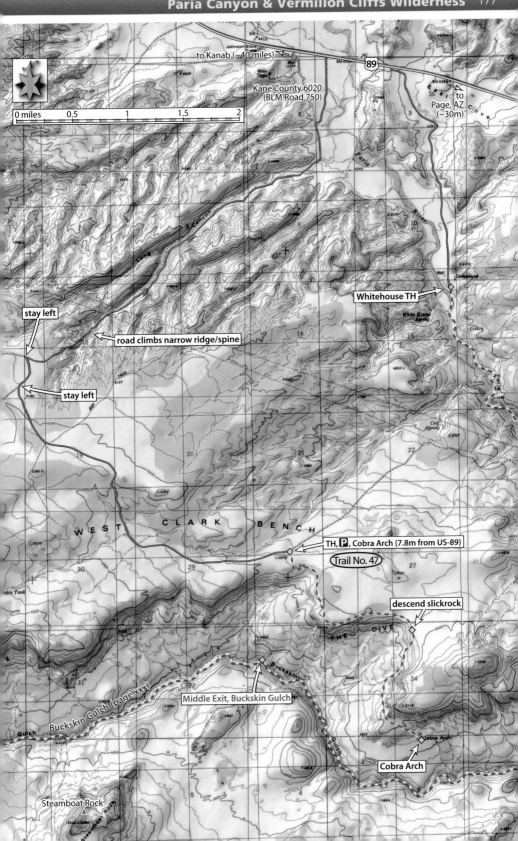

to Kanab (~40 miles)

89

to Page, AZ (~30m)

Kane County 6020 (BLM Road 750)

0 miles   0.5   1   1.5   2

Whitehouse TH

stay left

road climbs narrow ridge/spine

stay left

WEST CLARK BENCH

TH, P, Cobra Arch (7.8m from US-89)

Trail No. 47

descend slickrock

THE DIVE

Middle Exit, Buckskin Gulch

Buckskin Gulch (page xxx)

Gulch

Cobra Arch

Cobra Arch

Steamboat Rock

47 COBRA ARCH DETAILS

TRAILHEAD - Travel east on US-89 from Kanab toward Page. The road dips south just before the Cockscomb formation and then sweeps east at the turnoff for House Rock Valley Road. Set your odometer at this point and continue east on US-89 for 4.3 miles, where, just prior to crossing the Paria River, you will see a road on the right side of the highway. Turn right onto this dirt road and reset your odometer.

The road is Kane County Road 6020 (BLM Road 750). It's unmarked at first, but soon you will see a sign identifying it. There are many roads taking off from the main one, but ignore them, stay on the more heavily-traveled dirt road. The main road runs up Long Canyon, to the southwest, for a couple of miles and then breaks out of Long Canyon and continues south through another canyon. Soon it climbs a "spine" in the middle of the ravine, with long drop-offs on either side, then tops out on a plateau and arrives at another junction 4.2 miles from US-89. Stay left, keeping on the main road; keep left at the next fork, which is reached at 4.4 miles. A third fork is at 4.6 miles; once again, continue left on the same road. At 5.1 miles, there is an intersection; continue straight. The path becomes sandy with small ups and downs. It passes one deep wash at 6.4 miles that may require a 4WD to navigate. At 7.8 miles the road passes a barbed wire fence and just past this is a large juniper tree and a pullout where there is a register box. This is the trailhead.

TRAIL - Load up your pack, sign in and get ready to hike. The preferred route is along the top of the sandstone rim known as "the Dive." The trail leading eastward is not immediately apparent, but after hiking several hundred yards along the rim, a beaten path will be evident. Set your sights for the large sandstone buttresses that appear far in the distance. Cobra Arch sits just below the tip of the largest buttress, far to the east. Hiking along the trail is mostly gentle as it contours the rim, paralleling the basins below. The rim offers virtually no opportunity to descend for the first 2 miles, but once arriving at the back end of a large bowl, the cliffband exposes a weakness that allows descent into the desert valley below.

Bo Beck on Cobra Arch

BELOW THE RIM - Once below the cliffband, travel south, staying close to the now-elevating sandstone walls on hikers' left. Interesting balanced rock structures are passed, several washes are crossed and after a mile it will be necessary to ascend a tall sand dune. At the top of the dune is a level plateau and a 150-foot-high sandstone mountain. Walk around the mountain and begin travel southeast across the plateau until it descends to a group of small dome-shaped sandstone mounds. This diverse area of sunbathed, misshapen sandstone is highly photogenic. Cobra Arch is on the backside of this group of mounds. The arch is spectacular and the surrounding area offers shade where you can enjoy lunch and a break before the trek back.

GPS Coordinates
WGS84 Datum

Trailhead
37°02.663 N, 111 55.222 W

Scramble Down from Rim
37°01.916 N, 111 53.745 W

Cobra Arch
37°01.233 N, 111°53.754 W

Hiking along the Dive with Buckskin Gulch and Coyote Buttes in the Background

NORTH COYOTE BUTTES – THE WAVE ㊽

The Coyote Buttes area is hauntingly beautiful. The hike described here explores North Coyote Buttes and features a visit to the striped splendor at its heart: The Wave. The Wave is a gallery of gruesomely twisted sandstone, with formations resembling deformed pillars, cones, mushrooms and other odd creations. Deposits of iron claim some of the responsibility for the unique blending of color twisted into the rock, creating the dramatic rainbow of pastel yellows, pinks and reds.

This area sits deep within Paria Canyon at the bottom of Utah's Grand Staircase-Escalante National Monument. Though famed as a photogenic wonderland, the rocks and plants that create this beauty are fragile, so the BLM has designated this land the Coyote Buttes Special Management Area. This designation carries with it particular regulations, including a day-use-only rule and a visitor-permit system to manage visitation to the most popular destinations, including the Wave.

Bo Beck hikes the Wave, North Coyote Buttes, in a snowstorm

AT A GLANCE

Day Hike: No overnight camping is allowed inside the permit area.

Trail Distance: 5.5 miles to the Wave and back. 8-mile roundtrip from the Wire Pass parking lot to the Wave, Top Rock Arch, alcove, Melody Arch, dinosaur tracks and back.

Average Hiking Time: 6 hours for the round-trip to the Wave. Allow 8 hours for the Wave, arches, alcove and dinosaur tracks.

Equipment: Sticky-rubber hiking shoes. A least a gallon of water per person, especially in the hot summer months, and GPS. The BLM supplies a good map to the Wave with each permit. Optional Map: USGS 7.5´ Topographical Quads - Arizona-Pine Hollow Canyon and Arizona-Coyote Buttes.

Difficulty: Moderate to the Wave and the dinosaur tracks. Third-class scrambling to the arches and alcove. Good navigation skills are required.

Sun Exposure: Full sun. Dark red rock and sand reflect the sun, amplifying the heat.

Permits Required: For current information, see: www.blm.gov/az/paria

Kanab GSENM Visitor Center: Located at 745 E. & US-89, Kanab, Utah, 84741. Ph: 435.688.3200.

Paria BLM: Located on US-89, 4 miles east of the House Rock Valley Road turnoff.

Trail Conditions: The start of the trail is uphill and sandy, but most of the hike is over rock.

Trailhead: Wire Pass, which is located 35 miles west of Page, Arizona and 40 miles east of Kanab, Utah.

Trailend: Same as trailhead.

Best Season: Spring and fall. It's hot in summer. When the weather cooperates, this is a good winter hike.

Elevation Gain to The Wave: 325 feet.

Starting Elevation: 4,875 feet.

Wave Elevation: 5,200 feet.

Off the Beaten Path: Yes, but is slowly becoming more well-known. The permit system keeps visitor numbers down. Dogs are allowed with a permit. Dog permits do not use up any of the 20 hiking permits.

Restrooms: Vault toilet at Wire Pass Trailhead.

North Coyote Buttes

48 NORTH COYOTE BUTTES – THE WAVE DETAILS

1 WIRE PASS TRAILHEAD - From Kanab, drive 40 miles east on US-89. The turn onto House Rock Valley Road is on the south (right) side of the road. It is located between mile markers 25 and 26, just before a sweeping lefthand curve in the road protected by a guardrail. House Rock Valley Road soon becomes dirt (impassible if wet). Continue 8.5 miles to the Wire Pass Trailhead parking lot, located on the right side of the road. Display your parking permit in your windshield.

2 WAVE ROUTE - Walk across the road, to the east, and locate the hiking path. Sign in at the register box and read pertinent information. Soon the path drops into a Wire Pass drainage. Walk down the wash (east) for 0.6 miles. Look for the signed path of use on the right, exiting Wire Pass Wash. Hiking becomes steep for the next few hundred yards, as an old 4WD road is followed to the top of the ridge and to the second register box. Once again, stop and sign in at the register. Shortly after leaving the register box, there may be an indication that the trail splits. Take the lefthand fork for easier traveling. It continues east and passes large rock domes on the flats below. After passing the domes, the trail soon drops into a wash. It will be necessary to cross it and approach the slickrock ridge to the east. Continue east, up the slickrock ridge. Once on top, work down the east side (backside) of the ridge, but bearing to the south (hikers' right), and staying as high as is comfortable on the steep slopes of the ridge.

3 VERTICAL CRACK OR NOTCH - Looking south, a large, slickrock mountain comes into view. There is a long, vertical crack in the mountain. This crack becomes the landmark to steer toward for the next mile. The Wave is located beneath the mountain with the crack. Remember to stay as high as comfort allows, hugging the sandstone slabs on hikers' right.

4 TWIN BUTTES - As you continue south, two large buttes come into view. These are called the Twin Buttes, and come almost halfway through the hike. They are best passed by walking up the slickrock bowl and going around the right side. A wash is encountered 0.5 miles after rounding the Twin Buttes.

Melody Arch, North Coyote Buttes

5 MULTICOLORED DOMES - Peer across the wash and notice the multi-colored domes on the opposite side of the wash. These, and the less-obvious sandstone formations to the right are the Wave. Walk down into the wash, locate the dead juniper tree and the sandy path that leads up to the Wave.

6 THE WAVE - The area called Top Rock is a collection of white Navajo sandstone formations. The south end of Top Rock divides North and South Coyote Buttes. The Wave is a chasm located on the northwest edge of Top Rock.

7 TOP ARCH - Few hikers venture beyond the Wave. This next section involves 3rd-class scrambling. Only those experienced in slickrock scrambling should attempt to go to the arch and beyond. Work steeply up the sandstone, heading toward the right. Locate the arch at the top of the mountain. Find the easiest path to travel up the steep slickrock toward it. The arch is approached from the backside of the mountain. From the arch, the red cones of South Coyote Butte are visible.

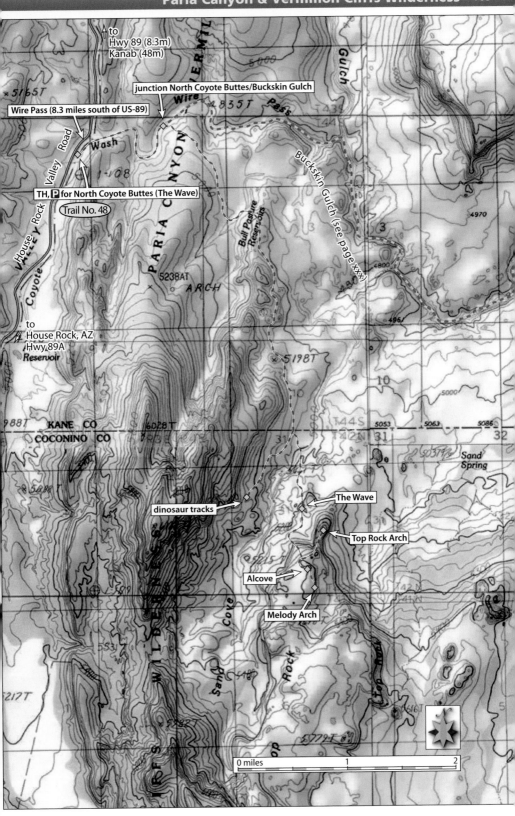

to
Hwy 89 (8.3m)
Kanab (48m)

junction North Coyote Buttes/Buckskin Gulch

Wire Pass (8.3 miles south of US-89)

TH, P for North Coyote Buttes (The Wave)

Trail No. 48

Wire Pass

Buckskin Gulch (see page xxx)

VERMIL

Gulch

PARIA CANYON

Bull Pasture Reservoirs

ARCH

to
House Rock, AZ
Hwy 89A
Reservoir

W House Rock Valley Road

Coyote Valley Road

Wash

KANE CO
COCONINO CO

dinosaur tracks

The Wave

Top Rock Arch

Alcove

Melody Arch

WILDERNESS

Sand Cove

Top Rock Cove

Sand Spring

0 miles   1   2

8 ALCOVE - This hidden treasure is rarely found by hikers. To locate the Alcove, return the way you approached the arch. This time stay to the left, hiking over crossbedded sandstone. In the Alcove, fine grains of sand have been tossed and turned, wielded by the wind, leaving a carefully sculpted creation assembled in its bowels.

9 MELODY ARCH/GROTTO/WINDOW - From the Alcove, scramble up and left of the alcove to attain the top. Once on top, travel southeast, following the maze of ridges and desert tanks, staying as high as possible. Steer toward the eastern edge of the caprock. Soon a chasm appears in front. Look down and into a grotto that contains a window and an arch: Melody Arch Grotto. Backtrack far enough to find an easy route down into a tank from where you can scramble out the backside and slide down into the grotto.

10 DINOSAUR TRACKS - From the Wave: The dinosaur tracks are on the northwest side of the large wash, across from the Wave. To locate them, cross back northward over the wash, retracing your earlier footsteps and travel up to the level ground on the north side of the wash. Hike to the west, staying against the steep slickrock mountain, as high as possible, to locate the tracks. They are found at the base of the steep slickrock slab to the north, and are in pinkish-colored rock, just before the slabs become seemingly impossible to ascend. The GPS coordinates given below are to one track; look around to locate more tracks, mostly within 100 yards of the first. There are nice views of the Wave from here. The footprints appear to be from small, bipedal dinosaurs, most likely Grallator (Megapnosaurus) and Anomoepus.

STATELINE CAMPGROUND - A convenient campground is on the House Rock Valley Road, 10 miles south of US-89. There are only 4 spots, so if you want to camp, get a spot early. It's first come first use. Two of the camp sites are in Utah and two are in Arizona. There is no water, but there are vault toilets.

COYOTE BUTTES SPECIAL PERMIT OFFICES - For information and permits for hiking in the Coyote Buttes and the Wave:

Arizona Strip Field Office: 345 East Riverside Drive St. George, Utah 84790. Ph: 435.688.3200
Kanab GSENM Visitor Center: 745 E. & US-89, Kanab, Utah 84741. Ph: 435.688.3200.
Paria Contact Station: South of US-89 between mile posts 21 and 22, between Kanab and Page.

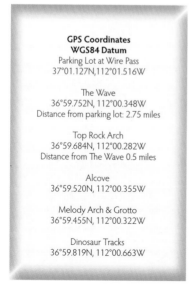

GPS Coordinates
WGS84 Datum
Parking Lot at Wire Pass
37°01.127N,112°01.516W

The Wave
36°59.752N, 112°00.348W
Distance from parking lot: 2.75 miles

Top Rock Arch
36°59.684N, 112°00.282W
Distance from The Wave 0.5 miles

Alcove
36°59.520N, 112°00.355W

Melody Arch & Grotto
36°59.455N, 112°00.322W

Dinosaur Tracks
36°59.819N, 112°00.663W

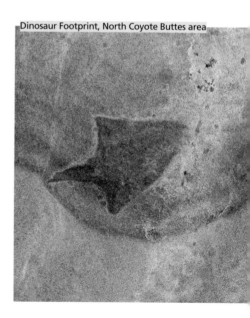
Dinosaur Footprint, North Coyote Buttes area

SOUTH COYOTE BUTTES

The Coyote Buttes Special Management Area sits between Utah's Grand Staircase-Escalante National Monument and the upper section of the Paria Canyon Wilderness Area-Vermilion Cliffs National Monument. This desolate land contains a disorderly collection of fantastically twisted and striated sandstone.

Hike No. 48 visited North Coyote Buttes. The trail presented here explores an area just a few miles to the south, accessed from a different trailhead. There is nothing here as famous as the Wave but South Coyote Buttes accesses a remote area with multitudes of beehive-shaped hills that appear to be enveloped in a sea of colorful petrified waves. Other formations have been contorted into caverns, arches, domes and fragile fins—all slowly crumbling as they continuously succumb to the forces of nature.

AT A GLANCE

Day Hike: Only day-hikes are permitted. Overnight camping is not allowed on the hiking route.

Distance: South Coyote Buttes is an exploration around an area rather than a hike leading to a destination, so the mileage will vary depending on how much you want to explore.

Average Hiking Time: It will take about 4 hours to see the main area of interest.

Difficulty: Moderate.

Sun Exposure: There is little to no shade and the sand reflects the sun, amplifying the heat. Carry plenty of water when you hike, and at least 1 gallon of water per person in the summer.

Permits Required: Walk-in permits are available for next-day hikes and are limited to six in a group. Apply for an online permit or pick them up in person. From March 15 to November 14 permits will be issued at the Paria Contact Station. From November 15 to March 14 the Contact Station is closed and permits are issued at the Kanab GSENM Visitor Center, located at: 745 E. & US-89, Kanab, Utah 84741. Ph: 435.688.3200

Paria BLM: Located on US-89, 44 miles east of the House Rock Valley Road junction.

Trail Conditions: A 4WD is required to get to the South Coyote Buttes trailheads. Be aware that even with a 4WD the main road, due to the clay content, can be dangerously slippery or even impassible if wet.

Trailhead: Paw Hole or Cottonwood Teepees.

Trailend: Same as trailhead.

Best Season: This is a nice hike in the spring, fall and winter

because the direct sun makes it too hot in the summer. Winter snow on the rock adds interest for many photographers.

South Coyote Buttes Elevation: 5,789 feet.
Cottonwood Teepees Elevation: 5,933 feet.
Paw Hole Starting Elevation: 5,950 feet.
Paw Hole Highest Elevation: 6,350 feet.
Off the Beaten Path: Yes.
Restrooms: Vault toilet at the Wire Pass Trailhead and another at the Stateline Campground.

Bo Beck hiking in the South Coyote Buttes

49 SOUTH COYOTE BUTTES DETAILS

HOUSE ROCK VALLEY ROAD - From Kanab, drive 40 miles east on US-89. Turn right onto House Rock Valley Road, located between mile markers 25 and 26, just before a guardrail and a sweeping lefthand curve. Set your odometer and drive for 17 miles. Pass the Wire Pass parking lot at 8.5 miles and then the Utah-Arizona state line, which also divides Utah's Grand Staircase-Escalante National Monument and Arizona's Vermilion Cliffs National Monument. At 17 miles, look for an unmarked turnoff on the left side of the road. If you get to the Honeymoon Trail sign, which is 18 miles from US-89, you have gone too far.

PAW HOLE TRAILHEAD - The first landmark, Lone Tree Reservoir, is just past the unmarked turnoff. The name implies a water supply but you will probably only see a single juniper tree sitting in a dry hole. Soon after this you should see a welcome sign for the Vermilion Cliffs National Monument, then farther down the road there is a sign for Coyote Buttes. The road is lined with junipers, sagebrush and purple, red, orange and white wildflowers. Parking for the Paw Hole Trailhead is 2.5 miles from the turnoff.

There are no established trails in this area. Please be careful where you walk. Do not climb or scramble on rocks in South Coyote Buttes that might get damaged or broken as a result. The features this area is known for—fragile mounds, strata, flakes and fins—are often extremely delicate.

PAW HOLE - From the parking area, look for the small, interesting arch on top of the first hoodoo. The climb to it is a 4th-class scramble which is not recommended due to fragile rock. The southeast side of the trailhead offers some nice formations and to the northeast there is a beautiful sandstone bowl at the end of the dunes. From the parking area, hike north-northeast, through the fence, heading for the buttes. There are no established trails, this route is more of an exploration around the rocks. The line on the map is a suggested route possibility. Hike around the bowl and along the sand toward the hoodoos to the northeast. Once you turn west, and topout on the ridge, House Rock Valley Road appears to the west and a variety of oddly shaped, upright rock structures become visible. Below and on the western slope the sandstone gets really interesting. If you take the route on the western edge of the butte there is some 4th-class climbing at the bottom of the cliff. Locate the angular-shaped grotto. Inside you will find fragile fins and soft sand. Take some time to explore the area before hiking back to the parking area.

COTTONWOOD TEEPEES PARKING - Reset your odometer. Drive east from the Paw Hole parking for 3.25 miles to Windmill Junction. Turn north (left) just prior to the windmill and other dilapidated structures nearby. Continue north through the gate and into the South Coyote Buttes Special Permit Area. Leave any gates as you found them. At 2.5 miles from the windmill, the road becomes impassible. Park your vehicle.

EXPLORING THE TEPEES AND COTTONWOOD SPRING - Both north and west from the parking area are large hoodoos: the Cottonwood Teepees. Hike over the desert sand and climb the nearest rock formations on the left (west) side of the road. Once on top, Cottonwood Spring can be seen in the wash to the north and below the formations. Teepees are visible both to the north and south of the slickrock plateau. Fragile, windswept layers of tangerine swirls prevail here, like an elegant, layered dessert. The vivid colors come courtesy of generous mineral deposits. Rounded domes and flat-capped stones fill this desert oasis and fossilized sand dunes present a wonderful display of weird patterns.

THE QUEEN - Head toward your vehicle; walk east to another cluster of hoodoos. Look for a particularly rounded, towering formation, the highlight of the sandstone formations to the right of the road. This rock has been dubbed, unofficially, as the Queen, due to its similarity to a chess-piece.

PERMITS AND CAMPING INFORMATION - Same as for North Coyote Buttes: see page 184.

GPS Coordinates, WGS84 Datum	
Turnoff US-89 onto House Rock Valley Road 37°07.567N, 111°58.612W	Windmill Junction 36°55.631N, 111°58.183W
Parking lot at Wire Pass 37°01.171N,112°01.483W	Cottonwood Teepees Parking 36°57.611N, 111°58.706W
Turnoff - House Rock Valley Road to Lone Tree Reservoir 36°54.872N, 112°03.096W	Cottonwood Spring Formations 36°57.901N, 111°59.481W
Paw Hole Parking and Trailhead 36°55.447N, 112°01.038W	The Queen 36°57.599N, 111°58.545W

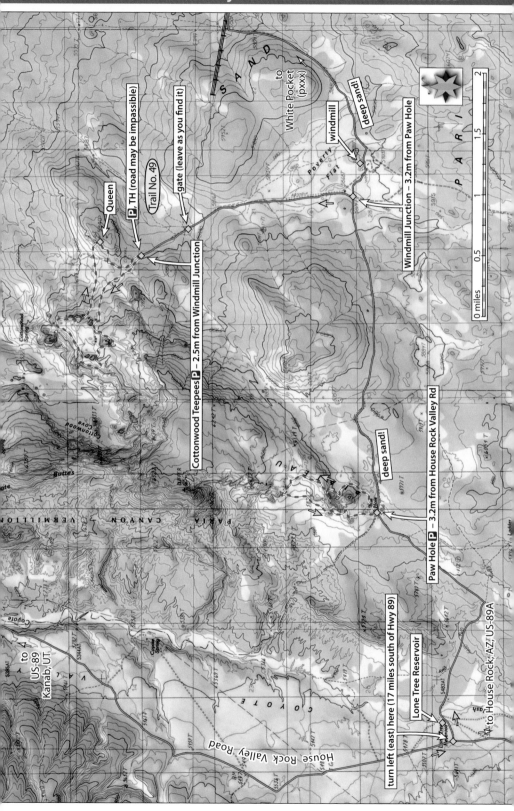

Queen

P TH (road may be impassible)

Trail No. 49

gate (leave as you find it)

to
White Pocket
(pxxx)

windmill

deep sand!

Cottonwood Teepees P – 2.5m from Windmill Junction

Windmill Junction – 3.2m from Paw Hole

deep sand!

Paw Hole P – 3.2m from House Rock Valley Rd

Lone Tree Reservoir

turn left (east) here (17 miles south of Hwy 89)

to House Rock; AZ/ US-89A

House Rock Valley Road

to
US-89
Kanab, UT

0 miles   0.5   1   1.5   2

WHITE POCKET ⑤⓪

While driving the sandy backroads of the Paria Canyon-Vermilion Cliffs Wilderness, a brilliant-white formation of twisted rock stands proudly above the desert and calls explorers to come near.

This brilliant-white formation is called White Pocket, a seldom-visited area of magical beauty. It is as stunning as the widely known and popular Wave. However, unlike the Wave, White Pocket, at the time of this writing, does not require a permit for enjoyment of its beauty.

On close examination the sandstone is multicolored, with hues swirled through the rock and thin strata. Exploration of the area by foot is endlessly satisfying. Whether spending just a couple of hours or an entire weekend, White Pocket will definitely be at the top of your list of special places.

Keep in mind that this is a fragile environment and the utmost care should be taken to preserve it. Stay on the slickrock when possible. Be careful not to snap off thin fins of rock or trample delicate vegetation. This pristine area should be saved for any and all that visit in the future.

AT A GLANCE

Day Hike: Yes.
Distance: 4-mile round-trip.
Average Hiking Time: 3 hours.
Equipment: Sticky-rubber hiking shoes, emergency supplies, 3 quarts of water per person, sun-protective clothing, map, compass and an optional GPS.
Difficulty: Moderate.
Sun Exposure: Full sun.
Permits: Not required.
Trail Conditions: Off-trail with sand and rock areas.

Trailhead: Off US-89 between Page, AZ and Kanab, UT in the South Coyote Buttes area.
Trailend: Same as trailhead.
Trail Access: Year-round, but if the road is wet or there is melting snow the road can be impassable. A 4WD is required.
Best Season: This is a year-round adventure as long as the road is drivable.
Elevation: 5,700 feet.
Off the Beaten Path: Yes.

White Pocket in winter

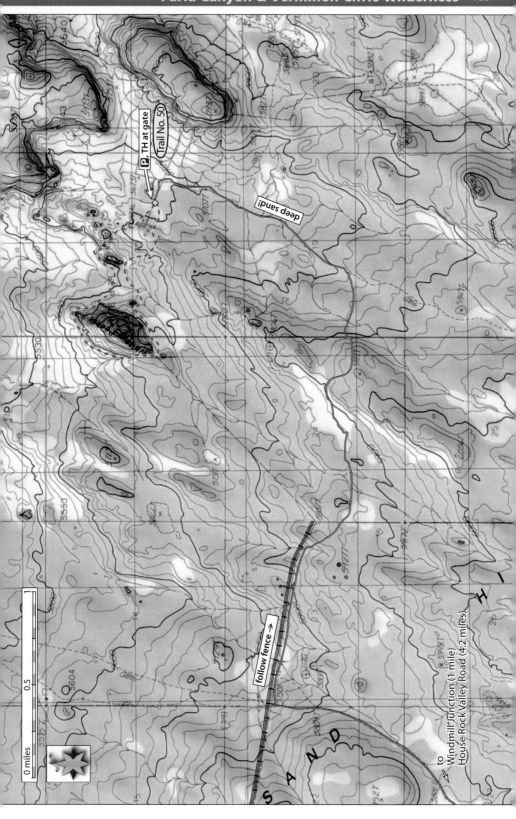

P. TH at gate

Trail No. 50

deep sand!

follow fence →

to Windmill Junction (1 mile)
House Rock Valley Road (4.2 miles)

S A N D

H I

0 miles   0.5   1

50 WHITE POCKET DETAILS

1 **DIRECTIONS FROM KANAB -** Drive east on US-89. After 40 miles, turn right (south) on House Rock Valley Road (see map page 171). Map on page 146–147, and area map page 7 may also be helpful. This junction is located between mile markers 25 and 26, just before the guardrail and a sweeping lefthand curve. Set your odometer, since the unmarked turn to the trailhead can be difficult to spot. The road soon changes to dirt (it may be impassible if wet).

Pass the Wire Pass parking at 8.5 miles from US-89. Continue south past the Utah-Arizona state line, which also divides Utah's Grand Staircase-Escalante National Monument and Arizona's Vermilion Cliffs National Monument. At 8 miles beyond the Wire Pass parking, look for a dirt road on your left. This is the same road that accesses the South Coyote Buttes Trail (see map page 187). The turnoff is unmarked, but it quickly leads to Lone Tree Reservoir. A sign located 0.2 miles after turning will verify that you are on the correct road.

2 **4WD ROAD -** Follow the "main" road east for 2.4 miles to the Paw Hole Trailhead. Beyond Paw Hole, the soft sand on the road becomes deeper and travel gets quite rugged. You may need to deflate your tires to prevent your vehicle from sinking into the sand and getting stuck. The road is similar for the next 3 miles to the windmill at Poverty Flat Ranch. The road passes through two gates, which you will need to close after passing through them.

Once at the windmill, travel northeast, passing the windmill on the left and an old barn on the right. The sandy road now heads toward a large water-tank that rests on a knoll. The sandy road gets deep as it ascends—be sure to keep up your momentum here. Follow this sandy road to the east and then north for 1.8 miles until it arrives at a corral and a fence. At this point the road will turn right and follow alongside a fence for a short time. It will then continue east for 2.8 miles before steering northeast for another 1.5 miles. The road ends in a deep-sand area by a lone juniper tree. This is the parking area and trailhead. The White Pocket monolith is visible during the drive at various times, and it can be seen a half-mile to the west from the parking area.

3 **TRAIL -** There is no formal trail established, wandering and exploring is the main fare. The map suggests one possible, recommended route.

Slickrock formations will lure and amaze with their unique colors and texture. Take time to look over the extensive formations and drop down into the valley. Most hikers will want to circumnavigate the monolith to the west. Enjoy, but remember to tread lightly and preserve the landscape as you found it. Leave only footprints.

Bo Beck in White Pocket

GPS Coordinates
WGS84 Datum

House Rock Valley Road and
Lone Tree Reservoir Intersection
36°54.876 N, 112°03.079 W

Paw Hole Trailhead and Parking
(South Coyote Buttes Permit Area)
36°55.394 N, 112°01.080 W

Gate 1
36°55.501 N, 112°00.369 W

Gate 2
36°55.613 N, 112°00.197 W

Windmill at Poverty Flat Ranch
36°55.561 N, 111°57.920 W

Corral at Fence Line
36°56.569 N, 111°56.713 W

White Pocket Parking
and Trailhead
36°57.328 N, 111°53.734 W

INDEX